Making Technology Work for Learners with Special Needs

Practical Skills for Teachers

Jean G. Ulman
Ball State University

Boston ■ New York ■ San Francisco
Mexico City ■ Montreal ■ Toronto ■ London ■ Madrid ■ Munich ■ Paris
Hong Kong ■ Singapore ■ Tokyo ■ Cape Town ■ Sydney

Executive Editor: *Virginia Lanigan*
Executive Marketing Manager: *Amy Cronin Jordan*
Editorial Assistant: *Scott Blaszak*
Production Administrator: *Won Jang*
Composition and Prepress Buyer: *Linda Cox*
Electronic Composition: *Omegatype Typography, Inc.*
Manufacturing Buyer: *Andrew Turso*
Cover Administrator: *Joel Gendron*

For related titles and support materials, visit our online catalog at www.ablongman.com.

Copyright © 2005 Pearson Education, Inc.

All rights reserved. No part of the material protected by this copyright notice may be reproduced or utilized in any form or by any means, electronic or mechanical, including photocopying, recording, or by any information storage and retrieval system, without written permission from the copyright owner.

To obtain permission(s) to use material from this work, please submit a written request to Allyn and Bacon, Permissions Department, 75 Arlington Street, Boston, MA 02116 or fax your request to 617-848-7320.

Between the time Website information is gathered and then published, it is not unusual for some sites to have closed. Also, the transcription of URLs can result in unintended typographical errors. The publisher would appreciate notification where these errors occur so that they may be corrected in subsequent editions.

Library of Congress Cataloging-in-Publication Data

Ulman, Jean G.
  Making technology work for learners with special needs : practical skills for teachers / Jean G. Ulman.
    p. cm.
  Includes bibliographical references (p.) and index.
  ISBN 0-205-40745-5 (pbk.)
  1. Children with disabilities—Education—Computer-assisted instruction.   2. Special education—United States—Computer-assisted instruction.   3. Computer-assisted instruction.   I. Title.

LC4024.U56 2005
371.9'04334—dc22
                                                                              2003070769

Printed in the United States of America

10   9   8   7   6   5   4   3   2   1   09   08   07   06   05   04

Photo Credits: Photos on pages 101, 102, 103, 105, 106, 108, 111, 112, 113, 114, and 115 courtesy of Jean G. Ulman.

CONTENTS

Preface   xi

PART ONE   Building Your Skills

1 Introduction   1

2 Word Processing   4
    Are You Typing or Typesetting?   4
    Exploring Your Word Processing Software   7
    Practicing New Skills   10
        Summary   12
    More Word Processing Features   12
        Preferences   13
        Formatting Characters   13
    Using Help   13
        Summary   15
    Producing and Using Symbols and Special Characters   15
        Dashing Around—The Hyphen, En Dash, and Em Dash   15
        Accessing Symbols and Special Characters   15
    Using Your Skills   16
        Summary   19
    What's Next?   19
    Key Terms   20

3 Graphics   21
    A Little Background   21
    Experimenting with Clip Art   22
        Arranging Images   22
        Modifying Images   24
        Summary   25

CONTENTS

Learning about Drawing Objects   26
- Exploring the Drawing Toolbar   26
- Using AutoShapes and Lines   27
- Producing Text Effects   31
- Summary   34

What's Next?   34
Key Terms   35

4 Spreadsheets   36

Exploring a Blank Spreadsheet   36
Making a Simple Spreadsheet   38
- Entering Data Into a Spreadsheet   38
- Creating a Formula   38
- Changing the Appearance of the Spreadsheet   39
- Printing a Spreadsheet   40
- Summary   41

Creating a Grade Book   41
- Creating a New Spreadsheet and Entering Data   42
- Using a Function to Create a Formula   42
- Copying the Formula to Other Cells   44
- Calculating Averages for Each Test   44
- Calculating the Overall Percentage for Each Student   45
- Exploring Chart Options   46
- Formatting the Final Appearance of the Spreadsheet   47
- Summary   49

What's Next?   49
Key Terms   49

5 Databases   50

Exploring a Database   51
- What Is a Form?   53
- What Is Sort?   53
- What Is Filtering?   54
- What about Dates?   56

Making Reports   58
- First Thirteen States Report   58
- The Largest and Smallest States Report   60
- Summary   61

CONTENTS   v

Creating a Database   61
Defining the Fields   62
Entering Data   62
Exploring Your New Database   64
Summary   66

What's Next?   67

Key Terms   67

6 Presentation Software   68

Exploring a *PowerPoint* Presentation   68

Creating a *PowerPoint* Presentation   70
Summary   72

What's Next?   73

Key Terms   73

PART TWO Integrating the Computer into the Classroom

7 Educational Software   75

How to Use Software in the Classroom   76
Reinforced Practice   76
Tutorial   77
Simulation   78
Problem Solving   78
Graphics   79
Reference   79
Teacher Utility   79
Student Utility   80
Authoring   80

Reviewing Software: Educational and Technical Criteria   82
Objectives   82
Prerequisite Skill   83
Accuracy   83
Use of Skills "Reinforcers"   83
Time Commitment   83

Independence   84
Pace   84
Usefulness   84
Flexibility   84
Screen Design   85
Documentation   85
Universal Design for Learning   85

How to Approach a New and Unfamiliar Program   86

Software Activities   87
Mini-Review   87
In-Depth Review   87

What's Next?   87
It's Mine; I Bought It!   87
How Much Can I Spend?   89

Key Terms   90

8 Internet   91

Web Accessibility   91

Searching and Using Web Materials   92
How Do You Find Things Out There?   92
What Can You Do with What You Find?   93

How Can You Use the Internet?   94
Communication   94
News and Current Events   94
Live Broadcasts   95
Reference   95
Research   95
Instruction   96
Assessment   96
Tools   97
Shopping   97
Entertainment   97

Structuring the Work Environment   98

What's Next?   99

Key Terms   99

PART THREE Making Adaptations for Learners with Special Needs

9 Making Adaptations with Hardware and Software 101

Simple Solutions 102
Keyboard and Mouse Shortcuts 102
Keyguard 103
Touch Screen 103
Mouse Devices 105
Other Aids 107

Software Solutions 107
Assisted Keyboard 108
Talking Word Processors 109
On-screen Keyboards 110
Word Prediction Software 111
Screen Enhancing Software 111
Writing Tools 112
Macro Programs 112

Specialized Alternative Devices 112
Alternative Keyboards—Fixed 112
Alternative Keyboards—Programmable 115
Switch Input 117
Speech Recognition 120

A Functional Assessment 122
Watch-Listen-Identify 122
Select the Least Restrictive Adaptation 123
Locate a Device 123
Use a Team 123
Try and Train 123

Study Questions 124

Key Terms 124

10 Customizing Curriculum Content 125

What It's All About 125

Designing the Custom Overlay 131
What the Student Sees 131
What the Computer Receives 131
What the Student Hears 131

viii CONTENTS

    Considering Complexity   131
    Planning the Overlay   132

11 How to Do It—Using IntelliTools *Overlay Maker*   135

Simple Talking Activities   135
    What the Student Sees   136
    What the Computer Receives   138
    Print, Send, and Test   139
    Summary   140

Simple Writing Activities   141
    What the Student Sees   145
    What the Computer Receives   145
    Save, Print, and Test   147
    Summary   149

What's Next?   149

Tips and Troubleshooting   149

12 How to Do It—Using *Discover:Create*   151

Simple Talking Activities   151
    What the Student Sees   154
    What the Computer Receives   156
    What the Student Hears   156
    Save, Print, and Test   157
    Summary   158

Simple Writing Activities   159
    What the Student Sees   163
    What the Computer Receives   163
    Save, Print, and Test   165
    Summary   166

What's Next?   166

Tips and Troubleshooting   167

13 *IntelliPics Studio*   169

Exploring Activities   170

Exploring Modes   174
    The Paint Mode   174
    The Design Mode   175

Making an Activity from a Template   176
    Plan the Activity   178
    Edit Buttons on Toolbars   178
    Add and Edit an IntelliQuiz Button   179
    Hide Author Mode and Save   180
    Summary   182

Making a Non-Linear Activity   182
    Create a New Document   185
    Add a Title with a Text Box   186
    Create, Name, and Label Additional Pages   188
    Design the Menu Page   188
    Create Buttons   188
    Make Buttons Link to Another Page   189
    Copy Buttons   191
    Add Text to the Content Pages   192
    Add Return Buttons to the Content Pages   192
    Add Images to the Content Pages   192
    Hide Toolbars and Save   193
    Summary   193

Create an IntelliMation   193
    Summary   196

Learning About IntelliQuizzes   196

Providing Alternative Access   196

What's Next?   197

APPENDIX A   Special Character Codes for Windows and Macintosh   199

APPENDIX B   Activities to Accompany Chapter 9   203

APPENDIX C   Keyboard Shortcuts for *IntelliTalk* and *Write:OutLoud*   209

APPENDIX D   Resources   213

Glossary   219

Index   223

PREFACE

This book arose from a need for hands-on computer experiences for pre-service teachers in a technology class that I teach. It is particularly useful for those who feel insecure or inadequate about their computer skills. Offering non-threatening carefully structured instructions for classroom-relevant activities, here is a book wherein the reader does not "read" the chapters; rather, the reader "does" the chapters.

Readers will be pleased to find exercises providing instructions for using popular productivity applications more effectively. For example, many people use word processors, albeit, with only minimal adequacy. That is, they can type, save, print, and have even learned to modify text style (e.g., bold, underline, italics, and size). But, they have never learned to use headers/footers, indent markers, multiple columns, and other useful features offered by even the simplest word processing software. Here chapters on word processing, graphics, spreadsheets, databases, and presentation software are self-paced and could be completed independently or in a classroom/lab setting. Only after becoming comfortable with their improved skills can teachers begin to incorporate computer activities into their daily classroom routines and address making adaptations for learners with special needs, as described in the remaining portions of the book.

The chapters are structured for reader success. There are lists of skills to practice and checklists for completed exercises. Each exercise closes with a summary; each chapter closes with a *What's Next?* section—how to continue building skills. Chapters 2–9 contain lists of Key Terms that are compiled in the *Glossary*. Key Terms are identified with ***bold italicized*** style when first mentioned in the chapters.

This book could be used as the primary text for a skill-building computer class in special education or general education. It could be a supplemental book in a technology class having a broader scope. Or, it could be a book that individuals use independent of any class structure—that is, practicing teachers could use these chapters at home to improve their computer skills.

Acknowledgments

The reality of this book has been driven by the needs of my teacher-education students for quality basic computer instruction with lots of practice. I want to thank each and every one over the years for their needs, their questions, and their accomplishments. Without them, there would be no book. My husband, Jerry, has read every word and completed every exercise; he has always been the first hurdle all text had to pass. With rapidly approaching deadlines, breakdowns occurred in our food acquisition and preparation system. Although not adept at cooking, Jerry, adept at hunting and gathering, discovered interesting new carryout opportunities. For your valuable feedback, encouragement, and support, I thank you. To my son James, CAD engineer extraordinaire, thank you for your work and advice with the images. Many thanks to Virginia

Lanigan, Special Education Editor at Allyn & Bacon. Your patient guidance and advice have been valuable. Finally, I want to acknowledge the reviewers' contributions to the final product. Thank you for making me look at things in different ways; and thank you for your valuable suggestions and criticisms—Beatrice C. Babbitt, University of Nevada, Las Vegas; Linda J. Hager, Clarke College; Rita Mulholland, California State University, Chico; Jennie I. Schaff, George Mason University.

Jean G. Ulman
Ball State University

PART ONE

Building Your Skills

CHAPTER

1 Introduction

The last ten to fifteen years have brought a technological revolution to our educational system. Where previously a computer in school was a rare occurrence, now there are computer labs, computers in resource centers, and computers on teachers' desks. Teachers can use computers to simplify their work with spreadsheets and other utility software, to create attractive documents, to conduct research, and most importantly, to enhance the classroom curriculum. Teachers are now expected (a) to be competent with these electronic tools; (b) to enhance the classroom curriculum with computer activities; and (c) to teach computer skills to their students. In special education there is an even greater need for competence with computers. The use of computers can empower learners with special needs to accomplish incredible feats that would be impossible without such computer assistance. Without question, the computer is rapidly becoming indispensable in our lives—both personal and professional. In short, computer skills are essential for today's teachers.

How does a teacher learn this new technology in order to use computers effectively in classrooms? Consider this: Did you ever ride a bicycle? What skills did it take to ride a bicycle, and how did you acquire those skills? Did you learn to ride a bicycle by reading a bicycle book or by watching someone else ride one? Not likely! You learned to ride a bicycle by riding a bicycle, and the more you rode the better you got. The same is true of computers. To improve your skills with the computer, you must use the computer. Reading about computers is not enough; nor is watching other people use one. You must do it yourself, step-by-step, steadily accomplishing increasingly complex tasks until you find that you are competent with the computer—a tool that will make your job easier and enhance the classroom experiences for the children that you teach.

Teachers need to be "computer adaptable"—to learn the basic concepts, acquire new skills, and find answers to their own questions regardless of the computer platform, operating system, or software that they encounter. They should become comfortable exploring software features and options, browsing menus, and searching the help files for answers. This book was developed to help teachers become competent and independent by building a solid foundation of basic computer skills and concepts employing widely used productivity software with all activities centered on educational uses—both utility and instructional. *Part One—Building Your Skills* addresses this need.

As your own skills develop and improve, you can then consider how to begin integrating computer technology into your daily classroom routine. *Part Two—Integrating the Computer into the Classroom* features educational software and the Internet. *Part Three—Making Adaptations for Learners with Special Needs* focuses on adapting the computer to provide computer access for persons with varying disabilities and also customizing curriculum content.

Readers beginning the chapters should have minimum computer competencies, such as using a mouse, navigating on the desktop, locating and opening software, and saving documents to an external data storage device. The book does not contain computer literacy information, such as bit/byte, RAM/ROM, input/output, what a hard disk is, and so on.

There is some basic information readers should gather about the particular computer system and software available in their settings—the computer model and its operating system, the version of Microsoft®Office®installed on the computer, the available printer and its location, and the kind of disk available for saving work.

What software, hardware, or peripheral devices are required to be able to work successfully with this book? Each section of the text requires the availability of different resources. For Part 1, *Building Your Skills* (Chapters 2–6) the student should have a version of *Microsoft Office* available. The book has been tested with *Office 97, 2000,* and *XP* for Windows computers and *Office 98, 2001,* and *v.X* for Macintosh computers. These chapters use Microsoft's *Word®, Excel®,* and *PowerPoint®.*

In Part 2, *Integrating the Computer into the Classroom,* a wide selection of educational software—both special education and general education titles—should be available for exploring and evaluating. Also, Internet access is necessary.

Part 3, *Making Adaptations for Learners with Special Needs,* supplies the reader with many different ways to make adaptations for both computer access and customizing curriculum. The activities accompanying Chapter 9 give the reader practice with computer adaptations. Suggested hardware/software to complete all of the activities include *Easy Access/Universal Access* (Macintosh) or *Accessibility Options* (Windows), a touch window, an assortment of different mouse devices, a programmable keyboard, word prediction software, an on-screen keyboard, and an assortment of alternative keyboards and single switches. It is not expected that all readers will have access to all of the suggested adaptations. However, there is at least one activity that all readers will be able to experience. Chapters 10 to 13 address customizing curriculum. Readers can practice these skills with either IntelliKeys or one of the Discover programmable keyboard options (Chapters 11 or 12). In addition, Chapter 13 teaches the basics of *IntelliPics Studio 3* with a focus on preparing customized instructional materials.

There are several documents that accompany the text that are necessary to successfully work through the chapters. Throughout the text, readers will be asked to open documents and then continue with instructions to modify them in some way. The documents are stored on an Internet site and can be downloaded from the following web address:

Macintosh: http://www.bsu.edu/julman/textdocuments.sit
Windows: http://www.bsu.edu/julman/textdocuments.zip

Download the documents before you begin *Chapter 2—Word Processing*. Store the folder, named *Text Documents*, in a convenient location so that the documents will be readily available to you as you progress through the chapters.

A few short years ago we could never have imagined that computers would have gigahertz processors, hundreds of megabytes of RAM, and wireless Internet connections. We cannot guess how much computer technology will change in the future. The skills you develop using this book—fundamental skills based on a conceptual approach—are not likely to become obsolete in the near future. With this book you will become competent and confident with the survival skills necessary to tackle unfamiliar computers, software, and peripheral devices in your efforts to make technology work for you and your students.

CHAPTER

2 Word Processing

The basic elements of *word processing* are covered in this chapter. Word processors are software applications, installed on computers, to enable the simplified production of printed text. There are many different word processors created by many different software publishers. Also, any one title, such as *Microsoft Word*, may have different versions as new editions released by the publisher update the capabilities of the software. When new versions appear, the toolbars, menus and menu items, shortcut palettes, and button bars may change. However, the basic elements of all word processors are the same, regardless of the software publisher or the current version of the program.

This chapter illustrates *Microsoft Word v.X*, the Macintosh version for OS X. However, the sample documents that you downloaded to accompany this text, for both Windows and Macintosh computers, will work with *Word 97, 2000,* or *XP* for Windows computers and also with *Word 98, 2001,* or *v.X* for Macintosh computers. The features of *AppleWorks* (Macintosh) or *Word Perfect* (Windows or Macintosh) are similar. All of the different word processing programs have their own specific features. Some are quite full-featured, even complex, enabling the most sophisticated text-editing capabilities. Others offer only the basics. All of them include the basic features of word processing covered in this chapter. Develop your word processing expertise with the activities in this chapter. Then, branch out with the software you have access to. Browse the menus, toolbars, floating palettes, and help files. Find out what else your software can do and begin to incorporate new skills into your repertoire of text-producing skills.

The objective of this chapter is to introduce you to the basic features of word processing using the version of *Microsoft Word* software available to you. You will browse the help files to learn word processing features. You will edit a *document* prepared by the author. Finally, you will create your own professional-looking newsletter.

Are You Typing or Typesetting?

Christopher Latham Sholes invented the first practical typewriter, marketed by the Remington Arms Company in 1874. As machine-produced text began to be accepted by writers, businesses, and the general public, a body of typing conventions to enable typed text to look typeset came to be accepted.

What's QWERTY?

The first typists did not touch type or even use all fingers. Early typists used the two-fingered hunt-and-peck method. Because of the way the early machines were constructed, the "arms" for each key would catch on each other and jam if the typist rapidly pressed letters next to each other. Sholes devised a method to move keys that were frequently pressed in succession, such as TH, away from each other so typists could produce text with fewer mechanical problems. The keyboard layout, called QWERTY (pronounced "kwer-tee"), after the first six letters on the top row, has persisted to this day, despite the fact that typewriters are mechanically different and typists use all ten fingers.

The advent of the computer age has brought to the general public computers with word processing software that enable the production of sophisticated typeset text. As typists make the transition from typewriters to word processors, they bring with them over one hundred years of typing practices—all created to simulate typesetting—and no longer necessary now because they can typeset. Just as the ***QWERTY*** keyboard has persisted one hundred years after it was no longer necessary, the old typing rules are still being taught and used.

Typeset text has features that typewriters cannot duplicate. The different font faces, sizes, and text styles in a newspaper or textbook cannot be created on a typewriter. The typewriter has a single set of uppercase and lowercase letters, numbers, and punctuation marks. Consequently, to simulate the italics of typeset text, typists substituted underlining. To underline with a typewriter, the typist backed up over the previously typed words and then pressed the underline character for each letter to be underlined. With no subscripts or superscripts, the typist learned to roll the typewriter platen to achieve the **H_2O** or **MC^2,** put plain letters in accented words like **résumé,** and spelled out **degrees** when writing **98.6°**. In addition, single and double quotation marks and apostrophes were all created with the foot and inch marks key as the typewriter cannot produce smart or "curly" quotation marks. When producing text with a word processing software the writer has access to all features of typesetting including special characters such as Σ, ¢, and ©, text styles **bold**, *italics*, ~~strike-through~~, and outline, and variously sized letters.

A convention, embraced by typists for the last one hundred years, has been to place two spaces after periods or other end punctuation. This rule developed because the typewriter font was monospaced; that is, every character was exactly the same width. Because the width of characters varies, the monospaced type of the typewriter has varying amounts of space between characters. In order for the reader of typewritten monospaced text to see a visual separation at the end of a sentence, two spaces are necessary. This age-old typing convention is no longer necessary and is, in fact, incorrect when the writer is producing text using a word processor with a proportionally spaced font. With a proportionately spaced font each character takes up only the amount of space it requires. Spacing between characters is uniform. The

PART ONE / Building Your Skills

> ```
> This example, written in a typewriter font (Courier) is monospaced.
> Notice that each letter is exactly the same width regardless of the
> actual size of the letter.  Examine the wasted space.  Also note
> that two spaces are required after each period to indicate that an
> actual space is there.
> 
> Sample line of 10 letter "i": iiiiiiiiii
> Sample line of 10 letter "m": mmmmmmmmmm
> ```
>
> Now look at this example written in a proportionately spaced font, Helvetica, designed for a computer. Each letter takes up only the amount of space that it actually needs. A single space after end punctuation is enough to visually separate sentences. Note the following phrase: Only one space is necessary after the colon, too. When using a proportional font face you never need to use two spaces after any punctuation mark.
>
> Sample line of 10 letter "i": iiiiiiiiii
> Sample line of 10 letter "m": mmmmmmmmmm

font face **Courier** is a computer font that is monospaced. Compare sentences written using **Courier** with sentences written with the font face **Helvetica** in the box above.

Many typists who move from typing to word processing do so without learning all the features of the word processing software. They continue to "type." A typist new to word processing is thrilled to learn that mistakes can be deleted with a press of a key. A spell checker can scan for typographical errors and automatically correct them. The capacity to save, edit later, and print multiple copies is almost a miracle! Gradually, the typist learns some of the features of word processing and begins to be trapped between typing and typesetting.

Scenario #1. The typewriter typist always starts a new page with a title and page number on the first line and continues using this method with the word processor—unfamiliar with the Header function. The typist, who is working with word processing software, places these "headers" on the top line of each page. With the new capacity to edit previously entered text, the typist edits the text, moving paragraphs around and adding words here and there. Now, the "headers" have moved to somewhere other than the top line of each page. The typist deletes them, typing them in again in the new locations of each page—not too bad a task if the paper is only a few pages, but what if it is not?

Scenario #2. A typist learns to set up a reference list with *hanging indents* (see Figure 2.1 for an example of a hanging indent) by pressing [RETURN] or [ENTER] at the end of a line and beginning successive lines of a reference entry with a [TAB]. Constructing references that way with word processing software may work until the typist decides to change the margins, type size, or font face, thereby altering the line length. See Figure 2.2 to see a "typed" reference after a typist changed the font size. In order to

CHAPTER 2 / Word Processing 7

> Male, M. (1988). *Special magic: Computers,
>   classroom strategies, and exceptional students.*
>   Mountain View, CA: Mayfield Publishing Co.
>
> Hanging Indent

FIGURE 2.1 Hanging Indent.

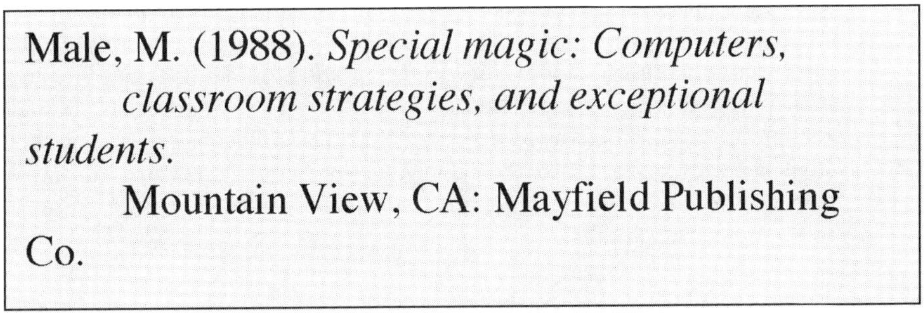

> Male, M. (1988). *Special magic: Computers,
>   classroom strategies, and exceptional
> students.*
>   Mountain View, CA: Mayfield Publishing
> Co.

FIGURE 2.2 "Typed" Hanging Indent after changing the type size.

repair the modified reference the writer must delete the tabs and paragraph returns and replace them in new locations.

Scenario #3. The typist is not aware of the subscripts, superscripts, or special characters that are possible with word processing software. Did you ever have to type **H2O** for H_2O? Did you ever type **H O** and then use a sharp dark pencil to put in the subscript? Have you ever used that sharp pencil to create the accent marks in **résumé**?

Typists must shed one hundred years of Typing 101 habits and practices and embrace typesetting to produce professional-looking documents with word processing software. As you begin adopting word processing habits, it really does not matter which word processing software you use. Most word processors have similar features—at least regarding the basics, which are the most important. For example, if you learn how to use the indent markers in *AppleWorks 6.0* to create hanging indents for references, you will have no difficulty using the hanging indents in *Word XP.*

Exploring Your Word Processing Software

Begin by becoming familiar with the look of the word processing software that is available to you. **Do this:** Locate the *Word* program on your computer and begin a new blank document.

Word is software with many features; for example, outlining, auto numbering/ bulleting of lists, tracking changes in manuscripts, capitalizing first words and proper nouns, indexing, spell checking, grammar checking, and autocorrecting commonly misspelled words. Some of these features are turned on, by *default,* and can become intrusive when they are applied if you do not want them. For example, a teacher is preparing a language arts worksheet for students to identify words that should be capitalized. She types:

Joe will be fishing on saturday.

Word immediately capitalizes "saturday" whether she chooses to capitalize it or not! It autocorrects and autoformats many options automatically. This means that you must somehow know what the options are and how to turn them off. As you begin to complete the exercises in this chapter you will start by locating and turning off most of the automatic options. Later, explore them and turn on the ones you find useful. **Do this:** From the Tools menu choose **AutoCorrect** or **AutoFormat** (depending on the version of *Word* you are using). You may see a large dialog box with tabs across the top labeled **AutoCorrect, AutoFormat As You Type, AutoFormat,** and **AutoText.** If you do not see these tabs, click on the **Options** button. A new dialog box with tabs across the top is revealed.

- Uncheck all **AutoCorrect** choices
- Uncheck all **AutoFormat As You Type** options *except* "straight quotes" with "smart quotes."
- Uncheck all **AutoFormat** options *except* "straight quotes" with "smart quotes."
- Uncheck all boxes on the **AutoText** tab.

You may or may not have already experienced the red and green "squiggles" that *Word* places in your text to identify words/phrases that may be misspelled or grammatically flawed. You can run the Spelling and Grammar checker (Tools menu) to find out why *Word* suspects an error. You can accept changes the software recommends, make your own changes, or ignore *Word*'s suggestions.

Take a few minutes now to explore the software features. From the **View** menu look for the list of toolbars. Open the **Standard** and **Formatting** toolbar (a check mark beside the name means the toolbar is open). Also open, from the **View** menu, the **Formatting Palette**—if that option is available in your version of *Word*. Look at the toolbars, formatting palettes, and menu options. Typically in the *Word* software, if you allow the pointer to linger on any toolbar button, the name of the button will be revealed. Another feature to watch for is a menu or palette that expands. Look for a small triangle-shaped arrow. Click on one and watch the menu expand. Try this out as you explore the software. Listed below are some specific options you should locate at this time. You will be using these features in the first activity.

- Font faces—names or illustrates all font faces available for use
- Size of characters—offers point sizes for characters (12 pt. is usually default)
- Text style—gives choices for bold, italics, underline, and other styles
- Text color—offers options for displaying characters in different colors
- Line spacing—gives choices for single spacing, double spacing, and others
- Alignment—allows centering, left/right aligned, or fully justified

CHAPTER 2 / Word Processing 9

See the illustrations in Figures 2.3, 2.4, and 2.5 of some of the toolbars, palettes, and menus.

When you have found the six features previously listed, you are ready to proceed with the following exercise where you will have an opportunity to experiment with them.

FIGURE 2.3. *Word 98* Toolbars—Standard and Formatting.

Screen shot reprinted with permission from Microsoft Corporation.

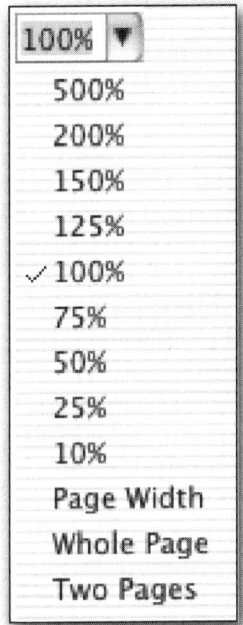

FIGURE 2.4 Expanded Zoom control menu from *Word 98* Standard Toolbar.

Screen shot reprinted with permission from Microsoft Corporation.

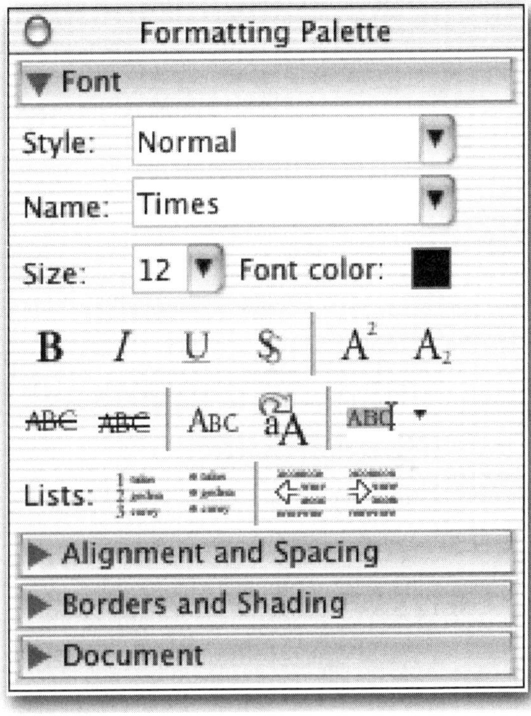

FIGURE 2.5 Formatting Palette from *Word 2001*. Notice the triangle-shaped arrows at the beginning of each heading. The Font menu is expanded. The Alignment and Spacing, Borders and Shading, and Document menus are not expanded. Clicking on the triangle will expand or contract a section.

Screen shot reprinted with permission from Microsoft Corporation.

Practicing New Skills

With a new blank document open in your word processing software, type the following text. Press [TAB] to begin each paragraph. Press the [RETURN] or [ENTER] key at the end of each paragraph, not at the ends of lines. When you reach the end of a line, the text will wrap to the next line automatically—called ***word wrap.*** Do not worry about the line spacing or how many words are on each line. Use the hyphen key alternating with spaces to make the tear-off line. Use [SHIFT] hyphen for the fill-in blanks. After the text is typed, you will use some of the features you just located to modify the appearance of the document.

Dear Parents,

We are planning a field trip to the Children's Museum on December 6. We will leave our building at 8:30 a.m. and will return by 2:00 p.m.

Although we are taking a school bus and don't require parents to drive, we would like parent chaperones to accompany our class. Dress your child in comfortable clothing and send a bag lunch. We will supply drinks for everyone.

Please complete the permission slip below, tear it off, and return it to me by December 1. Thank you,

(Press [TAB] twice) Ms. Teacher (Note: your name here)

- -

My child, _____, has/does not have (circle one) my permission to attend the Children's Museum field trip on December 6.

I can / cannot (circle one) accompany the class on this trip.

Signed by _____ (parent or guardian)

When the text has been entered, save the document on your personal data disk. Use a meaningful filename, like ***fieldtrip.doc*** or ***wp1.doc.*** If you are expecting to submit these

Using SAVE or SAVE AS

When you save a new untitled document the first time, a Save Dialog Box appears enabling you to give the document a file name and pick a location—usually your personal data disk—for it to be saved to. As you edit or add to the document and save changes using the **SAVE** option, the computer "invisibly" resaves the document with its new changes using the original file name and saved location, overwriting the document you saved the first time. Usually this is what you want to do. However, you may wish to save an edited version with another file name, preserving the original document, or you may wish to save the document in another location or on another disk. Use the **SAVE AS** option to change the name or location of the edited document because the **SAVE AS** option always brings back the Save Dialog Box.

documents electronically for a class, you may be instructed to add your initials to the filename; for example, *fieldtrip-jgu.doc* or *wp1-jgu.doc.*

You will be following a similar pattern in upcoming assignments: First enter all of the content; then save it; and finally, format the material for its finished version.

Format the Field Trip letter as follows:

1. *Changing the Text Style.* Select the text **Children's Museum** in the first paragraph by clicking in front of **Children's** and dragging to the end of **Museum.** Change the style of the selected text to bold.

2. *Changing Font Face and Point Size.* Select all text, either by dragging from beginning to end or by choosing **Select All** from the Edit menu. Set the font point size to 12. Also, set the font face for the entire document to New York or Times or any clear, easy-to-read font face.

3. *Changing Line Spacing.* Select all text again. Change the line spacing to double-spaced. Usually, by default, line spacing is single-spaced. Most word processing programs offer single spacing (1.0), one and a half spaces (1.5), and double spacing (2.0). Take care to select 2.0 and not 1.5. Also, be sure that you have not placed extra line spaces between paragraphs. If so, take them out.

4. *Adding a Centered Heading.* Move to the top of the document and click to place the insertion point in front of the first word. Type **Let's Go!** in front of **Dear Parents** and press [RETURN] or [ENTER]. Now the heading is on a line alone. Change the size of the heading to 18 point. Now, click any place in the heading text, if the insertion point is not already there. Locate the alignment icons and click on each of them to see the effect on the heading text. End up with the **Let's Go!** heading centered.

5. *Checking the Spelling.* Locate the spell check feature of *Word* in the Tools menu or as a button on the standard toolbar. Follow the on-screen prompts to correct any errors that the spell checker detects. Read the final text carefully to detect any errors that the spell checker does not identify; for example, *its* for *it's* or *your* for *you're.*

6. *Final Editing.* Look carefully at the completed document. Are there small corrections you could change to improve it? What about the dotted line—the tear-off permission slip? Did changing the font change that line length? If so, edit the dotted line so that it fits across the page on only one line. Finally, does the document fit the page? Balance empty space at the bottom by adding a few blank lines at the top. Save any changes.

7. *Printing the Final Document.* You may wish to print the final version of the field trip letter. Before you initiate printing, go to ***Page Setup*** accessed through the File menu. The options in **Page Setup** are determined by the printer you have available—so **Page Setup** options can vary. Open **Page Setup** now. Look at the choices for Paper Size and select **Letter** (assuming that 8½ × 11 sized paper is available to the printer). Also notice Page orientation. There are two orientations—***Portrait*** and ***Landscape.*** Choose Portrait (the vertical page orientation) for this document. Initiate printing by choosing **Print** from the File menu. By default the computer chooses to print one copy

of all pages of the document. If you wish to print more than one copy, or limit the pages printed, you can make the changes here. If there is a choice for Print Quality, choose a lesser, faster, or draft quality and click **OK** or **Print** to print one copy of all pages.

Field Trip Letter Checklist

- Text of letter is as instructed in the text and is carefully edited with no spelling or typographical errors
- Each new paragraph begins with a [TAB].
- **Children's Museum** (first paragraph) appears in bold.
- All text except title is a readable 12-point font size.
- **Let's Go!** is centered at the top of the page in an 18-point font size.
- Tear-off line is hyphen/space; fill-in blanks are underline characters.
- Document is double-spaced.
- Tear-off dotted line extends approximately from margin to margin.
- Document is centered on the page.

Summary

In this section you have:

- created a new word processing document.
- selected text—words and the entire document.
- changed the font face and font point size.
- changed text style.
- changed line spacing.
- changed text alignment.
- used the spell check feature.
- used **SAVE** or **SAVE AS**.
- selected paper size and page orientation.
- printed a document.

More Word Processing Features

As you gain experience with your word processing software you will begin to need more features that take you beyond typing into the world of typesetting. The activity introducing you to some of these features begins with one of the documents in the *Text Documents* folder you downloaded to accompany the textbook. If you have not yet downloaded the *Text Documents* folder do so now. See instructions at the end of Chapter 1. You need the *WP Features* document to continue with the next assignment. Open the document named ***WPFeatures.doc***.

Preferences

Preferences are choices you can make to customize your software. Many types of software, in addition to word processing software, have preferences that you can customize. Browse the *Word* menus now to locate **Preferences,** and open them. Look at all of the options you can configure—they vary with the software version. You do not need to change any preferences at this time, but be aware of which features you can modify.

Formatting Characters

Formatting characters are the normally invisible, nonprinting characters that show where spaces, tabs, and paragraph returns are placed in the text. If you have ever experienced spacing irregularities in printed documents, you will benefit from viewing the document with visible formatting characters. For the following activity you should show the formatting characters or "invisibles" as they are sometimes called. To show these characters, browse the **Standard** toolbar for a **Show/Hide ¶** icon. Click it to **Show** or **Hide** the formatting characters. If you cannot find the icon on the toolbar, return to **Preferences** (**View** tab) and turn on all of the **Nonprinting characters.** The visibility of the characters does not affect the spacing or printing of the document. Formatting characters will never appear in print.

Using Help

Software publishers are moving away from publishing print manuals to accompany their programs. On-line Help has become a feature that is accessible any time you have the software open. On-line Help is better than a printed manual because it is always at your fingertips and does not require any valuable desk space.

You should know what features are available as you begin to use unfamiliar word processing software. For example, the typist who did not know that text for a header was typed one time and automatically appeared at the top of each page obviously would not have looked to Help for information about headers. Most Help documents have an Introduction, New Features, or Basics in addition to Contents and Index lists and also the capability of searching for words or topics.

You will use the Help features of *Word* to find the answers to the questions in the *WPFeatures* document. You should be able to access the Help files from the Help menu or by clicking the Assistant "guy" in the floating window of *Word*. If you do not see the assistant, search the menus for a **Turn Assistant On** item and choose it. You can ask the assistant questions or go directly to Help Contents or Index. The on-line help files are extensive and detailed. Browse them, and also search to find answers to all of the questions in the *WPFeatures* document.

Insert the answers to each question into the *WPFeatures* document, beginning each answer with a new paragraph immediately following its question. Do not use [TAB]. Write answers in complete sentences and with enough detail that a printed copy of your document could serve as a guide to someone learning the features as you are now. Do not do any formatting at this time—no tabs or extra line spaces. When you have found and typed in all of the answers, save the document.

Use the following steps to format the document.

1. *Change alignment.* Double-space the entire document. (There should be no extra line spaces.)

2. *Add header text.* Add your name and a document page number to the header that are right aligned. Use automatic page numbering from the header toolbar.

3. *Change document margins.* Change top, bottom, left, and right document margins to ¾ " (.75).

4. *Change text style.* Select the text of each of the questions (not the answers) and change the text style to Bold.

5. *Indent blocks of answer text (not questions).* **Using the Right and Left indent markers from the Ruler,** change the margins of all answer text (not the questions) ½ " narrower than the currently set margins for the document.

6. *Inspect page, inserting a* **Page Break,** *if necessary.* Use Zoom to reduce the page image. If a complete question and answer are broken apart at the bottom of a page, insert a Page Break, just before the beginning of the question, to force the whole question and answer unit onto the next page. **Do not accomplish this by adding extra line spaces.**

7. *Check for errors.* Check the spelling and carefully peruse the document for other errors.

8. *Save and print.* Save any changes in the final document, and print one copy.

WPFeatures Checklist

- Answers to the questions are accurate.
- All spelling and grammar are accurate.
- Entire document is double spaced.
- All document margins—top, bottom, left, and right—are .75".
- Your name and page number aligned right appears in the header of all pages.
- Text of the numbered questions is formatted in bold; answers are not.
- Margins for the blocks of answer text have been narrowed by ½ " using left and right indent markers.
- Question and answer sets are not divided by natural page breaks.

Summary

In this section you have:

- examined Preferences.
- revealed hidden or nonprinting formatting characters.
- located Help documents.
- created a right-aligned header.
- numbered pages automatically.
- set document margins.
- used indent markers to adjust paragraph margins.
- used zoom to examine an entire page.
- inserted a Page Break.

Producing and Using Symbols and Special Characters

Dashing Around—The Hyphen, En Dash, and Em Dash

When typing practices developed to simulate typesetting, the hyphen key—used for hyphenating words or to break words at the end of a line—came to be used for other purposes, like making a dash. Striking two hyphens together typically makes a "typed" dash, like this: --. In typesetting there are actually two dash characters in addition to the standard hyphen: the *en dash* and the *em dash*. The en dash, which is the width of a capital N in the chosen font face, is used with duration or ranges. For example, "The flu symptoms may continue for 3–5 days" or "The meeting goes from 9:00–11:00." The em dash, the width of a capital M in the selected font face, has the purpose we more typically attribute to the dash. You may use it to indicate a change in thought or to equate similar ideas, as illustrated in the first sentence of this paragraph.

Accessing Symbols and Special Characters

Word has a feature that you can use to add special characters such as •, √, é, or the em dash or en dash. Both the Windows and the Macintosh versions of *Word* include features to access symbols and special characters. See this feature now by choosing **Symbol** from the Insert menu.

If you wish to use special characters in other software such as your e-mail program, a web page design program, or graphics software, there are still ways to produce symbols and special characters. Macintosh computers have a utility called *Key Caps*—accessed through the Apple menu or Utilities folder in OS X—that you can use to locate and then copy and paste special characters into your document. There are also key press shortcuts you can use to access these characters directly from the keyboard. On a Windows computer there is a Character Map utility—a program accessory from which you can copy and paste special characters into your documents. Also in Windows you can use the keyboard to produce the characters with key presses using numeric codes. Look at the lists of special characters and symbols and the various ways to produce them in Appendix A for both computer platforms. Use these characters at every opportunity to give your documents a professional, typeset appearance.

Using Your Skills

In the final word processing exercise you will create a school or class newsletter similar to the one illustrated in Figure 2.6. It is not necessary to have access to page layout software to make a simple one-page newsletter. In the illustrated example, the masthead (name of newspaper) is text placed in a header in a large font point size. The text is single-spaced with an extra paragraph return made between headings and text paragraphs. The font face for the headings is **Arial** in bold because a sans serif (no "feet" on the characters) font looks best for headings. The font face for the paragraph text is **Times**—a serif font with "feet" on the characters.

Use the steps below to make your own newsletter:

1. *Create a new* Word *document.*

2. *Make the masthead.* Open the header. Type the name of your newspaper—any name you choose—as text in a header. Center the header text, make it bold, and change it to a 72-point size or the largest size possible to keep the newsletter name on one line. If you need a size that does not appear in the list, type the numeral into the size box or choose **Other** . . . and enter your choice. As an option, but not necessary, you could place a border around the header text as in the illustration. Close the header.

3. *Set up multiple columns.* Use the **Columns** choice from the Format menu, or use Help to locate the column setup dialog. Choose two columns.

4. *Enter text for first column.* At this point, you will enter all of the text for both columns—not worrying about the spacing. Then, you will edit text, change alignment, and change spacing or font size to get all text pleasingly arranged on the newsletter. The first column will contain three items of news. You may use the text below or make up your own. The only criterion for the first column is that one of the news items uses the bullet character (•) and Tabs to create a list of at least four items. Use a *sans serif* font face such as **Arial** in bold for centered headings. Use a *serif* font face such as **Times** for the paragraph text.

> *Optional Text for Item #1.*
> Heading: Field Trip
> Text: Our class visited the Children's Museum last Monday. The trip was exciting, and everything went as planned. Kim's favorite exhibit was the dinosaur. Howie liked the hands-on magnet experiments best. Everyone is eager to return and explore more.

Optional Text for Item #2.

Heading: Parent Meeting

Text: The Parent Support Group will meet on Monday evening at 7:00 in the cafeteria just before Open House.

Optional Text for Item #3.

Heading: Food Baskets

Text: Our Hill Street School family is conducting a food drive to distribute holiday baskets to members of our community. Please bring or send any of the following items to the school office. The deadline is November 20. Do not bring perishable foods or items in glass containers. (First, use a [TAB] and then the Special Character called a Bullet (•) to precede each food item.) Canned fruits or vegetables, Canned meats, Canned soups, Boxed dinners, Boxed gelatin or pudding

5. *Enter text for second column.* You may or may not be at the top of the second column. At this time it does not matter. Just continue entering the text. After all text is entered and the formatting is adjusted you will establish the column break. For the second column, use the text below. Do not substitute this content.

Required Text for Item #4.

Heading: Food for Thought

Text: The computer bestows a special magic on children who have special needs by empowering them with a sense of independence and control (Male, 1988). As a powerful and versatile instructional tool, computers have enormous potential for altering the lives of exceptional children and providing them with opportunities for growth and learning. The value of the computer may be greater for exceptional youngsters than for any other population. It is widely acknowledged that computers enable ordinary people to do extraordinary things. They enable extraordinary people to do ordinary things (Trieschmann & Lerner, 1990, p. 1).

References

Male, M. (1988). *Special magic: Computers, classroom strategies, and exceptional students.* Mountain View, CA: Mayfield Publishing Co.
Trieschmann, M. & Lerner, J. (1990). *Using the computer to teach children with special needs: A guidebook of effective computer strategies.* Evanston, IL: National Lekotek Center.

6. *Save and edit.* Save the document now, before you change the formatting. With all the text entered, it is time to "fiddle" with document options. If your View—from the View menu—is **Normal,** switch it to **Page Layout.** Now, zoom out to 75% and look at the entire page.

- Set the margins for the whole document to one inch—top, bottom, left, and right.
- Does the **Food for Thought** item appear at the top of the second column? If not, place the insertion point just before the **Food for Thought** heading. Then

from the Insert menu select **Break** and then **Column Break** to force that heading to the top of the second column.

- Align text in the paragraph bodies, not the headings, to be fully justified—that is, all lines are of equal length. Sometimes this makes unusual spacing between words in some lines, but overall makes the document look more like a newspaper.

- Center the References heading. Use the indent marker to create small hanging indents for each of the two references, about ¼ to ⅜ inch.

- Examine the length of the text in the first column. The text should fill the column and be approximately the same length as the text of the second column. If it is not, you can add more text, add space between news items, or change the font point size of the headings. If you change the point size of all text, make sure the second col-

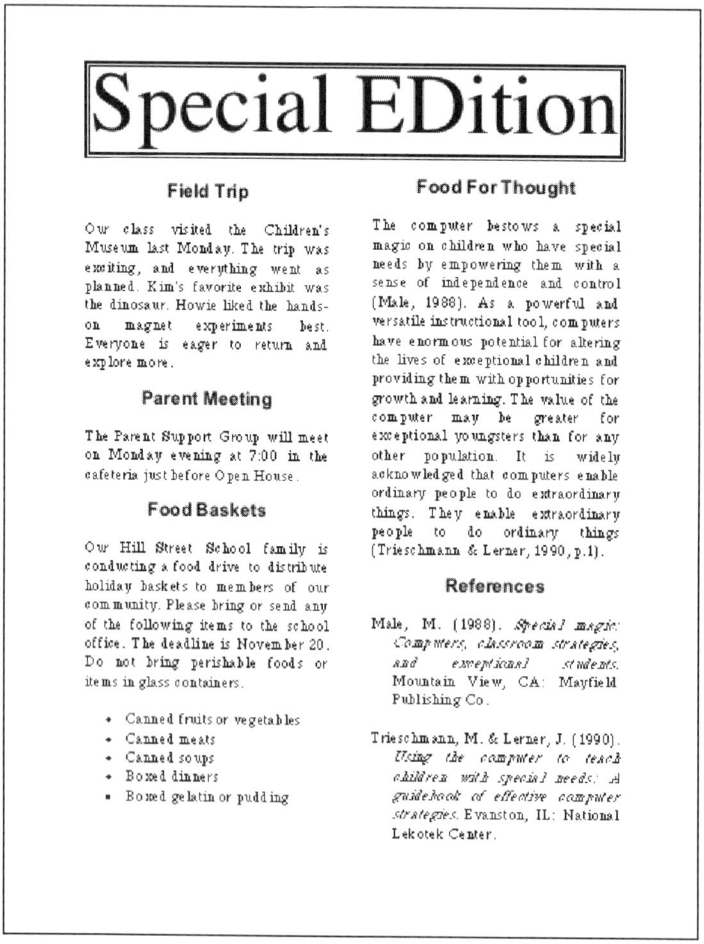

FIGURE 2.6 Sample classroom newsletter.

umn will still fit on the page. Experiment with these options, adjusting the text and spacing to make the two columns similar in length. See the sample newsletter document in Figure 2.6.

7. *Save and print the final document.*

Newsletter Checklist

- Name of newsletter is in a header, in 72-point size (or size to fit the header area), and bold.
- Body of newsletter contains two columns.
- Document margins—top, bottom, left, and right—are all one inch.
- Article headings use a sans serif font face and are bold.
- Paragraph text of the articles is a serif font face and single spaced.
- Three articles appear in the first column.
- One article contains a list of four items formatted with [TAB] and bullets.
- A column break appears at the bottom of the first column.
- The "Food for Thought" text with references appears in the second column.
- The "References" heading is centered, and the two references are formatted with hanging indents.
- Article text, including the reference text, is justified.
- Articles have been "adjusted" to balance the spacing, so that the two columns are approximately the same length.

Summary

In this section you have:

- created a document with multiple columns.
- located and used special characters.
- learned to distinguish between san serif and serif font faces.
- inserted a column break.
- created justified text.
- created hanging indents with the indent marker.
- adjusted spacing, alignment, and/or font face size to balance column lengths.

What's Next?

Some versions of *Word* allow you to convert a document to **HTML**. Look for **Save as Web Page . . .** or **Save as HTML . . .** in the File menu along with the more familiar Save options. Carefully proofread all HTML documents that you convert from *Word*. Sometimes you may discover unexpected character substitution that you will need to correct before you publish the document on the web.

Revisit the AutoFormat or AutoCorrect features. Explore what they do and how they can help you work more efficiently. Add those that make your work easier; turn off those that are intrusive.

What can you do to continue the transition from typing to typesetting? Here are some general principles:

- Press [RETURN] or [ENTER] only when you need to begin a new paragraph or to customize spacing.
- Never use two spaces after any punctuation mark.
- Use subscripts, superscripts, and special characters.
- Use en dash and em dash as necessary—not the hyphen.
- Use indent markers for references—never "fake" it with the [RETURN] or [ENTER] key and [TAB].
- Use bullets or dingbats—symbol characters in special font faces—for lists, not asterisks or hyphens.
- Use headers or footers and automatic page numbering.
- Proofread everything! Do not expect the spell checker to find grammatical errors.
- Explore the menus, button bars, toolbars, and palettes.
- Use the on-line Help to learn new features.

KEY TERMS

default	header	QWERTY
document	HTML	sans serif
em dash	landscape	serif
en dash	page break	word processing
footer	page setup	word wrap
hanging indent	portrait	

CHAPTER

3 Graphics

In this brief chapter you will explore some of the options in Microsoft's *Word* that will enable you to add pictures, drawing objects, and interesting text effects to your word processing documents. These instructions apply only to *Word* and assume that you have completed Chapter 2 using the *Word* software. With the graphics features offered in this chapter you will be able to create more interesting work sheets, letters, newsletters, and signs.

A Little Background

Before you begin working with graphics, you should understand how *Word* treats graphic images. A word processing document appears to be a sheet of paper. Seemingly, you start at the top and end at the bottom and that's it! It is not quite that simple. A word processing document actually has three layers, whereas a sheet of paper has only one. The text that you see is on the middle layer. Think of the layers as three sheets of transparent plastic. The layer on the back, or background layer, is for placing images such as watermarks. Have you ever seen a page with a pale image under the text? The **watermark** is actually an image placed on the background layer of the document behind or under the text layer. An image on the top layer floats over the text. In order to use graphics effectively with text, you need to learn the characteristics of the layers and how to achieve the effects you wish using text and graphic images on the different layers.

Look at the following examples to see the effects of graphics placed on different layers of a text document. In this paragraph an image has been moved to the background, behind the text. To make the text readable, the image has been lightened. This example is a watermark.

This second example has an image inserted into the text layer. The image appears in line with the text. A graphic image inserted into the text layer has the same characteristics as this letter M printed in a large font size. It functions just like a very large character in the line of text. Notice that these lines of text have irregular spacing. This is because the height of a character on the line exceeds the double-spaced line height.

In the example within this paragraph, the graphic image floats over the text. There are several different ways the image can be displayed. First, it can appear directly on top of the text, thereby blocking some of the text. The image can also be placed over the text, but the text can be made to "wrap" around it so that all text is visible. Text is wrapping around the cube image. The text is not blocked.

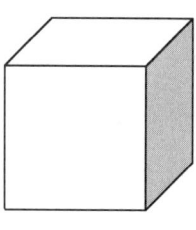

If you have experimented with manipulating graphic images in *Word* previously, you may have found it confusing. The basic skills you practice in the upcoming exercises should give you confidence to continue exploring and learning new features.

Experimenting with Clip Art

Word contains two different classes of graphic images—pictures and drawing objects. Pictures are graphic images that are brought into *Word* already made, such as photographs, image files, or **clip art**. Options for working with pictures are located on the **Picture** toolbar and are limited. Drawing objects are created or edited within *Word* using special tools located on the **Drawing** toolbar. Because pictures have fewer options—most of which also apply to drawing objects—the first graphic exercise will explore picture options.

This first exercise will allow you to explore the clip art collection built in to *Word* while you experiment with the attributes of pictures and the effects of placing them on the different document layers. Sources for images to place in your documents are endless. You could use photos from a digital camera, images captured from the Internet, or commercial clip art collections. You could draw your own, edit images acquired from another source, or take screen shots of anything you see on the screen. Regardless of the source of the image, the attributes of that image and the tools you will use to work with it will remain the same. For now, you will explore the clip art images built in to the *Word* software. The different versions of *Word* provide these options to you in slightly different ways with several sets of clip art images, arranged by category. Access to options for selecting and editing images also may vary slightly. If your software is not the same version as that used in these examples, browse the menus, toolbars, and help files to locate the appropriate options.

To experiment with integrating clip art into text, you need a text document to work with. Open the document from the *Text Documents* folder titled *Graphics1.doc*. To see images and work on them within your document, display the document in **Page Layout** from the View menu. Also from the View menu, locate and open the **Picture** and **Drawing** toolbars. As with other features of *Word*, if you let your pointer linger over these tools you can learn their names.

Arranging Images

Since you are going to insert a clip art picture into the open word processing document, go to the Insert menu, select **Picture,** and finally **Clip Art.** *Word* opens its Clip Gallery software, revealing a large selection of categories of clip art. Browse through the categories and look at some of the images.

An Image In-Line with the Text.   For this exercise, choose the Animals category. Browse the animals and choose one you would like to use. Click on the selected image, and then click on the **Insert** button. *Word* automatically places the picture into the text layer in line with the existing text; the image will appear in the text where you left the insertion point. The image you selected may be quite large. By the end of this exercise, you will have four copies of this image inserted into the *Graphics1* document—one in each paragraph; you will need to reduce its size to approximately one inch. (**Note:** Use the ruler along the top of the document as a guide. If the ruler is not visible, check **Ruler** from the View menu.)

While the image is selected you can make changes, just like you can with text that is selected or highlighted. However, unlike text, when an image is selected it is not highlighted; instead, it has "handles" on its corners and sides. **Do this:** Select the image by clicking on it. As you move across the image with your pointer, notice how the pointer changes when you move over one of the handles. Move to the lower-right corner handle. While the pointer icon is changed, grab the handle and "push" up and to the left to reduce the size of the image. Moving it by the corner reduces both its height and width proportionately. Continue on after you have changed the size of the image to about one square inch.

Experiment with the image as a part of your text. Grab it in the middle, not by one of the handles and move it elsewhere in the text. Notice that it pops into the text wherever the text insertion point is. Finally, move it into the first paragraph and leave it at the end of the first sentence. Save the document.

An Image Atop the Text.   You will continue exploring graphics by moving a copy of the same animal image to the top layer. First you must copy the image. Click on the image to select it, and then choose **Copy** from the Edit menu. Move the insertion point to the middle of the second paragraph and choose **Paste** from the Edit menu to paste a copy of the image into the second paragraph. At this point, the image has the same attributes as the one in the first paragraph. It appears to be a large character somewhere in the flow of the text.

In order to change image attributes, you must first select the image by clicking on it. Then, click the **Format Picture** button on the **Picture** toolbar. (**Format Picture** options can also be accessed by choosing **Picture** from the Format menu or by double-clicking on the desired image.) The format box should appear with tabs for selecting formatting options. Different versions of *Word* vary slightly in naming the tabs, but the options are the same. To move the image from the text layer, click the **Wrapping** or **Layout** tab (depending on the version of the software you are using). Look at the choices. The choice **In Line With Text** is the text layer—where the image is now. The choice **Behind Text** (or **None**) is the background layer. The other choices **Square** and **Tight** are for the top layer and provide two slightly different *text wrap* options—ways the text wraps around the image.

If you have moved the image behind the text, you may not be able to click on it again. The **Drawing** toolbar has a special tool for selecting objects—even when they are on another layer. The arrow tool, named **Select Objects,** will allow you to select an object that is behind the text. When you wish to return to the text layer, click on the **Select Objects** tool again to deselect it. Leave the image, approximately centered, in the second paragraph with a square text wrap. Save the document.

An Image Behind the Text. For the third activity in this exercise, you will place a watermark in the third paragraph of the *Graphics1* document.

Paste the same image into the third paragraph. This time you will move the image behind the text. As you did before, open the **Format Picture** options and select the option that places the image behind the text. So far, so good! The image is now behind the text; however, depending on the colors and contrast of the original image, you may not be able to see the text easily.

There are options you can choose to modify the image other than simply resizing, which you previously experienced. Select the image again, using the **Select Objects** tool from the **Drawing** toolbar, and open the **Format Picture** options. This time choose the **Picture** tab. You will see options in Image Control to adjust the brightness and contrast along with a dropdown menu for color options. First, play with the brightness and contrast. You can raise the brightness and reduce the contrast to create your own watermark. Now, open the dropdown Color menu. Notice that there is a choice for watermark. Choose this option. The software automatically chooses 85% brightness and 15% contrast. If you wish to change these watermark default values, you can. Just leave the image behind the text, still visible but light enough to easily read the text that flows over it. Save the document again.

Modifying Images

In the last activity of this exercise you will explore more ways to modify a clip art image. As before, copy and paste your animal picture—this time into the fourth paragraph. (Remember to deselect the **Select Objects** tool from the **Drawing** toolbar.) First, explore the "handles" on the selected image. Pull and push them to experience the results. The final effect on the image does not matter. That is, you could stretch your turtle into a giraffe as long as the document still fits on one page.

Note: The last image copied remains on the clipboard. If the image on the clipboard is from the first paragraph, clicking into the text of the third paragraph and pasting will place the pasted image at the insertion point in line with the text. If you copy the image from the second paragraph, then the pasted image will be on the top layer and may appear, not at the insertion point as it is no longer "text," but directly over the copied image. In this case, just grab the image and in moving it you will see that there is an identical image underneath.

Next, using the **Format Picture** options, place the image over the text selecting a square or tight text wrap. Now, with the image selected, open the **Format Picture** options again. This time choose the **Colors and Lines** tab. With these choices you can place a line around the image and fill the background with color. Play with these options. There are dozens of combinations to change the way the image is displayed.

The more recent versions of *Word* have additional features to enhance picture images including an effects gallery, shadows, and color adjustment. Other features include options to edit photographs, such as cropping, fixing red eye, and removing scratches. Depending on the options you have available, you can experiment with the picture in the fourth paragraph as you wish. Leave the image with a colored background and a dark line around it. Save the final version of the document.

Save and print the final document.

Graphics1 Document Checklist

- Original text is present and legible.
- All images are approximately one inch in size.
- Document is double-spaced and fits on one page.
- Animal picture in first paragraph is in-line with the text at the end of the first sentence.
- Duplicate image in second paragraph floats above the text (top layer) with a square text wrap.
- Duplicate image in third paragraph lies behind the text as a watermark.
- Duplicate image in last paragraph has a colored background, a dark line around it, and may or may not be distorted. The text wraps around it. Advanced editing features may be applied.

Summary

In this section you have:

- located the Drawing Toolbar.
- explored the Clip Art Gallery.
- modified the size of an image.
- copied and pasted an image.
- selected text wrapping options.
- used the Select Objects tool.
- created a watermark.
- experimented with background colors and lines around images.
- located advanced picture editing features.

Learning about Drawing Objects

The upcoming exercises will introduce you to some of the graphic options available when you are using drawing objects. Unlike pictures that are ready-made images, you create drawing objects, using the tools offered on the **Drawing** toolbar.

Exploring the Drawing Toolbar

The **Drawing** toolbar is packed with options that you will be experimenting with. The characteristics of drawing objects in different versions of *Word* are virtually identical. However, as illustrated in Figure 3.1, the **Drawing** toolbars of *Word 2001* and *Word 98* for Macintosh look very different. Dragging the tiny striped area on the lower-right-hand corner can also reshape Toolbars.

Begin a new document in *Word*. Open the **Drawing** toolbar. As with your previous experiences identifying toolbar buttons, you can let the pointer linger on the buttons to discern their names. Several of these buttons have extended menus attached to them. Look at the first item of each toolbar. The first tool is **Draw**. Whichever toolbar you have, press on the **Draw** button and browse the options there. You will use some of these options later. Close the **Draw** button options and locate the **AutoShapes** button. The button may be represented by an icon image of stacked geometric shapes, such as a circle, square, and rectangle. When you expand the **AutoShapes** button, you will see further choices that expand. Each of these individual shape menus—**Basic Shapes**, **Block Arrows**, and others—can be "torn off" of the toolbar. **Do this:** To tear off the **Basic Shapes** toolbar, Open **AutoShapes**, slide to the **Basic Shapes** choice, slide across **Basic Shapes** to its menu bar and let go. The **Basic Shapes** palette will remain open on your screen to provide easy access to its options. Look through the different choices on the **Drawing** toolbar to locate other tear-off palettes. Once open, palettes can be arranged on your screen, out of the way of your work, to provide easy access to all drawing tools. If you inadvertently initiate some graphic option that you did not expect, just cancel it or close its window.

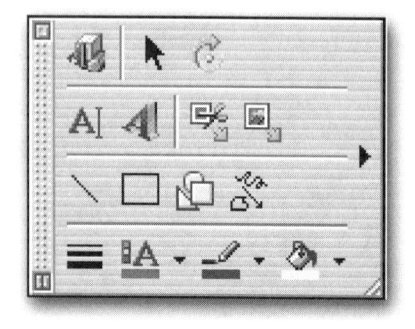

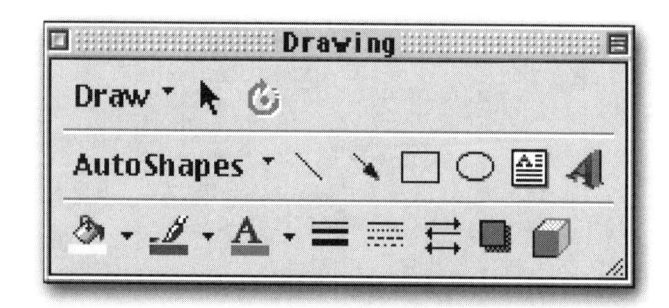

FIGURE 3.1 *Word 2001* Drawing toolbar (left) and *Word 98* Drawing toolbar (right).
Screen shot reprinted with permission from Microsoft Corporation.

Using AutoShapes and Lines

In this portion of the instruction you will begin with a new blank document. In each activity you will practice with the tools and features, ending up with an image on your document, deleting all the practice images. As you work through each section you will add another image to the "collection" ending up with a one-page document illustrating many of the drawing features of *Word*. See a completed sample document in Figure 3.4. Then, at the end of this section you will be given a choice of exercises to complete using the skills you have learned while exploring—putting it all together. The instructions are designed to give you only the most basic experiences with the drawing objects options. Try other options as you explore. If you inadvertently do something you do not want, you can select **Undo** from the Edit menu.

Unlike pictures, which are inserted in line with the text on the text layer, drawing objects automatically appear on the top layer of the document. Since that is the case, it is not necessary to have text in the document in order for you to experiment with drawing objects. To begin, you should have a blank *Word* document, the **Drawing** toolbar open, and the **Basic Shapes** palette "torn off" from the **AutoShapes** menu.

Drawing AutoShapes. From the **Basic Shapes** palette select the **Oval** tool. The text insertion I-beam turns into a drawing crosshair. Move to a spot where you would like to draw an oval. Click and drag to create an oval. As with pictures, you can manipulate an object's size and shape by pushing and pulling on the handles that are visible while the object is selected. Try this now with an oval. Click away from the oval; then click on it again to select it. Choose the oval tool again; draw another oval. Click on the **Rectangle** tool. Draw several rectangles any place on the document. Can you use the **Rectangle** tool to make a perfect square? Can you use the **Oval** tool to make a perfect circle? Try doing this before you read on!

Here is a really big tip! In order to make regular figures—that is, perfect squares or circles—press the [SHIFT] key after you select the tool and continue holding it until you have the shape completed. Now, make a perfect circle with the **Oval** tool and a perfect square with the **Rectangle tool.**

You should fully explore the other **Basic Shapes** tools in addition to those on the other AutoShape palettes—**Block Arrows, Callouts,** and **Stars & Banners.** (Note: Depending on the version of *Word* you have, you may have the **Lines** palette. At this time, ignore the **Lines** palette. You will explore line features later.) Learn how each tool responds to being drawn with the [SHIFT] key depressed. Notice that the **Callout** AutoShapes allow text to be placed within the shape.

You may have discovered that some of the AutoShape figures have an additional feature. **Do this:** Select the **Smiley Face** tool and draw a smiley face. While the smiley face is selected, notice that there is a small yellow diamond in the center of the smile. This "handle" can be adjusted. Pull or push on the adjustment handle to turn your smiley face into a frowning face! Several other AutoShape figures also have this feature. Try adjusting other AutoShape images to see the variations. Before you move on, fully explore the wide variety of shapes on the various **AutoShapes** palettes. What variations can you make both by holding down [SHIFT] while you draw and also by dragging the "adjustment" handles?

Modifying AutoShapes. Now that you have mastered drawing AutoShapes, look at some ways to modify their appearance. You may have a big mess on your document. Delete some of the images: While a shape is selected press [DELETE] or [BACKSPACE]. You do not need to save any work you have done so far.

First, you are going to experiment with shape **Fill Color** along with **Line Color** and **Line Style**. Draw any AutoShape, making it approximately two to three inches in size. On the **Drawing** toolbar, locate the **Fill Color** button. Next to the **Fill Color** tool is a drop-down color menu that you can open by clicking on the tiny black triangle. The selected color is indicated under the tool. Choose a color from the **Fill Color** palette to fill the shape you drew. To fill a previously drawn shape, click on the **Fill Color** tool (the paint bucket). When the tool is clicked, the selected shape fills with the chosen color. If no shape is selected, the color choices are not available. Choosing another color will replace the one you previously selected.

Line Color and **Line Style** refer to the line on the outside edge of any drawing object. To modify the line, first select the drawing object, then choose a color for the line and apply it by clicking on the **Line Color** tool. In addition to color, the width of the line can be modified. Locate the **Line Style** tool and browse the choices. Choose a six-point solid line.

There are some additional fill color and line color options that can be accessed at the bottom of the **Line Color** and the **Fill Color** palettes—**Patterned Lines** and **Fill Effects**. Select the AutoShape again and play with these additional features. If you have selected a wide line, the patterns will be more evident.

Drawing and Configuring Lines. In addition to shapes, you can draw lines with a variety of useful tools. Open the **Lines** palette and tear it off the toolbar. (Note: Depending on the version of *Word* you are using, the **Lines** palette may be one of the AutoShape palettes or it may be on the **Drawing** toolbar.) Make some space on your document. Now experiment with each of the tools on the **Lines** palette. The **Curve** tool requires you to click to change direction, and both the **Curve** and **Freeform** tools require you to double-click to end a line. What you previously learned about the color, width, and pattern options for lines around shapes also applies to all of the lines you have just created with the **Lines** palette. So you could make a wide double-pointed arrow colored with a red plaid pattern—try it! The possibilities are practically endless.

There is one additional feature of lines to consider. You have discovered that two of the **Lines** tools create arrows. However, lines created by any one of the six **Lines** tools can have arrow styles applied to them. Locate the **Arrow Styles** button. It may be on the **Drawing** toolbar or on an extension of the **Drawing** toolbar that can be opened by clicking on the tiny black triangle along the bottom or right edge, depending on how the toolbar is being displayed. First, select the line to which you wish to apply an arrow style. Then open the **Arrow Styles** choices and choose one.

Arranging Drawing Objects. Delete all previous practice on the page, as this time you will be saving your work. All of these next features can be accessed from the **Draw** button on the **Drawing** toolbar. Unfortunately, this menu does not tear off. Begin by drawing a circle, about one inch in diameter, and filling it with blue (a balloon). While the image is still selected, copy it (choose **Copy** from the Edit menu). Now choose **Paste** from the Edit menu to place a second blue balloon into your document. With the second balloon selected, change its color to yellow. Paste again, this time changing the balloon color to red. You should now have three balloons—blue, yellow, and red—probably overlapping each other.

Select the yellow balloon and move it back and forth across the other balloons. Then move each of the other balloons. Notice that the balloons seem to be on separate layers. The blue one is behind the other two. The graphic layer of the word processing document is actually "layers." Each drawing object you create resides on its own layer in the order that it is created. Experiment with this feature by selecting the yellow balloon. Open the drop-down **Draw** menu from the **Drawing** toolbar and expand the **Arrange** or **Order** submenu. The **Order** palette is also tear-off for easy access to these features. Moving an object forward or backward moves it one layer toward the front or toward the back. Moving an object to the back places it behind all other objects; conversely, moving an object to the front places it in front of all other drawing objects. Experiment with moving the balloons back and forth, overlapping each other. Leave the balloons with the blue and red balloons next to each other, nearly touching, and the yellow one on top and slightly above the others as illustrated in the following image.

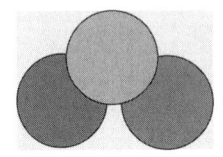

Using the **Curve** tool from the **Lines** palette, make strings for each of the three balloons.

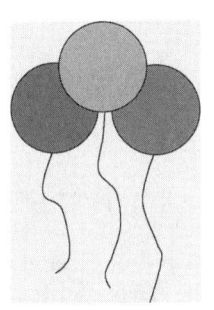

Grouping Drawing Objects. If you were to try to move the bunch of balloons to another location, or to copy them to use in another document, you may have a problem. There are six parts to the balloon graphic—three balloons and three strings with nothing holding the parts together. There is a special option available in the **Draw** menu, called ***Group,*** which enables you to "glue" or unite individual objects into a single image. Before you initiate the **Group** command, however, you must first select the elements you wish to unite into a single image. You may have noticed that if one object is selected, when you click on another object to select it, the first object becomes deselected. That is, only one object can be selected at a time. When you wish to use **Group** to unify parts, you need a way to select more than one object at a time. The method for this is easy. It is called Shift-Click. To use it, hold down the [SHIFT] key while you click on each element you wish to group. When you have all six elements of the balloon image selected, choose the **Group** option from the **Draw** menu of the **Drawing** toolbar.

Now, try moving the balloon image. You should be pleasantly surprised to find that you have a single image! If perhaps you missed a part, move the pieces back into position, Shift-Click the parts, and choose **Group** again. Any image that has been created of grouped parts can also be ungrouped. Notice the ***Ungroup*** option in the same menu. Move the balloons to the top of the document. The balloon image is the first image of the "collection" you will save for the drawing object activity. Save the document with the name *Graphics2* on your personal disk.

Flipping and Rotating Drawing Objects. The next experience with drawing objects will give you some practice with flipping and rotating. In order to have an image with which to experiment, you will create a fish using some of the skills you have previously practiced. The following step-by-step instructions will walk you through the steps for creating a more complicated image.

- Make a gold/yellow oval 1 to 1½ inches long (goldfish body).

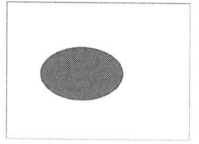

- Make a tiny black round circle to represent an eye.

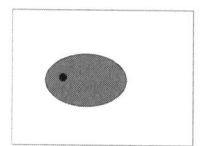

- Make a tail using the **Moon** tool from the **Basic Shapes** palette. Shape the tail as you wish.

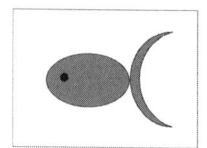

- Make fins using the **Moon** tool. Because you only want to see half of the moon, move each of the fins to the back, placing them behind the body.

- The basic elements of the fish are assembled. Now, Shift-Click all parts and **Group** them. Before you continue, check that all the parts are grouped and put together as you planned. If not, **Ungroup** and redo until the fish is perfect.
- **Tip:** If the "moon" fins appear in front of the fish body, Ungroup, move each one to the back, and Group again: Draw/Arrange/Send to Back.

To experiment with flipping and rotating, copy the fish; then paste it six times. Move the fish images around so they are no longer overlapping but remain close together. Select one fish. Open the **Draw** menu, slide down to **Rotate or Flip,** and tear off that palette for easy access. Experiment with each of the features with your school of seven fish. Notice that nothing seems to happen when you choose **Free Rotate.** The handles on the selected fish have become special handles that you can grab and drag to freely rotate the fish.

Use **Rotate or Flip** to modify each fish. The fish exercise completes this section. Save the document again.

Producing Text Effects

There are two techniques in *Word* to add interesting text effects to your documents—**Text Box** and **WordArt**.

Text Box. You will examine the Text Box first. The concept of a text box is simple. You draw a box and put text in it! Try this out. Select the **Text Box** tool from the **Drawing** toolbar or choose **Text Box** from the Insert menu. Your insertion point will turn into a crosshair. Drag a box (size does not matter as you can change it later). Type the information you wish to display into the box and modify text, as you like, using standard text formatting features from the **Formatting** toolbar or the **Formatting Palette.** The box has all the attributes of other drawing objects. That is, you can change the box color or pattern, the outside line width, color, or pattern. You can even group it with other drawing objects as illustrated in Figure 3.2.

The possibilities for text boxes within the documents you create are endless. You can place text anywhere you want on a page, free from the spacing restrictions of a

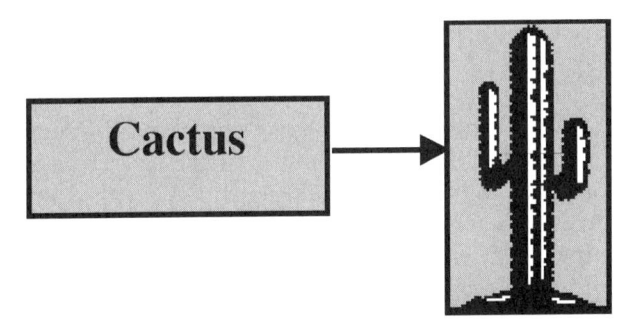

FIGURE 3.2 An image grouped with a text box and arrow.

traditional text format. From placing "sidebars" with extra information in a small box to creating labels that point to elements of an image, to signs you make to advertise a bake sale, car wash, sporting event, or a school play, text boxes free you to be creative in placing text on a page.

Next, you will use the **Text Box** you just made to label an image that will be similar to the "cactus" illustration. First, select any one of the **AutoShape** images and draw it on your document below the fish. Place this illustration below the fish. (**Note:** You can use a clip art image instead of an AutoShapes image. Although you know that clip art images do not have the same attributes as drawing objects, when clip art images are grouped with drawing objects, the unified object becomes a drawing object.) Take the practice text box you already have and format it to match the size, shape, or color of the image you placed below the fish. Type the name of the object into the text box. Next, draw an arrow to point from the text box to the image. Format each part to coordinate with each other pleasingly. Finally, Shift-Click the components and **Group** them into a single drawing object. Save the document.

Next, you will place three text boxes into the document to label the exercises you have already completed. Place a text box, formatted as you choose, beside the balloons. Include the following text:

> Make a circle by holding [SHIFT] down while drawing an oval. Unify the image parts using GROUP.

Place a second text box beside or under the fish. Put the following text in that box:

> Use ROTATE OR FLIP to modify drawing objects.

Place a final text box beside the text box labeled image. Use this text:

> Make labels with Text Boxes.

You will be adding one more element to this activity—a title created with **WordArt**. Since you will be adding the title to the top of the page, arrange the balloons, fish, and text box images to allow space of about two inches at the top of the page. Keep the entire activity on one page. If necessary, use Print Preview or the Zoom option to view the entire page. Save the document again.

WordArt. You can produce fancy effects with **WordArt** like the ones in Figure 3.3. Make a WordArt object now. Choose the **WordArt** button from the **Drawing** toolbar.
   Select a style from the WordArt Gallery, and enter the text: **Drawing Objects.** Move your WordArt object up to the top of the document. While the WordArt object is selected, the **WordArt** toolbar is available. Look at the choices there now. Most of them allow you to modify the style, the text, format, shape, and other word alignment options. Because WordArt is a drawing object, features you have already experienced (such as **Line Color** and **Fill Color**) also apply to **WordArt**. Experiment with other effects on the **Draw** menu from the **Drawing** toolbar; for example, **Shadow** or **3-D**.

CHAPTER 3 / Graphics   33

Fancy **Gradient** **Swoop**

FIGURE 3.3 Examples of WordArt.

When you have formatted the WordArt to your satisfaction, examine the whole page with **Print Preview** from the File menu. Check the document against the next checklist. Also see a sample page illustrated in Figure 3.4. Edit as is necessary, and save the completed document.

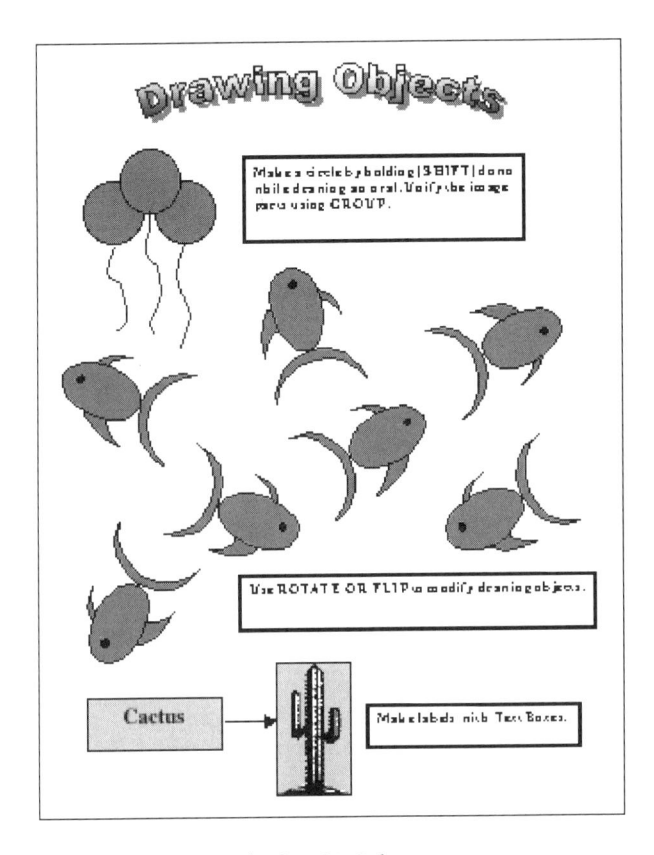

FIGURE 3.4 Sample *Graphics2* document.

Graphics2 Checklist

- A WordArt title, *Drawing Objects*, appears at the top of the page.
- Red, yellow, and blue round balloons are grouped with strings.
- Seven fish, flipped and rotated, are positioned below the balloons.
- An image, AutoShape or clip art, is united with a text box, containing a label for the image. An arrow points to the image.
- Three text boxes, each with text as described in the instructions, accompany the three images.
- The entire exercise appears on one page.

Summary

In this section you have:

- explored the Drawing toolbar.
- placed tear-off tool palettes on the screen.
- drawn basic AutoShapes.
- resized objects by pushing or pulling the "handles."
- used [SHIFT] along with a tool to make regular shapes.
- used Fill Color, Line Color, and Line Style to modify AutoShapes.
- explored the advanced options for Patterned Lines and Fill Effects.
- changed the layered order of drawing objects.
- grouped multiple objects to create a single image.
- rotated and flipped drawing objects.
- inserted, formatted, and grouped text boxes.
- created and modified WordArt.

What's Next?

You have explored the basics of using pictures and drawing objects in your word processing documents. There are ways the options could be combined that you have not explored. There are other features not covered in these instructions that you may wish to explore at another time.

Listed below are some activities for you to implement to get more practice using the graphic options of *Word*. Creating these documents will give you the opportunity to combine graphic features in different ways, in addition to giving you ideas on ways you can make more interesting, informative, and attractive documents. For each activity, use the entire page.

1. *Use AutoShapes, the Lines palette, and Text Boxes.* Create a diagram of an aquarium. Use a Landscape page orientation in Page Setup. Make several fish, rocks, plants, and round bubbles. Make small text boxes that label the four major elements—fish, rocks, plants, and bubbles. Place four arrows that point from each label to at least one of the images of that category.

2. *Create a class newsletter.* Use Portrait page orientation in Page Setup. Employ WordArt to make a large masthead at the top of the page for the name of your newsletter. Use Text Boxes to space the articles around the page. Place appropriate graphic images among the text boxes.

3. *Make a science diagram to illustrate the diagram* of a cell, the parts of a flower or plant, the parts of an insect, the solar system, or the food pyramid. Use Text Boxes and arrows to identify the parts.

4. *Make a sign that could be posted around the school.* Use Landscape page orientation. The subject of the sign could be a car wash, bake sale, sporting event, or school play. Include all of the information necessary for viewers to get to the event—date, time, place, and cost. Use clip art images and drawing tools to add illustrations that are appropriate to the topic. Use Text Boxes for large, clear text.

KEY TERMS

clip art	text wrap	watermark
group	ungroup	

CHAPTER 4

Spreadsheets

This chapter introduces you to the basics of ***spreadsheet*** software—software designed to manipulate numeric values. Spreadsheets are used to organize business expenses, calculate budgets, and predict profits. Simple spreadsheet formulas can automatically add columns of numbers and calculate averages and do any mathematical function instantly, easily, and neatly! The first impression most people have of spreadsheets is of an accountant crunching large columns of figures for a business. You might say to yourself, "This is not for me!" Do you keep a checkbook? Do you ever have to calculate grades? Have you ever kept track of trip expenses? Did you ever wonder how many red candies would be in the next bag of M&Ms? If you do any of these things, then a spreadsheet is for you too!

Spreadsheet software can be an incredible tool for educators both as a utility (grade books to make your job easier) and as an instructional tool (predicting red M&Ms in the next bag or constructing formulas to calculate the area of geometric figures). You will be developing two spreadsheets. The first, a simple activity you might use with students; the second is a grade book.

The spreadsheet software illustrated in this chapter is *Excel* from *Microsoft Office 2001* for Macintosh. However, the basics covered in this content are the same for other spreadsheet software including *Excel 2000* (Windows), the earlier (*Excel 97*-Windows, *Excel 98*-Macintosh), and newer versions of *Microsoft Excel* (*v.X*-Macintosh and *XP*-Windows).

Exploring a Blank Spreadsheet

Open the *Excel* software to reveal a new blank spreadsheet document. In most aspects it will be similar to the blank spreadsheet illustrated in Figure 4.1. *Excel* has powerful capabilities for complex problems so you may actually see a **Workbook** with multiple spreadsheets or worksheets. See the tabs along the bottom of Figure 4.1. In this chapter you will only deal with one spreadsheet at a time. So, if you have multiple sheets, just select the first one and ignore the rest.

If you do not see the cell name box or the formula bar above the first row of cells, choose **Formula Bar** from the View menu to reveal it. The **Formula Bar** choice should have a check mark beside it. From the list of toolbars in the View menu show **Standard**

FIGURE 4.1 A blank spreadsheet document in *Excel*.
Screen shot reprinted with permission from Microsoft Corporation.

and **Formatting.** Also show the **Formatting Palette** if you have that option. Move any toolbar that may be overlapping the **Formula Bar.**

The spreadsheet appears as a grid with columns across the top labeled with letters and rows down the left side labeled with numerals. Each little data box, or cell, is named according to its location (coordinates) on the grid. Move the mouse pointer over the grid and click in different cells. Watch the cell names appear in the cell name box in the **Formula Bar.** Also observe that the letter and numeral coordinates of the column and row headings for the selected cell are highlighted. You can also move around the entire grid with the arrow keys on the keyboard. Try navigating around the spreadsheet grid with the arrow keys.

Notice the toolbars and formatting palette, if you have one. Many of the formatting features you became familiar with in word processing are also available here. However, other features will look quite unfamiliar! Lingering on a button with your mouse pointer will reveal the button name. As with word processing software, extensive Help files are only a mouse click away. Use Help when you encounter an unfamiliar term or option.

Making a Simple Spreadsheet

Entering Data into a Spreadsheet

Click in cell B2 and type **98**. You can see what you are typing in the right half of the **Formula Bar** (View menu). Press [RETURN] or [ENTER] to enable *Excel* to accept the values. Your cursor should now appear in the cell below—B3.

> **Note:** It is possible that your cursor could have moved across to C2 instead of down to B3. Along with the [RETURN] or [ENTER], [TAB] can be configured to accept the information you enter and move your cursor to the next cell—either down or across the grid. In a case where you may be entering a considerable amount of data at one time, possibly horizontally instead of vertically, you can use the Preferences to determine which key accepts the new data and moves you ahead to the next cell in the direction you wish to move!

Enter the following values into the four cells of column B directly below the 98: **76, 58, 99, 82**. Next, click in cell B1 and type **What We Weigh**. Press [RETURN] or [ENTER]. You have created a list of children's weights. The students wish to learn what their total weight is and what their average weight is. You will learn how to do that next.

Creating a Formula

You have seen that whether you enter words or numerals into the grid, the characters you type appear in the cells. Next, you want to sum the values that appear in cells B2, B3, B4, B5, and B6 and place the total in cell B7. In order to place a formula that calculates a total or an average (or any other mathematical function) into a cell, you need to send a signal to *Excel* that what you are entering is not to be displayed. You do not want to see **B2+B3+B4+B5+B6** written in cell B7. You want to see **413** (the correct total) displayed in cell B7. The secret to typing a formula is the equals sign (=). Begin any formula with an equals sign (=), and the software displays the results of the formula, not the text of the formula.

Try it now. Click in cell B7. Enter a simple formula to calculate the total of the children's weights (type the cell references—B2, B3, etc.—into the formula, not the actual weights):

= B2+B3+B4+B5+B6

and press [RETURN] or [ENTER]. You should see **413** displayed in cell B7. If you do not, click in B7 and look carefully at the formula displayed in the **Formula Bar** at the top. Did you leave out the equals sign? Remember, **all** formulas must begin with the equals sign.

Now try this: Go back to cell B4, and replace the 58 with **62**. Watch the total change; the total should now be **417**. Presto! The formula remembers to add the contents of the cells—not the specific values.

Next, place a label in cell A7 called **Total Weight.** Also add a label to cell A8 called **Average Weight.** Do not be concerned at this time about sizes of the cells or length of the text labels. Then move to cell B8.

You will place a formula in cell B8 to display the average weight of the children. First, you will look at two ways to do this. Conceptually, the simplest way to calculate the average weight would be:

= (B2+B3+B4+B5+B6)/5

The formula above adds the five weights (note the parentheses) then divides "/" by **5.** You have already calculated the total in B7, so instead of the simple formula printed above, you could use this formula:

= B7/5

In this formula the software looks to see what is in B7 and divides that by 5. **Enter this formula.** It is simpler, and you are less likely to make a typing error. The average weight should be **83.4.** If it is not, click in cell B8, examine the formula in the formula bar, and make corrections. The answer could also differ if the weights of the children in your spreadsheet are not the same as those in this text.

Save the document now, if you have not yet saved it.

Changing the Appearance of the Spreadsheet

You can change the appearance of a spreadsheet document by formatting the cells using the formatting options you are already familiar with from word processing. Cells can be formatted individually, by row, or by column.

1. *Format Column B to be centered.* Click on the **B** at the top of the column to select the entire column. Find the alignment options from the formatting palette or toolbar and choose **Align Center.**

2. *Change alignment, point size, and text style of text labels.* Cell by cell, choose the text label cells—**Total Weight** and **Average Weight,** and make the text in each one display in bold with a fourteen-point font size and aligned right. **What We Weigh** is already centered. Change its style to bold and the font point size to fourteen. Also make the total and average cells (B7 and B8) bold.

3. *Change column width.* The label in cell B1 may now be wider (or taller) than the column, depending on the original column width, font face, and type size. Move your pointer to the **B** heading of the column. As you move over the right edge of the column, when your cursor changes to a double-pointed arrow, drag the column edge to the right to widen it. Also modify the width of column **A** if the labels are too wide for the column. Another way to change column width and row height is through Format menu options. If the row height is inadequate, choose Format menu, then **Row,** and **Height** to increase the row height enough to display the complete label. (You could also change column width through options in the Format menu.)

4. *Change number format.* Another dimension of formatting in a spreadsheet is number format. How do you want numbers displayed? Are they currency? Are they

percents? Do you want decimals to display one place, two places, or more? Format the cell displaying the average weight (B8) to one decimal place. Click in cell B8. You can locate number format from the Formatting Palette or the Format menu (Cells), depending on your version of *Excel*. Open that feature now and examine the choices. Experiment with some of the choices and watch the effect on the number displayed in B8. Leave the number in a number format displaying one decimal place.

Printing a Spreadsheet

1. *Add header text.* Before printing, use the **Header and Footer** feature (View menu) to add header text to your document. Sometimes the software offers you preset headers. If it does, bypass those choices, choose **Custom** and type your own name in the left section of the header. If you wish to change font face, size, or style of the header locate the text button from among the header tools. Then close the header box and choose **Print Preview** from the File menu to view the document with the header.

2. *Set the* **Print Area**. In most cases with a spreadsheet you need to determine what portion of the document you wish to print. If you have scrolled down or to the right, you may have seen that there are potentially many pages in the document. You should establish the print area **before** you initiate printing. Select from A1 diagonally down to the right to include the last cell you wish to print. In the case of the current project, drag from A1 down through B8. Look in the File menu, **Print Area,** and choose **Set Print Area. Note:** You must always highlight the cells **before** you set the print area.

3. *Show the column and row headings.* Examine the print options offered from the File menu, **Page Setup.** Notice that there are four tabs of options. Browse the features of each tab. In *Excel,* Page Setup has options to add a header or footer, print row and column headings, print the cell grid, and adjust document margins (in addition to page orientation and paper size, which you had previously located in this menu). Go to the **Sheet** tab and place a check mark next to the option to print the **Row and column headings.**

4. *Proofread and edit.* Use **Print Preview** from the File menu again to see how the finished spreadsheet actually looks. You should see the row and column headings this time. Save any changes you have made.

5. *Print the spreadsheet.* Print the final version. See an illustration of the finished spreadsheet in Figure 4.2.

What We Weigh Checklist

- Your name appears in a document header.
- Column and row headings are visible.
- Column widths have been modified to fit the text labels.
- **What We Weigh** label in cell B1 is bold, 14-point, and centered.
- Data in cells B2–B6 are accurate.
- Formulas in B7 and B8 are correct.
- Text labels in A7 and A8 are bold, 14-point, and right aligned.

```
Your Name

         |       A        |      B       |
    1    |                | What We Weigh|
    2    |                |      98      |
    3    |                |      76      |
    4    |                |      62      |
    5    |                |      99      |
    6    |                |      82      |
    7    |  Total Weight  |     417      |
    8    | Average Weight |     83.4     |
```

FIGURE 4.2 The final appearance of the *What We Weigh* spreadsheet.

Summary

In this section you have:

- examined a blank spreadsheet.
- typed words and numerals into spreadsheet cells.
- entered simple formulas for sums and averages.
- changed alignment and font size for data in cells.
- changed column width.
- changed number format.
- added header text.
- selected the Print Area.
- selected options to print row and column headings.

Creating a Grade Book

In the following exercises you will create a grade book for a few students. Then you will explore charting data and learn a better way to create formulas.

Creating a New Spreadsheet and Entering Data

Open a new blank spreadsheet document and enter all of the data into the cells indicated.

Cell A1: **Fall Semester Grades**
Cell B2: **Test 1**
Cell C2: **Test 2**
Cell D2: **Test 3**
Cell E2: **Total Points**
Cell F2: **Percent**
Cell A3: **Possible Points,** then **75, 75,** and **100** in cells B3, C3, and D3 respectively. (Do not type the commas.)

Next, skipping row 4, enter five student names in A5-A9 along with the three test scores for each of them into each of the test columns B, C, and D. Copy the student data from the following table. See the spreadsheet with data entered in Figure 4.3 or Table 4.1.

There are some cosmetic changes: to center the numerals, make the headings bold, and widen the columns to accommodate the text labels. You will make these formatting changes last, after all of the "working" parts of the spreadsheet are completed. Save the spreadsheet now.

TABLE 4.1

Susan	75	72	92
Eli	68	70	88
Thomas	74	72	94
Abigail	58	68	89
Hank	73	69	80

Using a Function to Create a Formula

In the first spreadsheet you made, you used a logical arithmetic equation to create formulas for adding numerals and calculating an average. There is a better and easier way to create formulas that you will learn now. First, inspect the spreadsheet. The first calculation you will make is to add the total points, including both possible points and actual points the five students earned. Use the following steps to sum these values using a function.

Locate Function. First click in cell E3, the cell where you want the first total to appear. This is the total number of points possible for the three tests. Next, open **Func-**

	A	B	C	D	E	F
1	Fall Semester Grades					
2		Test 1	Test 2	Test 3	Total Points	Percent
3	Possible Point	75	75	100		
4						
5	Susan	75	72	92		
6	Eli	68	70	88		
7	Thomas	74	72	94		
8	Abigail	58	68	89		
9	Hank	73	69	80		
10						
11						
12						

FIGURE 4.3 Grade book spreadsheet immediately after entering student data.

tion from the Insert menu. You will see a Function box listing all of the functions possible along with their categories. As you browse through them, you will see that you can execute just about any function you can imagine—and then some! Regardless of the software version you are using, categories of functions are similar. Select the **All** category. Locate, from the list on the right, the function to add values called **SUM**. Select **SUM** and click **OK**.

Use the SUM Function to Add Values. There are several ways to complete the SUM formula. In *Excel*, the software guesses a cell range to sum if there are cells adjacent to the formula cell that have values in them. It may select the three test scores in the

Note: The newer versions of *Excel*—*2000, 2001* or *XP, v.X*—have features (that you are not using at this time) that can assist you if you want to use the spreadsheet for database purposes. Sometimes, when you make a column or row of continuous text labels (like in this grade book), or when you save for the first time, the Office Assistant intrudes and asks if you would like help with list management. Just politely say "No," and continue! However, *Excel* may go ahead and turn your grade book into a database. You will know because you will see a thick blue line around all or part of the data, and you will also see little arrows in each of the cells across the first row. If this happens remove this feature: Open the List toolbar (from the toolbars in the View menu). Then open the **List** dropdown menu, from the List toolbar, and choose **Remove List Manager.**

prior three cells. If the cells that *Excel* has guessed are the correct ones, click **OK**. If *Excel* has not guessed cells or guessed incorrectly, type it yourself. Now, click in cell E3 and observe the formula in the function bar. It should be:

> = SUM(B3:D3)

Notice that it begins with an equals sign followed by the SUM function. Between the parentheses you will see **(B3:D3)**. The addition will begin with cell B3 and end with cell D3 and include all cells between. You should have a summed value in cell E3 that is **250**.

Variations on SUM. Adding values is one of the most frequently used mathematical functions in spreadsheets. Consequently, there are several different shortcuts to produce these formulas. First, you may see the Σ symbol on the toolbar. Pressing this button while you have the cursor in a cell will initiate placing a SUM formula in that cell. This saves the step of locating the **Function** menu item and choosing **SUM** from it. Another way to access the **SUM** function is to directly type the formula into the formula bar, ensuring that the cell in which you wish to display the **SUM** formula is selected. You can actually type the cell references into the formula bar, or you can begin the formula through the "(", carefully click in each cell you wish to include, close the formula with the ")", and press [Return] or [Enter].

There is considerable flexibility with spreadsheets and various ways to reach the same ends. The variations in ways to enter the SUM function apply to entering other functions as well.

Copying the Formula to Other Cells

In this step you will copy the formula down the column of grades to apply it to totals for each of the five students' test scores. First, click in the cell E3 to select it. When the cell is selected you will notice a very tiny box at its bottom right corner. This is called the **fill handle**. As you move your pointer over the fill handle, see the pointer change to a tiny outlined square with arrows on the corners. Carefully drag down to select the cells that include all five students' data.

You should now see totals for each student printed in the Totals column. In addition, you may see a zero displayed in cell E4. Ignore the zero for now. Click in each of the rows and observe how the formula has changed as it was pasted into each row. When the formula was copied to different rows, it adjusted itself to calculate the values in that particular row. This is called a *relative cell reference.* Relative means that the cell reference changes to reflect the row (or column) it has been pasted to.

Calculating Averages for Each Test

At the bottom of each of the three test columns you will place an average for the students' scores for each of the tests—cells B10, C10, and D10. First, in cell A10 place a text label **Test Average.** Move right to select cell B10 to place the first average formula. **AVERAGE** is a function just like **SUM**. Use **Function** from the Insert menu. Create a formula to average the values in cells B5 through B9. (Cell B3 should not be included because that score is not a student test score.) Create the Average formula now.

When you have successfully placed the correct average in cell B10 (69.6), use the same copy-formula method you used before to copy the formula across through cells C10 and D10. You should now have Row 10 displaying first a label, **Test Average,** followed by average scores for the three tests in the next three cells, B10 (69.6), C10 (70.2), and D10 (88.6).

Calculating the Overall Percentage for Each Student

Click into the cell where you wish the first student's percent score to appear—cell F5. Now, look at the spreadsheet data. How do you calculate percent? You could calculate Susan's overall percentage by dividing 239 (her total on the three tests) by 250 (the total possible test points) and multiplying by 100. Eli's percent is 226 (his total) divided by the same 250 possible points. The percent score for each student uses the total from cell E3 as the divisor. The percent formula you **could** enter for Susan is:

=E5/E3   Do not enter this formula!

If you used this formula and copied it down the column for each additional student, then the cell reference for the next rows would change as follows:

=E6/E4

=E7/E5

=E8/E6

=E9/E7

Keep reading!

With what you have learned about **relative cell reference,** it should be clear that in the formula you are about to make, you want the cell reference for the student total to change as you calculate for each student, but not for the 250 value. That value must not change. That cell reference cannot be relative.

In the whole column of percent scores formulas, the first cell reference should be relative; that is, it should change with the row numbers to reflect the grades of each different student. However, the E3 cell reference needs to be fixed. It must remain constant in each row. There is a different way to refer to a cell you wish to be a constant. It is called *absolute cell reference.* Absolute means that you want to use cell E3 in the first formula, and you want the same E3 to be the divisor in the formula that is copied to all of the cells. There is a special way to write the cell reference when you wish it to be absolute. You would write it this way: **E3,** placing a **$** in front of each character in the cell reference to define it as fixed or absolute.

Now click in cell F5, the location for Susan's percent score, and type the following formula:

=E5/E3

You should see a number (not in percent format yet) that represents the percent correct for Susan's total test scores. The score should be **0.956**. Do you remember how you accessed the number format back in the first spreadsheet you made? Click in the **0.956** cell and open the cell format option (Format menu, **Cells**); then select **Percentage** and set the decimal places to **1**. You should now see that Susan has a quite respectable grade of 95.6% on her three tests this semester. The percent format automatically multiplies by 100 for you.

Copy Susan's formula down to the other four students, as you did previously. The percentage format should be copied along with the formula. If it is not, set the format for each percent data cell to percentage. Now, click into the percent format cells for each student, observing the formulas in the formula bar. Observe how the relative cell reference changed, but the absolute cell reference remained the same—E3.

Proofread the Spreadsheet. At this point, examine the illustration in Figure 4.4 of the grade book up to this point. Compare the data to your document. Correct any errors and save the spreadsheet again.

Exploring Chart Options

Data in spreadsheets can be easily charted into a wide variety of chart options. *Excel* has a Chart Wizard; alternatively, you can initiate the charting process through a button on the standard toolbar. To chart all or any part of your data, you must select the range of cells that contain data you want to include in the chart **before** you initiate the charting process.

Do this: Select the range of cells to include the row of Test labels, Possible Points, and all the students' scores, including their names. **Do not** include the averages, totals, or percents. Next, initiate the charting process by clicking on the Chart Wizard toolbar button or by choosing **Chart** from the Insert menu. Follow the onscreen instructions and explore some of the charting choices.

To construct the chart, select a bar chart, labeling Series 1, 2, and 3 with the text: **Test 1, Test 2,** and **Test 3**. Move through the wizard screens without adding any other

	A	B	C	D	E	F
1	Fall Semester Grades					
2		Test 1	Test 2	Test 3	Total Points	Percent
3	Possible Poir	75	75	100	250	
4					0	
5	Susan	75	72	92	239	95.6%
6	Eli	68	70	88	226	90.4%
7	Thomas	74	72	94	240	96.0%
8	Abigail	58	68	89	215	86.0%
9	Hank	73	69	80	222	88.8%
10	Test Average	69.6	70.2	88.6		

FIGURE 4.4 The grade book with all data complete.

features. See the sample chart in Figure 4.5. Your chart may not look exactly like this one. However, it should be labeled with the students' names and the series should indicate Test 1, 2, and 3. The data should include the students' names, their three test scores, and the possible points. If you have inadvertently included totals, averages, or percents, select the chart, delete it, and start the chart process again.

While the whole chart is selected, pushing or pulling on one of the corner "handles" will stretch or squish the chart display. Adjust the chart size so data and names for all five students are visible. When complete, drag the chart to a position just below the last row of data.

Formatting the Final Appearance of the Spreadsheet

When you first entered the data, you left some things undone. Now is the time to clean it all up and make the spreadsheet neat and attractive. You have previously applied each of the formats that you need to use now. Format the grade book as follows:

- Change the text style of each label to bold.
- Widen columns to accommodate the width of the text labels.
- If you copied a formula through a blank cell, delete the zero.
- Center the columns containing numerical data.
- Add your name in header text.
- Go to Page Setup and change the page orientation to Landscape.
- Set the row and column headings to be printed (Page Setup, Sheet tab).
- Set the cell gridlines to print (Page Setup, Sheet tab).

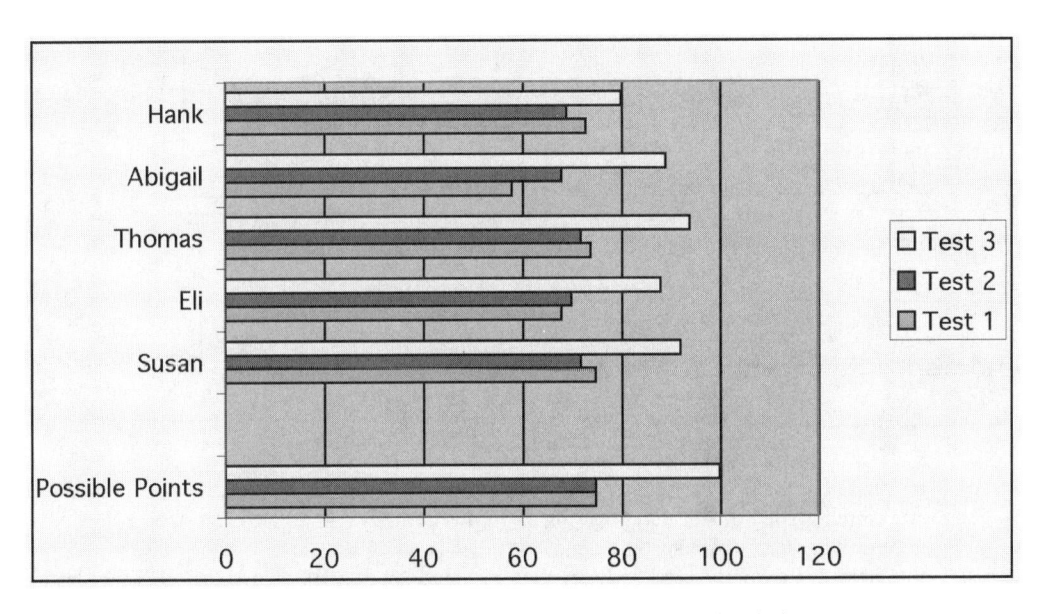

FIGURE 4.5 Example of one type of chart created from the grade book data.

- Set the Print Area to include all of the cells with data, in addition to the cells covered by the chart (otherwise some of the chart may be chopped off by the printer).
- Use Print Preview to see how your finished spreadsheet will look.
- Carefully proofread all aspects of the spreadsheet. See Figure 4.6 for an illustration of the completed grade book.
- Print and save the completed document.

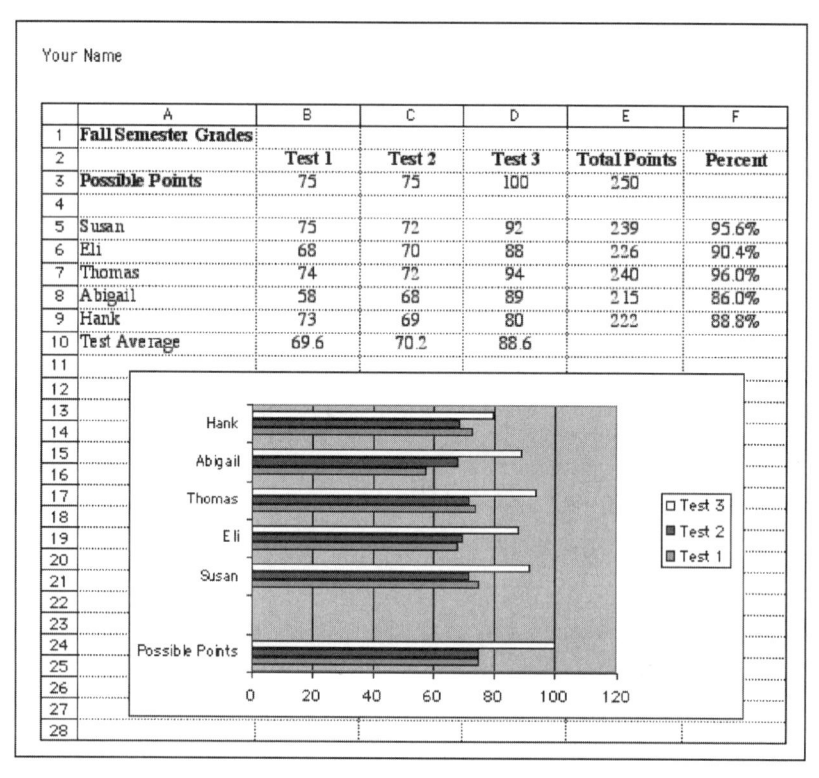

FIGURE 4.6 The completed grade book spreadsheet.

Grade Book Spreadsheet Checklist

- All data, both numeric and text, are accurate.
- Header contains your name.
- Printed grade book is in landscape orientation.
- Printed grade book displays row and column headings and gridlines.
- Printed grade book displays a complete chart beneath the data.
- Charted data includes students' names and test scores and possible points; series labels are Test 1, Test 2, and Test 3.

Summary

In this section you have:

- entered data into a grade book spreadsheet.
- used functions to calculate SUM and AVERAGE.
- explored various ways to enter function formulas.
- learned about absolute and relative cell reference.
- formatted numbers as percents.
- explored charting options.

What's Next?

Hopefully, with this introduction to spreadsheet software you have gained some insight into how spreadsheets can make your job easier. As a utility, a spreadsheet can make you a better grade book. As an instructional tool, the use of spreadsheets can supplement your instruction by helping students make calculations and predict outcomes.

Return to the Help files. Read some of the basics. Explore the menus. Search for explanations of unfamiliar terms. Explore features to display spreadsheets in different ways, such as show cell outlines or hide row and column headings. Use spreadsheets to keep track of books children read, bake sale profits, or school fundraisers. Any time you think a task might be easier if you plotted it out on a grid, try a spreadsheet. Continue to make and use simple spreadsheets. Soon you will discover that spreadsheet software has become an indispensable classroom tool.

KEY TERMS

| absolute cell reference | relative cell reference | spreadsheet |

CHAPTER 5

Databases

A *database* is a system for collecting, recording, sorting, and selecting large amounts of information. Software publishers offer database software with varying features, options, and complexity. Database software for commercial use can be extremely detailed, providing complex features unnecessary for the needs of most teachers. *Microsoft Excel* offers features within the spreadsheet software that allow the spreadsheet to function as simple database software. Hence, before you continue working in this chapter, you should have completed Chapter 4 Spreadsheets.

Here are some examples of how you might use databases in the classroom. First, a database of student information could be helpful. You might want to record the child's name, parents' (guardians') names, home address, home phone, and work phone. Because it makes your job easier, you could call this type of database a *utility*. We could call another database *instructional*, because you could use the data to enhance the instruction in your classroom. An example of an instructional database might be a list of all fifty states, their capitals, their area in square miles, the date they became a state, and other information.

You might already have student information stored on index cards—one card for each student. In database talk, a single card comprises a *record.* Each of the categories you place in a record is called a *field.* The fields for the student record could include **Student name, Parent name, Address, Home phone, Work phone.** In a database all records are comprised of the same fields.

If you have only 10 or 12 students, then data stored on index cards may work for you. But imagine this situation: A resource teacher in a large middle school serves 40 children. Some of them come to her classroom for classes throughout the day; a few of them spend most of the day there. Most of the students spend their class periods in inclusive classrooms—she rarely sees them, but she may prepare or administer tests for them. For all of the students, she coordinates their assistive technology: that is, she assigns computers, adaptive keyboards and other **peripheral** devices, and special-purpose software. She also supervises their use of computer adaptations, instructing them in use, modifying configurations, and maintaining the hardware. She has established a database of student information that she refers to daily. The record for each student includes: homeroom, their location each period of the school day, type of service she provides, and devices they use. She uses the database to sort students into individual homerooms to prepare notes to send home; she also sorts to locate all of the students using a particular device—for example, AlphaSmart keyboards—to recall them for servicing. The database has become a valuable tool enabling teachers to accomplish their jobs more efficiently.

Exploring a Database

The best way to begin learning how a database might be useful to you will be to explore one. You will first explore a states database prepared by the author, learning to find, sort, and filter data and to print portions of the data for reports. You will learn what the characteristics of the data must be for it to be recognized by *Excel* as a database. Finally, you will develop a simple database of your own.

Open the document **StatesDB.xls** from your *Text Documents* folder. You will be exploring the most basic options for data management within the *Excel* spreadsheet software. Before you move ahead, you will locate the tools you need to manipulate data. All of the options presented in this chapter are available in all versions of *Excel* from *97/98* up to the newest *XP/v.X*; however, the tools to access these features are not the same.

First, open the View menu and from the toolbars list choose the **Standard** and **Formatting** toolbars. Also show the **Formatting Palette** from the View menu, if you have that option. Finally, open the **List** toolbar from the toolbars menu, if you have one in the version of the software that you are using. (If you do not have the **List** toolbar, you will access the tools another way.) You will know that your version of the software uses a list management system if it has a **List** toolbar. You will also see **List** in the Insert menu and have access to a **List Wizard.**

Older versions of the software do not have a List toolbar, **List Manager,** or any way of defining a collection of spreadsheet data as a database. *Excel 97/98* treat the data as a database only when you begin to use database features such as sorting and filtering data. However, the older software versions have all the same capabilities as the newer versions. All features contained on the **List** toolbar can also be accessed through menu options. Look at the illustration of the **List** toolbar in Figure 5.1. If you do not have the **List** toolbar, you will locate similar options from the software menus, as you explore the states database.

FIGURE 5.1 List Toolbar.
Screen shot reprinted with permission from Microsoft Corporation.

The next thing to do is to make sure that the **AutoFilters** option is turned on. If **AutoFilter** is on, you will see tiny arrow(s) at the right edge of each spreadsheet column as illustrated in Figure 5.2. To turn on **AutoFilter** if you do not have **List Manager** options, open the Data menu, choose **Filters,** and then select **AutoFilter.** The **AutoFilter** selection should have a checkmark beside it. If you have the latest version of the software with the **List Manager** features, click on **AutoFilter** from the **List** toolbar. You may also have to click on **Visuals** (on the **List** toolbar) to make the arrows at the top right edge of each column visible. **Visuals** simply places a border around all data previously determined to be a database and permits the showing and hiding of the **AutoFilter** indicators.

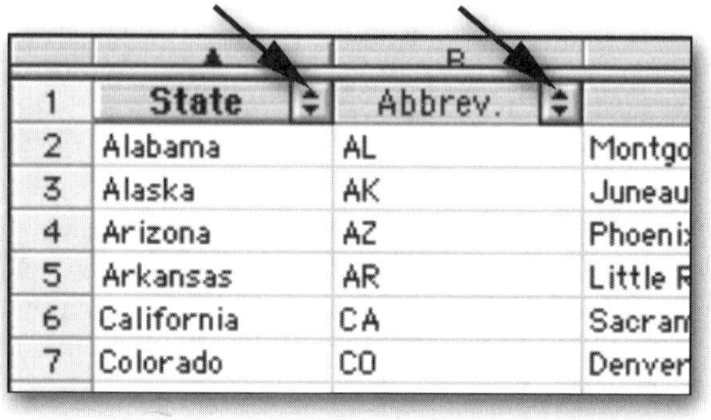

FIGURE 5.2 Data portion showing the **AutoFilter** indicators in Row 1.

Screen shot reprinted with permission from Microsoft Corporation.

When you can see the arrow(s) at the right end of each column name along Row 1 of the spreadsheet you should continue.

Look at the data in ***StatesDB.*** You will find information about all 50 states, including state name, zip code abbreviation, state capital, area in square miles, date the state entered the Union, the state bird, and the state flower. The names placed across the top of the columns in Row 1 define the *fields.* Each row contains information representing a single index card or ***record.*** In other words, each state **record** exists on a separate row. There are no blank spaces, no blank cells, and no leading spaces (that is, spaces added with a spacebar) in cells that contain text. You will consider spacing in databases later when you create a new database.

StatesDB is an instructional database. As you begin working with it, imagine your students sorting and filtering data to answer some of the same questions that you will be answering. In some cases, the students do the research and enter the data into a database after the teacher has set it up, thereby practicing research skills. As you learn some of the features of database management using the ***StatesDB*** document, you will be able to:

- print a list of the first thirteen states to enter the Union along with their dates.
- locate which state capitals have *City* in their names.
- determine how many states have designated the Northern Cardinal as their state bird.
- discern how many state names begin with the letter *M* and what their postal code abbreviations are.
- sort the states by size and identify the five largest and five smallest in area.

Throughout the exercises you will be completing with the states database you will not be making any permanent changes to the data. At any time you can stop and return to the chapter. You do not need to save any changes.

What Is a Form?

A data form is a representation of a single record in an index-card format. From the Data menu choose **Form.** When you open the form view of the database you will see complete data for one state. Buttons on the form allow you to do simple searches for information, edit and delete data, browse through all records, restore data you might have changed, add a new record, and finally, to close the form view.

Experiment with this now. Click on the **Criteria** button. You will see a blank form; click in the **Capital** field and type "Atlanta." Then click on **Find Next.** The software locates the Georgia record for you. Also, it is very easy, when entering large quantities of data at one time, to type into the wrong row when you are working in the familiar spreadsheet grid. **Form** is a good view to be in when entering data or having children enter data initially because entering data into the wrong row is impossible. Explore the form view, then close it and continue.

What Is Sort?

The states database comes to you sorted alphabetically by state—*Alabama* is first and *Wyoming* is last. As with the spreadsheet, data can be numeric or text; numeric data can be formatted different ways, like currency, percent, or dates. Data can also be sorted alphabetically or numerically in ascending or descending order. You could sort the states in descending order; that is, *Wyoming* first and *Alabama* last. When any sort is undertaken, the software determines that the data in each row remains together and should be treated as a unit. Otherwise, if you sorted the states alphabetically in descending order, sorting only the state names, the rest of the data would remain in the original order and the integrity of the data would be lost (for example, State: Ohio; Abbrev: FL). Use the following instructions to sort the database in descending order, alphabetically by state.

From the Data menu select **Sort.** If your version of *Excel* does not have the List Manager features, a box may pop up to inform you that it has detected additional data that probably should be included in the sort. If this happens, tell *Excel* to **Expand the selection.** The **Sort** dialog appears as illustrated in Figure 5.3. **Sort** allows you to sort on up to three different dimensions at one time. For this first sort you will be using only one. Click the arrows at the end of the first **Sort by** box and select **State.** Make sure that **None** is selected for each of the next two **Then by** boxes. Notice that you can sort in ascending or descending order. Click the button next to **Descending** and then click

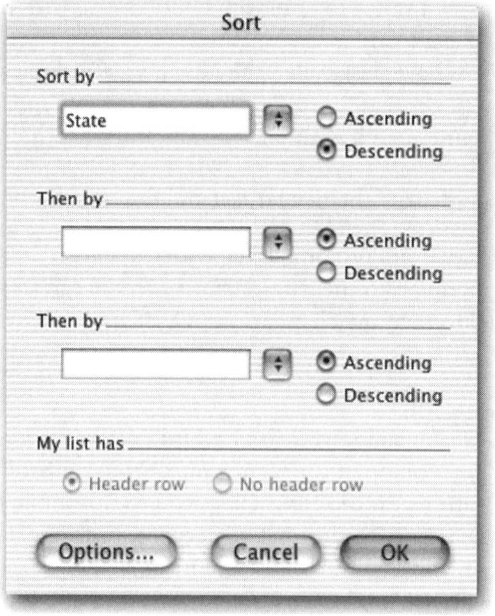

FIGURE 5.3 **Sort** dialog box showing a sort by **State** in **Descending** order.

Screen shot reprinted with permission from Microsoft Corporation.

OK. It happens quickly! Look across the data; notice that the data for each record "stuck" together (e.g., State: Ohio, Abbrev: OH), and the order of the states has been reversed. **Note:** If, by some chance the data are scrambled, continue reading.

Experiment by sorting the data by different fields both in ascending and descending order. If you inadvertently mess up the database (allowing the records to get scrambled) close the document—**Do Not** save any changes—and open a new copy of the database from the *Text Documents* folder. In exploring, sorting, and filtering data you may be seeing only portions of the data. However, unless you purposefully delete data, all data are still in the document (although some may be hidden at one time or another).

You have learned that sorting is rearranging. When you sort data, the fields in each record stay together and the entire database of data is sorted. You cannot choose to sort only portions of the list.

What Is Filtering?

When you wish to examine only portions of the data, you must apply a filter to "filter out" records you do not want to consider. For example, if you want to identify only the states that have Northern Cardinal as the state bird, you should not have to see the birds for all other states. Filtering selects portions of the records to view at one time, hiding all other records temporarily. Let's use the bird example and isolate the states that have Northern Cardinal as the state bird.

Move your pointer to the top of the State Bird column. Click and hold over the **AutoFilter** arrows to see what is in that menu. The tops of the **AutoFilter** indicators from two different versions of *Excel* are illustrated in Figure 5.4, with *Excel 98* on the left and *Excel 2001* on the right.

The newer versions also contain the Sort Ascending and Sort Descending features that you just accessed from the Data menu. It is simply a shortcut for two of the most frequently used options. Otherwise, the menus are identical. Notice that below the "Custom" entry is a list of each discrete entry for that column. Since most of the entries in each of the fields are unique, the bottom of the list may not be visible. You can see the entire list in the bird field, however. The list is much shorter because many states have the same birds. To view only the states that have Northern Cardinal as the state bird, one way would be to choose Northern Cardinal from that list. All states containing that entry will be in view; all other states will be hidden. **Try this now.** Choose Northern Cardinal from the **AutoFilter** list.

The first time you do this may be scary! What happened to the data for the other 43 states? Let's get it back quickly and then look at some other aspects of filtering. Look carefully at the **AutoFilter** arrow(s) at the top of the **State Bird** column. They should have turned blue. The color change indicates that the data have been filtered from this column. Return to the **AutoFilter** indicators for the **State Bird** column and select (**Show All**) or (**All**). Data for all fifty states will be visible again. Notice also that the **AutoFilter** arrow(s) at the top row of the State Bird column are no longer blue.

Filtering is a powerful feature of data management. **Try this:** Go to the different data fields and try another **AutoFilter** choice—(**Show Top 10**) or (**Top 10**). Each time you filter the database, return to the blue indicator and restore the list by choosing (**Show All**) or (**All**). What happens? Try to show the top ten records in each of the fields. You have probably determined that you cannot do this. The reason is because of the kind of data that each field represents. A field that is designated as numerical can have a "Top 10" filter. If the data are strictly text, it cannot. When you need to filter text data, there are other ways, which are accessed through the **Custom Filter** or **Custom** selection on the **AutoFilter** menu shown in Figure 5.5.

FIGURE 5.4 *Excel 98* (left) and *Excel 2001* (right) **AutoFilter** menus.

Screen shot reprinted with permission from Microsoft Corporation.

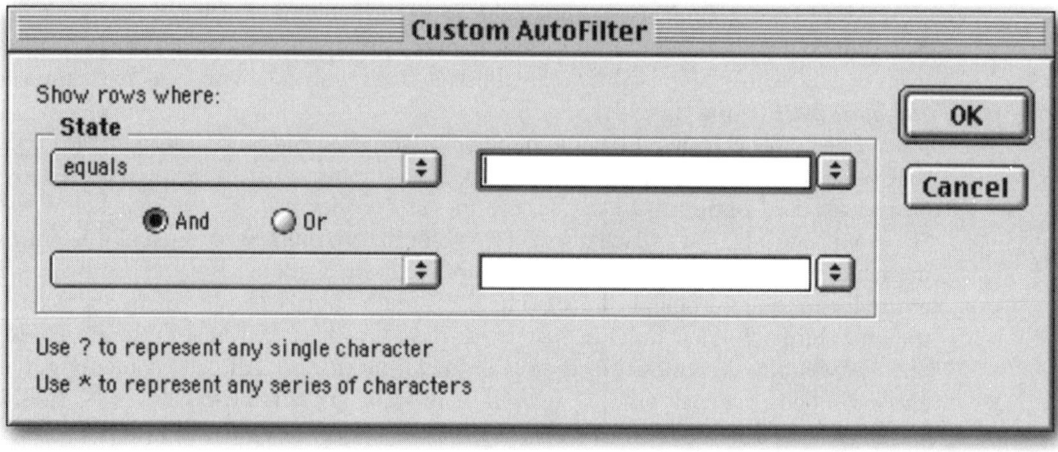

FIGURE 5.5 Custom AutoFilter options.
Screen shot reprinted with permission from Microsoft Corporation.

Look at how to filter text data now. Begin by clicking at the top of the **State** column and choosing **Custom** from the **AutoFilter** menu.

With the filter you see here, you could type *Pennsylvania* into the box and locate the row "where **State** equals *Pennsylvania*." This is somewhat limited because it would be easy enough just to sort the state list alphabetically and locate *Pennsylvania* that way. Where you see *equals*, hold your mouse button down and observe the choices that are hidden in that dropdown menu.

The **Custom AutoFilter** dialog illustrated in Figure 5.6 shows other choices you can make that will add power to the filtering process. For example, if you wish to find all states that begin with the letter *M*, choose **begins with** from the list and type *M* in the blank. Try it now. Show the records for all the "M" states. This is easy! To return to show all records again click the **AutoFilter** arrows at the top of the **State** column and select **Show All** or **All**. Perhaps you would like to know if the flowers for any of the states are any variety of rose. Activate the custom filter options in the **State Flower** field and filter with "**contains** *rose*." You should be viewing four states that contain *rose* in their state flower. After answering the "rose" question, return all records to view.

What about Dates?

You have looked at sorting and filtering records based on whether the data were text or numbers. Dates are a special kind of data in *Excel*. When you worked with spreadsheets, you learned how to change the format of cells to percentage or text. You learned to display differing numbers of decimal places. When you choose a particular format for a cell or group of cells, you might also select a text format or a date format. Because *Excel* is primarily a spreadsheet, capable of quite powerful calculations, the date format has some

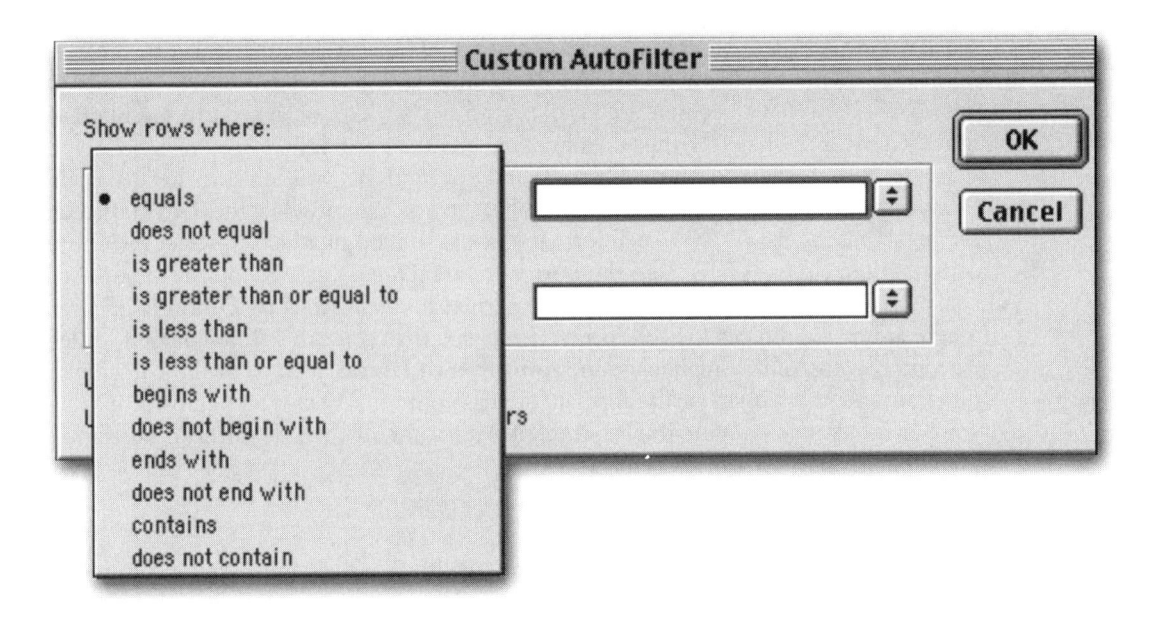

FIGURE 5.6 **Custom AutoFilter** choices.

Screen shot reprinted with permission from Microsoft Corporation.

special characteristics. The software actually takes a date, such as "3/4/98" or "March 4, 1998" or "98/3/4" or "4 March 1998," and turns it into a number, internally. So, you may see a date (in your choice of format) in a cell, but the software sees a number it can use to calculate time. For business purposes this is a good thing. An accountant or business manager may need to determine the volume of orders per week or month. If dates are formatted with the date format and not simply text, then the software can ascertain, say, how many days passed between orders—a necessity in the business world.

To simplify business calculations, *Excel* has developed an ingenious method for converting dates to numbers. Dates in *Excel* begin January 1, 1900 (Windows) or January 1, 1904 (Macintosh). *Excel* assigns a "0" to that date. Then, January 2 of that year is assigned "1," January 3 is "2," and so on through the ensuing months and years. January 1, 2004 is 36525 (Macintosh) or 37987 (Windows).

However, the date format is not always appropriate for instructional databases like the ***StatesDB***. When a field (column) is formatted as a date, if you were to attempt to enter July 4, 1776, the software may tell you that it is not a valid date, or it may simply enter it as you type it, treating it as text and not a date. If all fifty dates had been entered with a date format, dates prior to 1900 would remain as text, unrecognized by the date format. Those after the January 1 start date for *Excel* would have a different format. It would be impossible to accurately sort a field having two different data types. When you wish to use a date field in which dates will not be used for calculating or in which some dates fall before 1900, give the field (column) a **General** format, which is defined as neither text nor numbers. Nominal data such as telephone numbers, social security numbers, and postal codes are not typically treated as numerical data. That is, we usually do not calculate with them. In the *StatesDB* to circumvent this peculiarity with *Excel*, dates have been entered looking somewhat like social security numbers—first the year, a hyphen, the month, a hyphen, and then the day.

Because the data format is **General** and not numeric, you can sort the "dates" in ascending or descending order (alphabetically) but you cannot select the **Top 10** (which requires numeric data). To see cell format, click at the top of a field to select the entire column, then choose **Cells** from the Format menu. Do this now to look at the options using the **Admitted to Union** field. The format for **Admitted to Union** is general. There are many choices for cell format, even one that you can define yourself, called custom. Because of the hyphens in the **Admitted to Union** data, you will be unable to make any major changes in the format for that column. When you begin formatting your own database documents, experiment with some of these features to customize your documents.

Making Reports

A report is a printed portion of a database, filtered to remove unwanted records and sorted in a desired order. Among the many possibilities, an example of a report from this database is a list of the first thirteen states to enter the Union, in the order they entered the Union, with only the **State Name** and **Admitted to Union** fields visible. Another possible report is a list of the five largest states, with the largest at the top, followed by the five smallest states with only **State Name** and **Area/Square Miles** fields revealed. Following the steps below, create and print each of these reports.

First Thirteen States Report

1. Sort the database by the **Admitted to Union** field in ascending order. Delaware should appear first, Hawaii last.

2. Filter the list to eliminate all states after Rhode Island. Look at the date for the fourteenth state, Vermont: 1791-03-04.

   Note: Observe that the 13th state is in Row 14! Row 1 has the column headings.

   Use **Custom Filter** to "<u>Show rows where</u> **Admitted to Union** <u>is less than</u> 1791-03-04" (the date that the fourteenth state, Vermont, was admitted to the Union). With this selection, you should see only the complete records for the first thirteen states, beginning with Delaware and ending with Rhode Island (the other thirty-seven records are hidden). So far, so good!

3. Hide the fields that you do not wish to include in the report. For this report you only want to print the thirteen state names along with their **Admitted to Union** date. This is a new skill, but an easy one. When you worked with spreadsheets in the last chapter, you had to define the area you wished to print by selecting **Print Area** from the File menu. In looking at the area you wish to print for this report, see the

Note: If you inadvertently hide the wrong columns, you can **Unhide** by (a) selecting the two columns to the left and right of the hidden columns, (b) return to the Format menu, (c) choose **Columns,** and then **Unhide.** If you have hidden the first column, do this first: Choose **Go To** from the Edit menu, and type **A1** into the Reference box and click **OK.** Then go to the Format menu, **Columns,** and **Unhide.** This will reveal the "lost" first column. At this point, you may still have hidden columns. Use the first method to **Unhide** the remaining hidden columns.

two fields (columns) that intrude between the desired fields. You only need to hide these two columns. Those columns after **Admitted to Union** will be excluded when you set the **Print Area.** Click at the top of the column **Abbrev.,** and drag right to also include the column **Capital.** While the two columns you want to hide are both selected, from the Format menu, select **Column,** and then **Hide.**

4. Add header text with your name and a report title (in a fourteen-point font face)—**The First Thirteen States.** If you have forgotten how, open **Header and Footer** from the View menu. Using the **Custom** text option, place your name on the left side and the title in the center.

5. Use the Portrait page orientation; do not print cell gridlines or row and column headings.

6. Drag to select the area to be printed, and set the **Print Area** (File menu). Before initiating printing, inspect the final product in **Print Preview.**

7. Print the report.

8. Restore all of the data. To **Unhide** the hidden columns, select the two columns that were originally on the either side of those that are hidden. Use the instructions in the previous **Note** to **Unhide** any hidden columns. Return to the **AutoFilter** buttons for the **Admitted to Union** field and **Show All.** The order of the data does not matter. From the File menu, return to **Print Area** and choose the option to **Clear Print Area.** With all data visible again, you are ready to prepare another report.

First Thirteen States **Checklist**

- Header has name on the left and title (fourteen-point font face) in center.
- First thirteen states, in order of admission to Union, appear in first column.
- **Admitted to Union** field is to the right of the states; dates are accurate—match the states.
- Page is Portrait orientation; there are no cell gridlines or row and column headings.
- **State** and **Admitted to Union** fields are the only fields printed.

The Largest and Smallest States Report

1. Sort the database by the field **Area/Square Miles** in descending order. You should see Alaska (largest in area) at the top and Rhode Island (smallest in area) at the bottom.

2. In order to show only states that are larger than the sixth largest (the largest five) and all states that are smaller than the forty-fifth (the smallest five) you will filter using two conditions. Look at the sorted list of fifty states. Count off the five largest. The sixth largest is Arizona—114,000 square miles. Scroll down to the bottom of the list. Identify the five smallest. The sixth smallest is Massachusetts—8,284 square miles. Scroll back to the top of the document so you can see the **AutoFilter** indicators. Initiate **Custom Filter** for the **Area/Square Miles** field. You will "Show rows where **Area/Square Miles** is greater than 114,000." Continue to the next condition, after clicking **OR** to "Show rows where **Area/Square Miles** is less than 8,284." Click **OK**. You should see a list of ten states, five large followed by five small, in order of size from largest to smallest. If you do not, return all records to view and try again.

3. For the printed report, you will print the ten state names along with the **Area/Square Miles** field. As for the first report, hide the columns you do not wish to print. (Refer back to Step 3 of the **First Thirteen States** report, if necessary.)

4. Edit the document header to entitle this report **The Largest and Smallest States.** Use a fourteen-point font size for the title. Remember that the header is part of the document, not a part of the report. Consequently, if you do not change it, your new report will be printed with the title of your previous report.

5. Use the Portrait page orientation; do not print cell gridlines or row and column headings

6. Set the **Print Area** and **Print Preview** as you did before.

Note: Regarding using **AND** or **OR** in filtering for multiple conditions. You wanted to find the largest states *and* the smallest states. However, the conditions to satisfy whether or not one of the two criteria are met in this situation is **OR**. If you are not sure that the criteria will display what you expect, express the criteria in a complete sentence using the field name, like this:

> Alaska is a state which has an area greater than 114,000 square miles **AND** Alaska has an area less than 8,284 square miles.

It cannot be both! This is definitely a situation for **OR**. Read the sentence again using **OR** in place of the **AND**. It works! To illustrate further, place any state name in the sentence. If you were to read the sentence for each of the fifty states, the five largest and five smallest would be selected. All other states would not be included. An example where **AND** is useful might be where you want to find states whose bird was a Northern Cardinal **AND**—out of the states which have Northern Cardinal—that also has Magnolia as its flower.

7. Print the report.

8. When the report is successfully printed, **Clear Print Area, Unhide** the hidden columns, and **Show All** records again.

The Largest and Smallest States **Checklist**

- Header has name on the left and title (fourteen-point font size) in center.
- First column lists the five largest states followed by the five smallest states—*Alaska* first and *Rhode Island* last.
- The second column displays **Area/Square Miles;** data are accurate.
- Only fields printed are **State** and **Area/Square Miles.**
- Page is Portrait orientation; there are no cell gridlines or row and column headings.

Summary

In this section you have:

- distinguished between the purpose of a utility and an instructional database.
- identified database *fields* and *records.*
- explored database Form features.
- located the **AutoFilter** option.
- explored sorting order—both ascending and descending.
- used **AutoFilter** to select a subset of data records.
- used **AutoFilter** to restore all records to view.
- considered data categories of text, numbers, and dates.
- temporarily hidden fields, using **Hide,** to prepare a report.
- used **Unhide** to restore hidden fields to view.
- set and cleared **Print Area.**

Creating a Database

Your final database experiences will center on developing your own database. Since your previous database experiences have been using a database designed for an instructional purpose, this time you will work with a utility database—a tool to make your job easier.

If you are using an *Excel* version with List Manager, you can tell the computer that the material is a list. The List Manager (a) recognizes that the rows must stay together as records, (b) frames the list to isolate those cells from any others that may not be in the database, and (c) provides a toolbar with quick access to frequently used tools. A List Wizard can walk you step-by-step through naming the fields and identifying the data types.

In *Excel* versions with List Manager, starting a new spreadsheet with words in the top row and selecting **List . . .** from the Insert menu opens the List Wizard that helps you define a database. With other versions there is no obvious way to define list properties while creating the database. *Excel* recognizes the data to be a database (list) when you begin to sort or filter the data. Because of the differences in defining a list among the different versions of *Excel*, the process for creating a new database is slightly different, although the final result will be the same.

Defining the Fields

The first step in creating your own database is to decide what fields you will need. This utility database organizes useful data you may need about the students in your classroom. Data are listed in Figure 5.7 for five imaginary students. You may use these data or you may use data of your own. If you decide to design your own database, include at least child's name, birth date, and a minimum of five other fields.

Entering Data

Excel recommends that certain guidelines be followed when entering data that is to be treated as a database. The guidelines are important whether you have list management capabilities or not.

- Place only one data list on any single worksheet.
- Do not leave blank cells.
- Do not put spaces into any cell before or after data. Use alignment options from the formatting palette to alter spacing within cells.
- Place the field names across Row 1. Format the text for Row 1 with some feature like bold, a larger sized font, or a cell border—or, alternately, use **AutoFormat**.

Now, begin a new spreadsheet document. Regardless of the version of *Excel* you are using, use the following sequence:

1. Begin Row 1 by typing in the field names. Select the whole row and make it bold or display a larger-sized font face.
2. One by one, select each column and identify the type of data the field represents. See the recommended types in parentheses with the field names in Figure 5.7. This can be accomplished through the List Wizard or by choosing Cells from the Format menu.
3. Fill in the data for each student. You can do this through the grid layout or with the Form layout. **Note:** If you see **####...** in place of the data you enter, the column is not wide enough to display your entry. Drag that column wider to display the data properly.
4. Save the document on your disk when the fields are defined and all data have been entered.

Name (text)

Birth Date (date)

Parent/Guardian (text)

Street Address (text)

City/State/ZIP (text)

Homeroom (number)

Devices (text)

Andrea Melton	Lacy Smith	Hank Ellis
April 6, 1992	September 14, 1992	April 18, 1993
John and Susan Melton	Elizabeth Smith	Jack and Mollie Ellis
36 Andrews Lane	244 Elm Street	319 W. Whitely Ave.
Maintown, IN 47473	Maintown, IN 47476	Maintown, IN 47473
112	114	228
AlphaSmart	AlphaSmart	IntelliKeys
Eric Johnson	Tony Murray	
October 11, 1990	February 10, 1991	
James and Alice Johnson	Anthony Murray	
2218 Central Ave.	718 Ash St., Apt F2	
Maintown, IN 47473	Maintown, IN 47476	
228	112	
None	Keyguard	

FIGURE 5.7 Data for the class list database.

Exploring Your New Database

Whether you have used the data provided in the text or your own data, you have a new utility database of class information. Before you go any further, select all data and turn on **AutoFilter** from the Data menu (Filters). This should initiate any list management features of which your *Excel* version is capable. (If the List Wizard is activated, follow the steps to turn all data cells into list data, placing the data at the top of the sheet A1.)

In this section you will sort the data, examine some features you may want to change, and print a simple report. This database is small, unless you have added more than five records. In "real life," of course, a class database would contain more records (more students) and probably different or additional fields. Imagine that there are records for forty students in your database. The fields you include and how you plan to sort and filter the data become more important when you have to manage more records.

Sorting by Student Name. Let's examine what you have created so far. First, examine the student name field. Sort the database by student name. What happens? Are you able to sort the list alphabetically by last name? After sorting, check the data to make sure that the records did not get scrambled. If the data are scrambled, close the document **without saving** and open the version you saved previously.

> **Question:** What do you need to be able to sort the list by last name?
>
> **Answer:** You need a column (field) that contains only the last name
>
> or
>
> you need to re-enter the children's names into the Name field, with the last name first.

When you plan fields for a database it is important to consider how you intend to use the data. Will you need to alphabetize by last name? Do you need to see birth dates by month? Do you want to see homeroom lists? In the following sections you will modify the database two different ways to make this class list more useful.

Editing the Name Field. Return to the class database and edit the name field so that the children can be sorted alphabetically by last name. Edit each name cell to place the child's last name first (e.g., **Melton, Andrea**). Do this now. Sort the data again by Name. Can you sort the students by last name now? Save the document.

Why might you have included the birth date field? Is it to determine who are the oldest and youngest students or arrange students in order chronologically by age? Is it so you can be prepared for birthdays when they come up throughout the year? If you formatted the birth date field as dates, then you can sort them in ascending order. Sort the birth date field in ascending order now.

What is the result of the sort? You should see the records sorted by age, oldest first. Now, if you are planning to recognize birthdays each month, it would be nice if you could see all the January records, February records, and so on, in groups. Perhaps you could apply a custom filter to your birth date field to "Show rows where **Birth Date** begins with April." Try this now for April or any other month, depending on the set of data you are using. Do you see a blank database? Do not be surprised by the results! To restore the data, return to the AutoFilter button for the Birth Date column and **Show** or **Show All.**

Do you remember the explanation earlier in the chapter about how *Excel* handles dates? If not, look back there now. Your birth date field is not text. If you want to know all birthdays for each month, then the date format is not very useful for these data. You may need to have the information in the Birth Date field as it is formatted now. Perhaps you need birth dates for test forms or Individualized Educational Program (IEP) documents. However, it is not useful to help you recognize birthdays each month. The secret is to trick *Excel* into seeing only text when it "sees" the dates! Then the data can be sorted in ascending or descending order based on alphabetical order, not by ages.

Adding a Birthday Field. First, add another field to your database. Click on the **Birth Date** column to select it. From the Insert menu choose **Columns.** A new blank column will appear next to the selected column. Type **Birthday** into Row 1 of the new column. Next select the whole column and set the format to **Text** before you enter any data (Format menu, **Cells**).

Entering Birthdays. Before you begin typing in birthdays, you need to determine how you want to sort the data. For example, if you use this format—Apr-18, then sorting will place the months in alphabetical order—April, August . . . September. There is nothing wrong with this. In fact, it is a good format, especially if you prefer seeing the "Apr" instead of a numerical representation of the month—"04." **Read on.**

An alternate way to represent dates as text is numerically—January is "01," February is "02," and so on. The April 18 birthday is written—04-18. Sorting birthdays that are numerical (although in text format) yields a list that begins in January (01) and ends with December (12). **Keep reading on!**

There is one final point to make about how to keep *Excel* from turning your text dates into its own date format. Regardless of how you format the cells in a column, if *Excel* perceives the data as dates it converts them to a numerical value. The secret to entering the dates is to type them in a format that *Excel* will treat as text. Here is the trick! Use a hyphen between the month and day as illustrated in the previous paragraphs. January 18 is **01-18** or **Jan-18** (April 6 is **04-06** or **Apr-06**). If you decide to use the numeric version, keep all months and days as two-digit. Remember, these data are alphabetical—not really numerical—even though you may be using numerals. Numerals that are treated as text are not recognized for their numeric value. This means that "10" will appear alphabetically before 2 or 3 because it begins with "1." The numbers will sort properly as months if you make all months and days two digits with zeros.

Now, convert the birth date for each student to the format of your choice—either **Aug-22** or **08-22** (**Apr-06** or **04-06**)—and type them into the new **Birthday** field. You now have two different fields with birth dates—different formats for different purposes.

Making a Birthday Report. Sort the database by the new birthdays field in ascending order. If you used the Apr-06 format, the birthdays will appear alphabetically by month with April at the top. If you used the 04-06 format, the sort will yield the months in their numerical order. See the illustration in Figure 5.8 to see both versions of the data sorted by birthdays.

Set up the spreadsheet to print only the Name and Birthday fields. Add header text with your name at the top left and a title "Class Birthdays" in the center in fourteen-point text size. Do not print row and column headings or gridlines. The reports may differ because of the method used to enter the birthday dates.

Print the report.

Name	Birthday
Melton, Andrea	Apr-06
Ellis, Hank	Apr-18
Murray, Tony	Feb-10
Johnson, Eric	Oct-11
Smith, Lacy	Sept-14

Name	Birthday
Murray, Tony	02-10
Melton, Andrea	04-06
Ellis, Hank	04-18
Smith, Lacy	09-14
Johnson, Eric	10-11

FIGURE 5.8 Sample data sorted by **Birthday.**

Class Birthdays Checklist

- Header has your name on the left and title (fourteen-point font face) in center.
- First column lists the student names, last name first.
- The second column displays **Birthday.** All other columns are excluded.
- Data are sorted alphabetically by the Birthday field (either a-b-c or 01-02-03).

Summary

In this section you have:

- created a new database.
- examined list guidelines.
- set up the fields (columns) and data types.
- determined that the purpose for a field can determine how it is configured.

- edited previously entered data.
- inserted a new column.
- explored creative ways to represent dates.

What's Next?

Where do you go from here with database management? When using *Excel* as a database as you have done in this chapter, you worked almost exclusively with sorting and filtering data. You did no calculations as you had done with *Excel* in the previous chapter. In the states document there were no formulas, no fields that were calculated, nothing even vaguely recognizable as spreadsheet data. When you begin to combine the features of spreadsheets with the sorting and filtering capabilities you have just learned, you will begin to recognize the incredible power that *Excel* can offer a teacher.

Looking back at the states document, there are other fields you could add to enhance your students' experiences with research and data handling. You might add a field with a formula that calculates, from the sum of the states' area in square miles, each state's percentage of the total land area of the country. You might add a field for population figures from the latest census. Then you could determine population per square mile, comparing population density among different states.

As you continue working with database management, explore more features. Try more complex filtering. Add fields that can be calculated. Think creatively about how to provide your students with better activities to enhance your classroom instruction. Finally, browse the Help files for ideas you may wish to incorporate into your *Excel* skills.

KEY TERMS

database
field

peripheral device
record

CHAPTER

6　Presentation Software

This chapter introduces you to the basics of ***presentation software***—software designed to help you integrate graphics and text into appealing presentations. Skill with presentation software is invaluable to you as a teacher, whether you are making a presentation at a committee meeting or teaching children new concepts. It is recommended that you complete both the word processing and graphics chapters before embarking on this chapter. Many of the tools and toolbars used in *PowerPoint* are identical to those introduced in those previous chapters.

The software illustrated in this chapter is *PowerPoint* (Macintosh v.X version), another component of the *Microsoft Office* suite. The basics covered here are the same as earlier versions of the *PowerPoint* software including *PowerPoint 2000* (Windows), *PowerPoint 2001* (Macintosh), the earlier versions (97-Windows, 98-Macintosh), and newer *Microsoft PowerPoint XP* for Windows. The newest versions of the software have additional features including new graphics, animations, and templates. The basic features of the software included in this chapter can be completed with any of the previously mentioned versions of the *PowerPoint* software.

Typically you would use a data projector to display your *PowerPoint* presentation. However, if your group is small, you could "gather round" a large monitor for an effective presentation. If you do not have a data projector available, you can print *PowerPoint* slides as overhead projector transparencies. You can also save your presentation as an html file and view it through a web page!

Exploring a *PowerPoint* Presentation

To begin exploring a *PowerPoint* presentation, open the prepared presentation in your *Text Documents* folder titled *ThirteenAreas.ppt*. This presentation describes the characteristics of the thirteen areas of disability recognized by IDEA. The document should open into the version of *PowerPoint* that you have available. If *PowerPoint* seems to open but the *ThirteenAreas.ppt* document is not visible, try this: Open your *PowerPoint* software, open the File menu and choose **Open . . .**, and finally navigate to the *ThirteenAreas.ppt* document on your disk to open it.

Regardless of the version of *PowerPoint* that you have available, the basic options and features are similar to the other versions. The first thing you will do with this presentation is to run it and see it as a viewer would. Later, you will look at how the presentation was created, and finally, you will make your own *PowerPoint* document.

As with other *Microsoft Office* applications, you will find a myriad of menu options, toolbars, and help files to aid you in the development of your *PowerPoint* skills. From the View menu, expand the **Toolbars** submenu and open the **Standard, Formatting, Animation Effects,** and **Common Tasks** toolbars. If you have the option for **Formatting Palette,** open that also. Drag the toolbars and palettes you have just opened to convenient positions on the screen.

The first options to locate in your version of *PowerPoint* are the ways you can view the material you are working on for your presentation. Open the View menu and notice the top few choices—**Normal** (older versions has **Outline**), **Slide, Slide Sorter, Notes Page,** and **Slide Show.** Because these options are used so frequently, you will find small icons at the bottom left of your document window. Move the cursor slowly over each icon at the bottom left of the *Thirteen Areas* document to discover these menu choices in an easily accessible location.

Now, in any order you choose, try each view—except for Slide Show. When you are ready to begin the slide show, you should watch for slide transitions and animations. Slide transitions are things that happen as you move from slide to slide. Animations happen with text or images on each slide. While in the slide show, you can use the right arrow key, the spacebar, or the mouse button to move through the slides. You can stop the slide show at any time by pressing the **[esc]** key on your keyboard.

While the slide show is in progress you can also access a contextual menu—*right click* for Windows and *[ctrl] click* for Macintosh. Access this menu and look at the options. **Pen** (in Pointer Options), might be especially useful when using *PowerPoint* for instructional purposes. In earlier versions this feature was called *Electronic Chalk.* When **Pen** is turned on, you can draw with a tool directly onto the slide. You could underline or circle any elements on the slide that you wish the viewers to take particular note of. Play with this feature, too. Run the slide show as many times as is necessary to explore these features.

When you have completed the slide show, look back at the View menu and those various options at the top. Locate the option to view notes. Look at the notes attached to the *Thirteen Areas* presentation. The notes supplement the main points illustrated on the slides. They also help you keep on target as you deliver a presentation. You can include notes along with images of the slides on printed handouts, enabling students to pay more attention to the lesson and less time to writing their own notes. A printed handout like this becomes a useful instructional aide, especially to accompany a slide show that is presenting new material to students.

At this point, explore the options for printing that are available to you based on the specific printer you have, the computer system you are using, and the version of *PowerPoint* that you are using. You can look at **Page Setup** and the **Print** dialog box from the File menu. In addition, you may find options for printing in **Preferences** (File menu or *PowerPoint* menu). For example, initiate printing as you might if you want to print a word processing document. However, do not actually print the document. Take some time now to explore the choices in the Print Dialog box—look for the *PowerPoint* options here to print four (or more) slides per page, print notes, print outline, and others.

You have seen a *PowerPoint* slide show and examined ways to produce printed versions to meet various needs you may have, based on the purpose of the presentation. The next step will be to examine how the slide transitions and text animations were created. Go to the first slide of *Thirteen Areas*. Choose **Slide Transition . . .** from the Slide Show menu. While the Slide Transition dialog box is open, examine the transition choices from the menu. Also note other options available from this location to customize your slide show. To locate the text animation feature, first select one of the lines of text below the slide title. Then, open the Slide Show menu again and observe the animation choices. These choices are "grayed out" or unavailable unless you have selected text that you may wish to have animated. At this point, play with each of these features. Choose different effects. Change anything you wish. Run the slide show again to observe the effects.

The last feature of *Thirteen Areas* to examine is the design template that, in this document, appears to look like a spiral notebook. Choose **Slide Design . . .** from the Format menu. Older versions of *PowerPoint* may offer the design option as **Apply Design . . .** from the Format menu. Notice that you can apply a design to all slides in the document or only the particular slide you were viewing when you opened the format option. Experiment with these designs as you did with the transitions and animations.

Creating a *PowerPoint* Presentation

It is time for you to make your own *PowerPoint* presentation. Before you open the software to a new blank document, you should plan your topic and break it down into sequential slide segments. For this exercise, plan a presentation of at least six slides. You may choose any topic you wish that would be appropriate to present to your colleagues, classmates, or children you are teaching. Listed below are several ideas from which you may select:

- Information about a famous person.
- The history of deafness.
- An explanation of the Americans with Disabilities Act for people who are unfamiliar with it.
- An outline of chapter content from any textbook you might present to colleagues, classmates, or children you are teaching.

Select your topic. Use scratch paper to plot out the content you want to include on each slide. Do not try to include too much material on each slide. Remember, especially if you are using a projector, that the audience must be able to see the material. If the text is too small, or there is too much material on an individual slide, then you are reducing the visibility and the effectiveness of your presentation. When you have planned the content of your presentation, you are ready to create your slide show.

You could take several different approaches to completing a *PowerPoint* presentation. For this first project use the following method. First, you will enter the content into all of the slides and save the document. Then, you will experiment with slide design, animations, and transitions to complete the presentation.

Now, open the *PowerPoint* software and begin a new blank document. When you begin a new presentation, *PowerPoint* offers you preformatted slide layouts. Look carefully at each of these. They offer preformatted headings and layouts for images and text lines. You can select one of these or choose a blank layout. With a blank layout, you can place headings, images, or text boxes wherever you choose. However, even with the layout templates you can move, add, or delete the slide elements as you choose. Layouts with clip art offer the built-in clip art gallery to select images from. Layouts with pictures are designed to use images from outside of the *PowerPoint* application—images you may have saved as separate documents. So, at this time, depending on the content you have decided to use, select one of the layout options. (**Note:** Skip the title slide at this time; you will be instructed to add one later.)

Make your first slide by clicking into the boxes and adding your material. If you choose a layout that includes images, you can select clip art from the Clip Art Gallery or add images from another source. When that slide is complete, you might want to view your slide with the slide show option. When you are ready to continue, add a new slide by opening the Insert menu and choosing **New Slide. . . .** Notice that you get the layout options again so you can select different layouts for each slide, depending on the nature of the content you are presenting. Continue typing in your text and adding new slides until you have completed entering the content for all of the slides. Save the *PowerPoint* document now.

Run the slide show. At this point, the presentation is one of the dullest, boring slide shows ever! It is time for the fun part—adding a slide design, slide transitions, and animations. As you experiment and explore all of the options, run the slide show to test the results. Although it is possible to incorporate a myriad of options into a single presentation, try to limit the effects to a few uniform actions throughout the presentation. You want the viewers to focus on the content, not wonder which effect will appear on the next slide!

The first feature to add to your slide show is **Slide Design** in the Format menu. Slide Design is the overall look of your slides. The *Thirteen Areas* document used the Notebook design, in which each slide looked like a page in a spiral notebook. Different versions of the software offer varying choices for Slide Design. Locate the Slide Design option for the version of the software available to you. Experiment with the different designs. Select one to apply to your presentation.

The second feature to add to your slide show is **Slide Transitions.** What will happen in your slide show when you move to another slide? Slide Transitions can be established individually for each slide or can to be applied to all slides in the document. Look for **Slide Transitions . . .** in the Slide Show menu. As before, experiment with the choices, running the slide show each time to examine the effects on your slides. When you have selected Slide Transitions for the slide show, move on to the next step.

The third feature you will experiment with is **Animations.** Animations are applied to individual objects, such as text boxes or images. Each individual text entry within a single box will be affected by the animation applied to that text box. Beginning with the first slide, locate the Animations feature for your version of *PowerPoint* and experiment with the choices. If your version of the software offers **Animation Preview**, try using it. The preview feature displays a thumbnail image of the slide along with any applied animations. Move through your slides, adding animations where appropriate, depending on the content you are presenting. Save the document again.

The last visual element to add to your presentation is a title slide. Create a new slide, choosing **Title Slide** from the layout choices. Place a title on the new slide along with your name. Add a slide transition to the new slide. However, do not add any text animations. This slide should appear, in its entirety, when the slide show begins.

Notice the number of the title slide. It is probably not in first place, where you will want it to appear. From the View menu choose **Slide Sorter**. When the thumbnail views of your slides appear, drag the title slide to the first place. Run the slide show to assure that the title slide appears first, and that the slide transition into the first content slide (Slide 2) is as you wish. Save the document again.

The final element you will add to the document is Notes. There are several purposes for having notes accompany *PowerPoint* documents. One purpose is to provide notes for you to follow while you are speaking. Another purpose is to give viewers copies of the notes. How you write the notes and what you include depends on how you expect to use the slide show. From the View menu select the view that displays the notes. Add notes for each of the content slides. Save the document again.

Give your presentation a final view. Does the content "flow" as you planned? Is all the content accurate? Do all animations and transitions provide the effects you expected? Examine all elements critically and make any changes you think may be necessary to "polish" your final product. Again, save any changes you make.

Slide Show Presentation Checklist

- Document contains seven cards—six content and one title.
- Title card appears first.
- Content is presented logically.
- A Slide Design has been selected.
- A Slide Transition has been implemented for each slide.
- Animations have been added for individual text lines.
- Each content slide includes notes.
- All spelling, punctuation, and grammar are accurate.
- Text is easy to read—easily readable font face and adequate size.
- All content is accurate.

Summary

In this section you have:

- examined a completed *PowerPoint* document.
- planned a slide show on paper.

- chosen slide layouts for new slides.
- entered text/images into slides.
- applied a Slide Design to a presentation.
- chosen Slide Transitions for your slides.
- applied animations to text boxes and/or images.
- added a title slide.
- sorted slides to move the title slide to Slide 1.
- added notes for your slides.

What's Next?

You have covered some of the basics of *PowerPoint*. What can you do to learn more features that can enhance your future presentations?

Explore the menus you have been using. What else is in the Insert menu? Experiment with inserting pictures, charts, tables, and movies. What other features can you explore from the Slide Show menu? Can you set up a *PowerPoint* slide show to run automatically during an open house event?

Browse the Help files. Examine topics that are unfamiliar to you. Do not be afraid to experiment with new features. Each time you develop a *PowerPoint* slide show, try to incorporate new features to improve your skills and enhance your presentations.

KEY TERMS

ctrl-click   presentation software   right-click

PART TWO

Integrating the Computer into the Classroom

CHAPTER

7 Educational Software

There are thousands of software programs specifically intended to enhance classroom instruction, engage learners, and provide resources beyond those directly available in traditional classroom materials. As a teacher, you are obligated to choose the software wisely that you want your students to use. What does the software do? Why are you using it? Does the software meet the individual needs of the learner? Equally important, how do you use the computer and associated software programs with the students in your classroom? Are students using the computer for research or reference, to learn new skills, to practice previously learned concepts, or purely for entertainment?

Each semester when I begin educational software exploration in my classes, I ask for a show of hands in reply to the following question: "During your years in grades kindergarten through high school, did you ever have a computer in the classroom that was used only by the children who finished their work first?" Most students raise their hands. What does this suggest? Well, it suggests that many teachers do not know how to integrate computer activities into language arts, social studies, science, or other subject areas. This is not to say that all teachers relegate use of the computer to free time activities for the brightest and fastest learners. Indeed not! Today's teachers are discovering innovative and creative ways to incorporate computer activities into their daily classroom routines. However, our pre-service teachers are not products of a technology-proficient public education system. Most of today's pre-service teachers began their formal education from thirteen to seventeen years ago. What was the status of computers in the schools then? How technologically proficient were most of those classroom teachers? What kinds of models did those K–12 teachers set for our current teacher education students? In light of this probable shortcoming, the purpose of the present chapter is to explore strategies for integrating the computer into the classroom curriculum and to help you learn how to evaluate educational software programs.

How to Use Software in the Classroom

Practically all educational software can be grouped into nine different categories based on their use. When you can determine what category a program fits into, you will have a better idea about how to integrate that program into your classroom routine. Later, when you begin to look at software, you will be asked to classify each software program into one of the nine categories. Described below, the nine categories are as follows:

- Reinforced Practice
- Tutorial
- Simulation
- Problem Solving
- Graphics
- Reference
- Teacher Utility
- Student Utility
- Authoring

Reinforced Practice

The first category of software to examine is ***reinforced practice.*** It is placed first in this list because most educational software fits into this category. *Reinforced Practice* means that the software reinforces previously taught material. The program does not attempt to teach any new material; rather, it strengthens skills that the learner has already acquired. When you look at new and unfamiliar software and you determine that any particular title is indeed reinforced practice, you immediately know that you must teach the concepts first and then give the students opportunities to practice the new content using the software. It is a well-established fact that learners have varying learning styles, have different learning speeds, and respond to educational materials in different ways. Reinforced practice software provides another option for allowing learners to practice new skills using software with features customized to their needs. *Stanley's Sticker Stories* from Edmark Reading (now Riverdeep Interactive Learning, Limited) offers learners an enticing environment to practice writing with interesting backgrounds, creative clip art "stickers," and entertaining sound effects. Learners can create their own stories, guided by Stanley.

Many educational games fit into the category of Reinforced Practice. Games rarely teach new material. Typically, games include levels or screens to complete and a scoring system. Games may even be competitive with multi-player features. Educational games can be an effective way to reinforce concepts taught using more traditional methods, allowing learners another avenue to practice newly acquired skills. An excellent example of an educational game is *Word Munchers* (also *Word Munchers Deluxe*) from The Learning Company. *Word Munchers* is an arcade-style game wherein the learner commands a "Muncher" to hop around on a screen comprised of a grid of blocks, each block containing a word. The "Muncher" must hop on (munch) each word containing a specified vowel sound before the evil Troggle jumps out to catch him. Successful completion of one screen leads to another. This program is obviously reinforced practice. It does not attempt to teach vowel sounds or word recognition. Instead, it gives learners practice in pronouncing vowel sounds, rewarding them for the correct pronunciation, all in a fun arcade game format. *Word Muncher Deluxe* adds the content of vocabulary, sentence structure, and grammar to the time-proven *Word Muncher* format.

An important issue with educational games is to be careful to detect games that are not educational! Make certain that software programs, which are obviously games, are indeed providing reinforced practice for previously taught concepts.

Tutorial

Unlike the preceding category, **tutorials** teach new concepts. When you use tutorial software, you are expecting the computer to teach the concepts. Some examples of tutorial software are *Simon Spells* and *Simon Sounds It Out* from Don Johnston Incorporated, *Balanced Literacy* from IntelliTools, Inc., and the *Thinkology* series from Broderbund—*Accuracy, Logic,* and *Clarity. The Secret Writer's Society* from Learning Upgrade LLC teaches learners to write effective sentences and paragraphs using the five-step writing process. In most cases, with tutorial software, the software has a management system that keeps track of an individual learner's progress and success with the material. The *Thinkology* series comes with a teacher's manual containing worksheets to be copied that are useful both to orient the student to the materials and to provide paper/pencil follow-up to the computer experiences. Tutorial software can present new material in small, programmed steps; reinforce correct responses; remediate errors; and compile a learner performance profile.

There is another type of tutorial software that deserves special mention—software that enhances computer skills and helps teach learners how to use the computer effectively. Programs such as *Creature Chorus* from Laureate Learning Systems, Inc. help learners with special needs or very young children to use the mouse or touch window. R. J. Cooper & Associates publishes *Joystick (and Mouse) Trainer* to help learners with special needs to develop skills with input devices using simple maze games. See a sample game in Figure 7.1.

If we expect children to become computer proficient at earlier and earlier ages, we must also teach them keyboarding skills earlier than ever before. Many different keyboarding programs are available for children today. Software such as *Mavis Beacon Teaches Typing for Kids* from The Learning Company (Riverdeep Interactive Learning Limited) offers short, simple, repetitive lessons to help orient young keyboarders to our sometimes-confusing QWERTY keyboard.

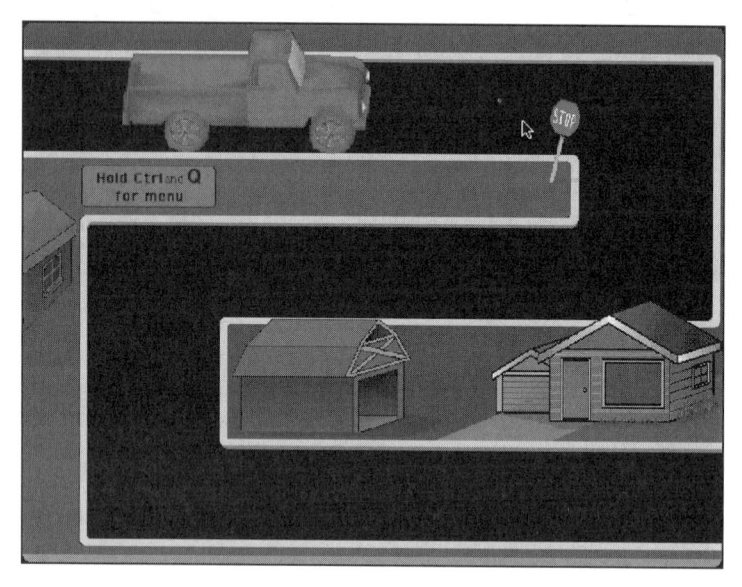

FIGURE 7.1 A sample maze from *Joystick (and Mouse) Trainer.*
© R. J. Cooper & Associates.

Simulation

Simulations are software programs that simulate some aspect of real life. The classic simulation program is *The Oregon Trail* from The Learning Company. In *The Oregon Trail*, an 1840s family is traveling by wagon from Missouri to Oregon. The student must make decisions to help the travelers arrive safely in Oregon (e.g., what to take, when to leave, how fast to move, how much food to use, how to cross streams and rivers, and how to deal with illness, among others). Simulations are undoubtedly games! However, they offer special features that other educational games do not. Simulations offer learners opportunities to make virtual real-life decisions and observe the likely consequences of those decisions. In classrooms, simulation software can provide opportunities for students to engage in learning activities cooperatively as they solve the problems together. Other simulation programs that are appropriate for K–12 learners include *Oregon Trail II* and *Amazon Trail* from The Learning Company and *SimAnt* and *SimTown* by Maxis. With *SimTown* learners can place streets, buildings, and people. They can provide places for work, school, and entertainment.

Problem Solving

Problem solving software programs give students the opportunity to solve instructionally relevant problems. So how does this category of software differ from simulations? True, simulations do solve problems, but the situations in simulations involve real-life settings and focus primarily on decision-making. Whereas, for instructional purposes, problem-solving situations are more contrived. A great problem-solving program is

Puzzle Tanks, a classic arithmetic program by Sunburst Technology. Students must fill, empty, and transfer liquids between different storage tanks to reach target amounts. The problems increase in difficulty and are suitable for learners in all of the elementary grades. With younger learners, the problems can be worked cooperatively. Also by Sunburst is *Factory Deluxe*. Activities in this program sharpen geometry, visual thinking, and problem-solving skills. The five learning environments provide experience in spatial learning and sequencing and improve students' problem-solving skills.

Graphics

Software that falls into the graphics category includes all programs that students can use to create and manipulate images, including paint and draw programs; page layout programs; photo editing software; and programs with templates for greeting cards, banners, and other graphics products. **Graphics software** allows learners to express their creativity without having the eye–hand coordination and fine motor skills that would be necessary using paper and pencil. Learners can explore shapes and colors, illustrate their own stories with clip art, and create awards and greeting cards. For learners with even minor motor impairments, graphics software offers a tremendous empowerment enabling them to create and display creative endeavors that equal or surpass those of their peers without disabilities. *Kid Pix Deluxe* by The Learning Company and *Print Shop Deluxe* by Broderbund are time-tested graphics programs for classroom use.

Reference

Software that falls into the ***reference*** category are electronic versions of more traditional printed reference materials such as a dictionary, thesaurus, and encyclopedia. Some of the major benefits of using reference materials in an electronic format are: searching is so much easier; illustrations can be enlarged for easier viewing; text can often be spoken; and complicated concepts can be animated or illustrated with video clips. In addition, the digital information is more current and more conveniently updated than text versions—especially for encyclopedia. The *American Heritage Dictionary for Children* from Houghton Mifflin is an exceptionally full-featured, attractive, and enjoyable implementation of a more traditional reference.

Teacher Utility

Any software program that makes the teacher's job easier could be considered a ***teacher utility***. Utilities are much more efficient ways to do things than with paper and pencil. As examples, word processing and spreadsheet software are clearly utility software. Other programs that may fit into this category are IEP programs, *Behavior Objective Sequence* from Research Press, grade-book software, database software, and programs that allow you to create your own worksheets, such as crossword puzzles.

A remarkably useful program is *Boardmaker* from Mayer-Johnson, Inc. *Boardmaker* provides thousands of the Picture Communication Symbols in digital format for inclusion on ***communication boards,*** daily schedules, sequencing boards, and language development activities. The images can be pictures only, words only, or pictures with words.

Student Utility

Student utility software is similar in function to teacher utility software, but designed to be used by students. They include word processors, spreadsheets, and database programs specifically designed for use by children. Student utility software often has fewer, less complex features than teacher utility software, but provides the essence of the program utility. *IntelliTalk II* from IntelliTools, Inc. is excellent talking word processing software for young learners and learners with special needs. Another talking word processor is *Write:Outloud* from Don Johnston Incorporated. *ClarisWorks for Kids* from Apple Computer, Inc. for children aged from six to twelve, delivers an appealing, easy-to-use package with a word processor, database, spreadsheet, and graphics program. The software offers clip art, video clips, and a wide assortment of templates to help children begin more complex projects. *Inspiration* from Inspiration Software, Inc., for students from Grade 6 through adults, is software that helps learners plan, organize, outline, diagram, and write. For learners from grades K–5 the company offers *Kidspiration* with similar features. The illustration in Figure 7.2 is a Water Cycle sample document from *Inspiration*.

Essentially, the programs in the student utility category offer learners alternatives to traditional paper/pencil activities. All students can benefit from the availability of electronic tools that enhance their creativity, productivity, and capabilities. Access to student utility software can empower learners with special needs to accomplish work comparable to that of their peers in general education classes.

Authoring

This category is an interesting one. ***Authoring software*** provides teachers with the tools to create their own instructional materials, without knowing how to actually

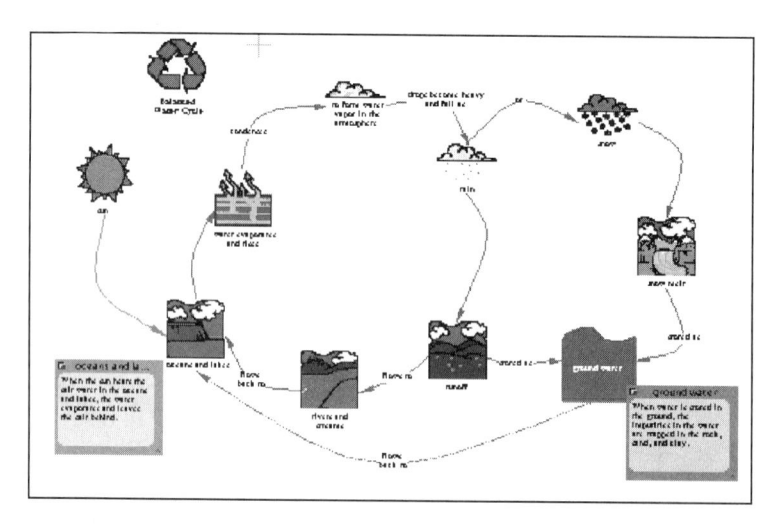

FIGURE 7.2 Water Cycle document from *Inspiration*.
Diagram created in *Inspiration®* by Inspiration Software®, Inc.

program the computer. Authoring programs are like software construction sets. One example of authoring software is *HyperStudio*® by Sunburst Technology, Inc. With *HyperStudio* you can make lessons for students and presentations for meetings or classroom use. Young children can use it to make research reports, book reports, creative writing, and similar activities.

IntelliTools, Inc. has integrated their three authoring tools—*IntelliMathics 3*, *IntelliTalk 3*, and *IntelliPics Studio 3*—into a single cross-platform suite of tools for preschool through middle school classrooms. Called *Classroom Suite*, the new software offers the versatility and ease-of-use of the older programs, adding spell checking and word prediction features, among others, to already powerful authoring environments. The flexibility of the user interface, accessibility options, and levels of complexity make the software accessible to users with varied physical abilities, instructional levels, and learning styles. IntelliTools, Inc. offers free downloads of teacher-made activities for these programs at the Activity Exchange on their web site. *Fun, Two, Three!* activity sets include templates and tutorials for *IntelliPics Studio*. IntelliTools describes *IntelliMathics* as a problem-solving tool with on-screen manipulatives. See an *IntelliMathics* screenshot in Figure 7.3.

The same *IntelliTalk* that provides learners with talking word processing capabilities offers teachers activity templates, palettes of pictures, and a locked text feature for the creation of on-screen worksheets, among others. A teacher can offer students selected images on palettes that learners can click to insert words into their documents. See the money palette in Figure 7.4 from *IntelliTalk II*.

In sum, when you can examine an unfamiliar software program and determine the category it best fits into, you are well on the way toward using that software effectively

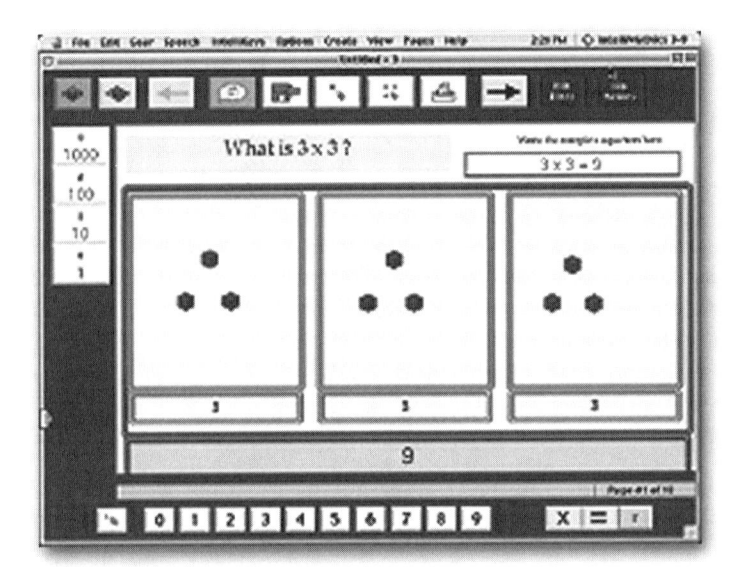

FIGURE 7.3 An *IntelliMathics* Base Ten Blocks template.
Used courtesy of IntelliTools, Inc.

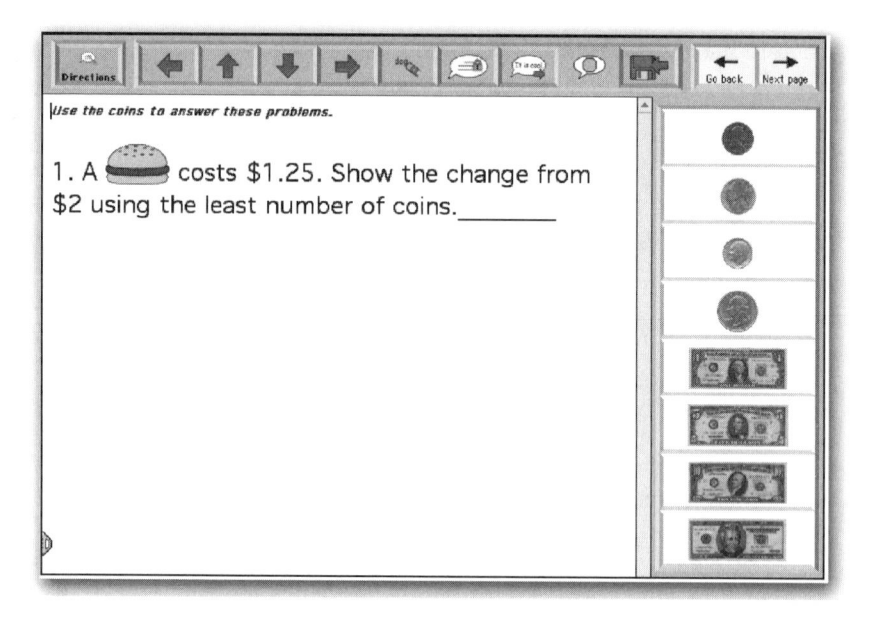

FIGURE 7.4 A money activity template from *IntelliTalk II*.
Used courtesy of IntelliTools, Inc.

in your classroom. The software you use should enhance your curriculum, support the various learning styles and skill levels of the learners in your classroom, and enrich the classroom experiences of all students.

Reviewing Software: Educational and Technical Criteria

As a classroom teacher, you probably will have access to software that others in your school acquired. How will you know if the software is appropriate for the learners in your classroom? What features are good? Which ones are not? How should you approach an unfamiliar software program—what should you look for? The following section will give you some tools to help you make these decisions. Consider the following educational and technical criteria when previewing and making decisions about unfamiliar software programs.

Objectives

Are the objectives stated somewhere in the printed materials that accompany the program? If not, can you examine the program and determine what they are? Does the program appear to meet these objectives?

Prerequisite Skills

What prerequisite academic skills do your students need in order to use the program successfully? For example, will they be able to read the words on the screen? Will they need particular arithmetic skills? In addition, physical skills may be necessary to use a program. Does the program require the learner to use the keyboard or the mouse extensively? If you have students with any physical impairment, how will they use the program? What about sound? Is sound an integral part of the program? Are instructions spoken? Can a student who is deaf use the software? As you preview the program, note what prerequisite skills and capabilities—both academic and physical—your students will need.

Accuracy

How accurate is the material? Examine the content for errors. A few years ago I borrowed a program on U.S. presidents for my classes to preview. A student discovered that one of the presidents was matched to an incorrect vice president! Errors like this are not common, but they are inexcusable! Also look carefully at the sentence structure, grammar, and spelling in on-screen text.

Use of "Reinforcers"

What happens when learners make correct or incorrect answers? Clever use of graphics and sound can make the computer an incredibly effective teaching tool. However, improper design or use can reinforce wrong answers. A reinforcer is an event that occurs immediately following a student's response that increases the likelihood of a similar response in the future. The program should reinforce correct responses. What would happen when the learner makes an error and the performance feedback is more appealing than what happens when the answer is correct? In effect, the software is reinforcing wrong answers! As you preview software, notice what happens for both correct and incorrect responses. If possible, watch a student who is using the program to see his/her response to the computer-supplied feedback. You will soon observe if the learner is being inadvertently reinforced for wrong answers.

Time Commitment

How long does the program take to run? Are there small freestanding segments? Are there stopping places? Can you save the student's performance at any point and return later? Classroom time is valuable. Can you allow the time the software takes? The first version of *The Oregon Trail* (by MECC) for the old Apple II computers had no option for saving. When you began the game in Missouri, you could seldom arrive in Oregon in less than an hour! What happened if you were in Kansas and it was time for lunch? Obviously, few students had opportunities during the school day to actually complete the trail. Thankfully, this is not true for more recent versions of *The Oregon Trail*.

Independence

Do you expect the learner to use the software independently? Look carefully at each program you preview. Are there any instructions for the learner—written or oral? If there are instructions, are they too complicated? Will the learner understand the instructions? Does the program require periodic teacher intervention? Does the program compile a user profile of correct and incorrect answers, or must the teacher record the student performance? Is the software such that, once the learner understands the instructions, it can be operated independently?

What about navigation? Are menus consistent throughout the software? Are options located on the screen or in inaccessible menus? Does the learner access options with keyboard or with mouse? Will the program be accessible to your learners?

Pace

How is the pace of the program controlled? Does the program repeat missed questions? Does the program supplement the instruction if answers are incorrect? Does the software provide prompts or does it move on regardless of the success of the learner? Will the program move ahead more quickly if the learner makes rapid and accurate responses? Marblesoft markets a set of programs that should be a benchmark for instructional software. The *Early Learning I, II,* and *III* and *Mix 'n Match* programs provide tutorial instructions for learning colors, number recognition and sequence, letter recognition and sequence, shape recognition, and beginning addition and subtraction. The teacher can configure all features for individual learners ahead of time. The program can present content with the teacher's specified difficulty level, deliver teacher-specified reinforcers for correct answers, pace the presentation of content based on the teacher's choice, and even back up to lower levels if too many errors are made. *Early Learning* "remembers" configurations for each learner, in addition to the learner's performance—not just how many answers are correct or incorrect, but which ones! See sample screens from the *Early Learning* series in Figure 7.5.

Usefulness

How useful is the software? Can you accomplish the same thing with paper and pencil? Is it "busy work?" If so, then maybe you should not use your valuable computer time and resources for this software. Games such as Tic-Tac-Toe, Dot-to-Dot, and similar paper/pencil games have not transferred usefully to the electronic medium.

Flexibility

How much flexibility has been built in to the software? Can the teacher access different skill levels? Can sound and graphic sequences be selected or turned off? If the program is a game format with points, can the teacher select the number of points necessary to win? Software that delivers the most flexibility has the greatest use in a classroom for learners with special needs.

FIGURE 7.5   *Early Learning* sample screens.

Screen Design

What do you see when you look at the program screens? Is what you see pleasing to look at? Is it easy to look at? Is the screen cluttered? Are words easy for the students to read? Is text in all capital letters (hopefully not)? Is there good contrast for learners with visual disabilities? Are there multiple areas on the screen demanding the learner's attention or one major area on which to focus? How will the appearance of the screens affect your students? Many learners have a difficult time focusing their attention on important areas of the screen. When there are multiple colors, objects, and animations all on the screen at once, many learners, especially those with attention and focusing problems, are unable to use the software successfully.

Documentation

Documentation is the name for all printed or digital materials that accompany the software programs. At the very least, the documentation should explain how to install and run the program. Beyond that, it should clearly state the program objectives and prerequisite skills. Does it explain and describe all of its activities? Does the manual explain how the content fits into the classroom curriculum? Does it suggest activities to orient the students to the content, or provide follow-up worksheets, paper/pencil activities, and topics for discussion? Teachers are more likely to use software successfully if it includes adequate documentation.

Universal Design for Learning

There is a growing movement toward designing usable products and friendly environments to accommodate the needs of people with diverse abilities. This movement—called ***universal design***—is defined as "the design of products and environments to be usable by all people, to the greatest extent possible, without the need for adaptation or specialized design" (definition from: http://www.design.ncsu.edu:8120/cud/univ_design/princ_overview.htm, August 3, 2003). The efforts of a group of architects, product designers, engineers, and environmental design researchers at the Center for Universal Design have culminated in an essential set of guidelines: *The Principles of Universal Design.* To illustrate the application of these principles, imagine the sidewalk beside a city street with a curb cut added to enable persons in wheelchairs to traverse the street. Is this accommodation useable only by persons in wheelchairs? What about the people on bicycles, people pushing strollers, people walking with canes, or people with poor balance or poor vision? People with diverse needs can benefit from the curb ramp. Why not build all sidewalks with ramps to accommodate the needs of everyone?

Teachers need universally designed educational materials to allow learners with diverse needs to access the general education curriculum. Instead of the teacher making "curb cuts" in the general education curriculum, developers of educational materials should be designing flexible, customizable materials with built-in adaptations. Essential elements of universal design for learning include the need for multiple modes of representation for learners who learn best from auditory or visual presentation, the need for multiple levels of complexity, and the need to allow learners to use their preferred mode of control. See the Center for Applied Special Technology (CAST) web site for more about universal design for learning (http://www.cast.org). Marblesoft's *Early Learning* series and the IntelliTools *Classroom Suite* are examples of instructional software that exemplify the universal design principles.

How to Approach a New and Unfamiliar Program

You will soon to be given opportunities to preview educational software. There is one more issue to consider before you do this. How do you approach an unfamiliar program? Well, first, you should **Be Yourself.** Open the software; try to quickly figure out what the features are. Then, as you begin to have questions, go to the documentation to find the answers. Gradually, you should cover all of the topics in the previous section until you are comfortable with the interface and the program features. Remember to read the manual carefully. Do not expect the software to somehow intuitively teach you how to use it.

Often this is as far as a reviewer goes. But, do not stop here! **Be a Good Student** next. Try to put yourself in place of the learner for whom the software was designed. Try to answer correctly and properly. Remember that the software is designed for children, so you should have no trouble in making the correct responses.

Finally, **Be a Poor Student**! Yes, make wrong answers deliberately. Find out how the software handles errors. You have been trained for years to make correct answers, and sometimes it is difficult to intentionally answer incorrectly. But the learners in your classroom are just beginning. They will make mistakes, and you need to know how the software responds.

Software Activities

The following activities will give you some practice in previewing educational software to determine its potential use with grades PreK–12 learners, both general education and special education.

Mini-Reviews

Preview ten software titles. Take notes on the following information:

Name of Program:

Software Category: Pick the SINGLE software category that best describes the program. The categories are: reinforced practice, tutorial, simulation, problem solving, graphics, reference, teacher utility, student utility, and authoring.

Descriptive Paragraph: Write a paragraph describing the program, giving enough information to describe it to someone who has never seen it. Include appropriate age or academic grade level and academic content area. Identify universal design principles that you observe.

Classroom Application: Describe how you might use this program in the classroom to enhance the learner's educational experiences. Use the software category to help you decide the best use for the program.

My Impressions: Tell what you think of the software, any criticisms you have of it, or any aspects of it that you particularly liked.

In-Depth Review

Select a single software program for which you would like to do an in-depth review. Print a copy of the *SoftwareChecklist.pdf* document from the *Text Documents* folder and complete it for that program. Try to answer all of the questions; however, because the evaluation form has been designed to encompass many varying types of programs there may be questions that do not apply to the particular program you have selected. If you encounter items that do not apply, write "N/A" for Not Applicable in the blank.

What's Next?

It's Mine; I Bought It!

When you or your school buys a software program, what exactly does the law entitle you, the end user, to do with it? Can you give it away? Can you share it with another classroom? Can you copy it for backup purposes? Can you give your backup copy to a neighbor? Can you put the program on all of the computers in the lab so everyone can use it at the same time? Can you run your single copy through the computer network so everyone can have access to it?

In most of the situations above, the answer is a definite "No!" Which situations are "No" and why? First, a little background: When you purchase a software program, what you are actually purchasing is nothing more than the right to use it. You do not own the software; the company that holds the copyright owns the program. Most commercial software is called *proprietary*—owned by a company. This legal provision is similar to copyrighted printed materials. Copyright law prohibits you from copying more than a short segment of a copyrighted text for distribution to others. When you purchase proprietary software you are purchasing the right to use that one copy. The law says that you can make a single *archival copy* for backup purposes—in case your original becomes damaged.

Then, can you loan your backup copy to another classroom? No, you cannot, because two copies would be in use at the same time. Can you give away your copy? Yes, you can give the software away as long as you also give away the license or registration and any backup copy you made. Can you place the software on more than one computer? No, more than one copy would be in use at the same time. What about a network? The same holds with a network: If you have purchased only one copy, and more than one copy of the software can be used at one time, then it is illegal.

So what can you do if you want to use more than one copy of a particular software program that is proprietary? Well, you could purchase as many copies as you need; however, that could get quite expensive! Most software publishers, especially publishers of educational software, offer educators special deals called lab packs, network versions, building licenses, or site licenses. All of these options offer the educator multiple copies at greatly reduced rates. In the case of lab packs, generally the license is for five or ten or fifteen copies. The educator gets one set of documentation and then as many copies of the software as is requested. Network versions are offered much the same way as lab packs. Sometimes, a building license can also be purchased so that the software can be used on any computer in that building with no limit on the number. This is an appealing choice for a school when a particular software title is in great demand by many classrooms. A site license is similar to a building license; however, a site may be a larger institution. Here is the bottom line: Buy one copy; use one copy. Any additional use could be deemed *software piracy*.

Are there other kinds of software for which the use of multiple copies is not so restrictive? Yes there are! Two additional kinds of software are *shareware* and *public domain software* (often called freeware). Shareware is software in which the software developer chooses to distribute the software. Since there is little or no overhead (printed manuals, catalogs, advertising, among others) the cost is kept down. Shareware programs are freely distributed or can be given to as many people as you wish and used on as many computers as you want because this is the developer's primary means of advertising and distribution. How can a software developer survive economically this way? Usually the shareware program you receive from someone or download from the Internet is not complete. There are several different ways to achieve this. First, you could acquire the complete shareware program, but it only works for a limited amount of time (a few minutes, a few days, or even a few weeks). Then a message will appear reminding you that your trial period has expired, and if you wish to continue using it you can send the fees to the developer. Another pattern for shareware is that when you download the program and begin to use it, you discover that only a few features are available—just enough, the developer hopes, to hook you on the program. If you want full access to all features, you must send in your money (through mail or Internet) to receive a registration number to "unlock" all of the features. Typically shareware fees are reasonable, usually from $5 to $30. There are excellent educational shareware programs available. One of the best ways to acquire shareware is to download programs from a reputable Internet source—one known for quick downloads of virus-free software.

Public domain software or freeware is another format for educational software. These programs are also freely distributed and can be freely used on any number of computers. Public domain refers to the legal designation for material that is not copyrighted. There are no copyright restrictions on the distribution or multiple use of public domain software (although others are prohibited from selling it or otherwise making a profit from it). Often public domain software includes simple computer utilities, clever add-ons to commercial software, or small programs with a relatively narrow focus. However, often software like this has great application in classrooms when teachers are striving to meet the varied needs of learners. You can locate public domain software much the same way as you find shareware.

How Much Can I Spend?

Throughout this software chapter you have considered many of the features of educational software that someone has already purchased. The day may come, hopefully sooner than later, when someone will remind you that the money allocated for software MUST be spent! What additional consideration should you make when purchasing educational software programs?

First, when browsing on-line catalogs, web sites, or print catalogs, keep in mind the computer you are purchasing the software for and its attributes. Not all software is available for both Windows and Macintosh computers. Not all software is made for every operating system that these two popular platforms use. And software has differing requirements for both disk space and RAM. You need to know the following information about your computer before shopping for software:

- Computer platform (Macintosh or Windows)
- Operating system (Windows 95, 98, 2000, XP; Macintosh 8, 9, 10; or others)
- Hard disk space (How big is your hard disk, and how much space is available?)
- Available RAM (How much RAM does the computer have?)

Many publishers offer demonstration versions of popular software titles at little or no cost—often only postage and handling. The demonstration version is usually a short segment of a single aspect of the whole program. For example, *Wheels,* by R. J. Cooper

& Associates is an arcade game for children with special needs in addition to a joystick trainer for potential electric wheelchair users. The learner battles it out with pie-throwing clowns to exit school-building mazes through nine increasingly difficult levels. The first maze of the Easy level is available for both Macintosh and Windows computers free from R. J. Cooper's web site. Both IntelliTools, Inc. and Don Johnston Incorporated offer demonstration CDs of some of their most popular software.

Finally, when shopping for software, as with other catalog shopping, use care in making these important decisions. You would not hesitate to purchase *The Oregon Trail* or *Print Shop Deluxe* if you had a need for either of these programs. They are well known and have excellent reputations. What about a title that you find appealing but are not sure of? Be wary of overblown advertisements! Can you ask someone who may have used it? Can you ask the company for a demonstration copy? If at all possible, "test drive" the software yourself before purchasing it. Once you receive the program and open the seal, it is yours!

Continue browsing new and unfamiliar software. Keep searching for software that complements your classroom materials and curriculum and the learning styles of the learners entrusted to you. Integrating the computer into the daily activities of your classroom takes a dedication that, in the long run, is well worth the effort.

KEY TERMS

archival copy
authoring software
communication board
documentation
graphics software
problem-solving software

proprietary
public domain software
reference
reinforced practice
shareware
simulation

software piracy
student utility
teacher utility
tutorial
universal design

CHAPTER

8 Internet

What is the *Internet*? What is the *web*? The Internet is an electronic communications network linking computers around the world. The World Wide Web (WWW or simply "the web") is that portion of the Internet accessible through computer software called ***browsers***.

What is the Internet? Well, it is good and bad, terrible and terrific! The Internet can be time-consuming or it can be timesaving. You can own it or it can own you. You can check your e-mail, locate a recipe for key lime pie, research a medical condition, play word games with people around the world, buy and sell anything, learn about desert animals, find out the meaning of a word, check the weather forecast for any city in the world, see movie previews, get breaking news, check tonight's television schedule, take a virtual field trip to the Smithsonian—and this is just scratching the surface.

Then there is a darker side: There is wrong information, questionable "facts," pornography, and controversial material; there is cheating, swindling, gambling, stalking, spying, identity theft, and all the information you never wanted to know about hate groups. There are annoying pop-up advertisements, unsolicited advertisements ("spam") in your e-mail, links that go nowhere, pages that load too slowly, and viruses that eat your hard drive.

What types of materials are on the Internet that you might want to use in your classroom? What makes a web site accessible to persons with disabilities? How do you locate useful web sites? What rights do you have to material that you find on the Internet? How can you incorporate use of the Internet into your classroom curriculum? How can you keep learners on task while they are online? How can you keep learners from accessing undesirable materials? These questions and more will be covered in this chapter.

Web Accessibility

Many people with visual disabilities use software that reads the screen to give them access to what appears on the monitor—a great adaptation for all-text applications. What if that person wants to browse the web? How does the software that reads text on the screen interpret an image it encounters? The answer is: "It does not!" An image-rich page may come through to the person who is listening to the page being read as

"Image . . . Image . . . Image. . . ." What can the web page designer do to make the page more easily accessed by users with special needs, whether they are visual, hearing, motor, intellectual, or language impairments? In the example of screen reading software attempting to "read" images, the page designer can offer alternative text for each image. So, instead of the users hearing "Image . . . Image . . . Image . . . , they could hear "Image of a sailboat . . . Image of a dog with six puppies . . . Image of a young boy in a wheelchair."

Web content should be accessible to persons with all disabilities. The World Wide Web Consortium (W3C) has established accessibility guidelines. Follow the link for *Accessibility* from the W3C Web site (http://www.w3.org/) to explore the documents there. This list highlights some of the recommendations:

- There is text alternative to visual images.
- There is text or sign (ASL) alternative to auditory content.
- Page does not rely on color.
- There are obvious navigation cues.
- The user has control of all moving, scrolling, or animated content.
- The page is clear and simple.

Another interesting and useful web site called *Bobby* is a service that evaluates the accessibility of web pages. An online version is available from the Bobby web site (http://bobby.watchfire.com/). Individuals or organizations that require frequent page testing can subscribe to the service. The online version offers free evaluations for single pages.

As you begin selecting web sites for learners to use, keep the accessibility guidelines in mind. Select only sites that your learners with disabilities can fully access.

Searching and Using Web Materials

How Do You Find Things Out There?

There are millions and millions of web sites on the Internet. How can you find the information that you seek? The answer is to use a ***search engine.*** A search engine is analogous to the card catalog in a library with one big exception: A single card catalog in a library typically includes references to all materials in the library. How easy it would be to find resources on the Internet if there were a single search engine with links to all possible web sites. As it is, there are many search engines, each with only small portions of possible web sites included. This would be like having a huge library with many small card catalogs, each one listing only a small portion of the whole collection. Much of the collection in this hypothetical library would not be listed in any of the catalogs. To find some of the materials you would have to walk around the stacks, browsing!

On the Internet you can initiate a search with the search button on your Internet browser software toolbar or enter a search engine's specific web address. Each search engine has its own particular rules for defining advanced searches and limiting search text to improve the search results. Look on the search page for a help button or more information on advanced searches to improve your search skills.

Exercise 1. Initiate a search with any search engine for any topic. Some of the popular search engines are:

- All the Web (http://www.alltheweb.com)
- AltaVista (http://www.altavista.com)
- Ask Jeeves (http://www.ask.com)
- Dogpile (http://www.dogpile.com)
- Excite (http://www.excite.com)
- Google (http://www.google.com)
- InfoSeek (http://www.infoseek.go.com)
- Lycos (http://www.lycos.com)
- Web Crawler (http://www.webcrawler.com/info.wbcrwl/)
- Yahoo (http://www.yahoo.com)

The length of time it takes to complete a search is based on both the speed of your Internet connection and your search topic. If you have chosen a broad topic, the search engine may be compiling a list of hundreds or even thousands of "hits." Look at the results of this search. Often the list of web sites (**URLs** for Universal Resource Locator) that you receive from a search is arranged in order of most relevant first. Next, try a search with another search engine for exactly the same topic. Compare the results. Among sites on both lists you may find many duplications; there may also be sites unique to each list. Because of this, when you need to locate a variety of resources, you should conduct searches with more that one search engine to increase the likelihood that you will locate useful resources.

What Can You Do with What You Find?

When you have located the material that you seek, what are you allowed to do with it? Can you use images or documents you download from the Internet in your classroom when you are creating your own materials? Can you use text you locate on the Internet in the documents you write? Can you build your own web page from the "pieces-parts" you collect from other sites?

There are two issues here: first, *plagiarism.* Plagiarism is attributing the use of text, images, and even ideas, from other sources to yourself. In all cases where you use material that is not originally yours, you must give credit to the creator of that material—whether the material is from a page in a book or an image captured off the Internet. Any time you create documents, images, or multimedia work using material from another source—not original material, whether it is copyrighted or not—all sources must be given credit. Otherwise, you are committing plagiarism.

The second issue is copyright. Copyright law protects most material you find on the Internet. Some web sites have obvious copy protection—clearly placed statements informing you of what your rights are. On others, your rights to copy are not so obvious. If you want to use material but are not sure whether it is copyrighted or in the public domain, contact the web master for the site and ask.

Only the owner of a copyrighted work has the right to reproduce the work, distribute copies of the material, modify the work in some way, or display it publicly. What restrictions are placed on the material you find on the Internet? How can you make use of copyrighted material? In brief, if you wish to distribute, display, reproduce, or modify it in some way, you must get permission from the owner. There are, however, exceptions to the rights of the copyright owner that are called "***Fair Use.***" Fair Use allows others to use portions of some copyrighted materials for reviews, reporting, teaching, and research, among other limited usages. As a classroom teacher you can use many copyrighted materials for teaching purposes without getting permission. This is Fair Use; copyright law is complex. The United States Copyright Office web site offers detailed information on what types of materials are copyright protected and what constitutes Fair Use. For further information see: http://www.lcweb.loc.gov/copyright/

How Can You Use the Internet?

In the educational software chapter you placed software programs into categories that helped you decide how they might best be used in the classroom. By examining different uses of the Internet, we can do a similar analysis of how to use the Internet in the classroom.

Communication

The Internet can be a conduit to everywhere! We can chat with people and e-mail people all over the world. E-mail and chats are becoming valuable educational experiences for developing effective communication skills. Imagine learners collecting weather data through e-mail communications with children in other parts of the world, charting changes and comparing weather conditions between the locations. Imagine children photographing and drawing local flora and fauna and exchanging these images with children in another part of the world. Imagine pen pals (e-pals) in distant lands sharing their experiences with foods, pets, and entertainment. Imagine homebound students interacting with teachers and classmates using inexpensive web cams. Furthermore, for learners with special needs, Internet communications open a whole world of social interaction and expression.

News and Current Events

The web sites of television networks, television stations, radio stations, and newspapers provide breaking news, current affairs and issues, editorials, and current weather. Some sites archive past articles for future research. Whether the source is local, national, or international, the latest news and weather is only a mouse click away.

Exercise 2

1. Locate one web site that carries international news headlines.
2. Locate one web site that posts news headlines for your state.
3. Locate one web site where you can find current weather conditions for any United States city.
4. Locate a web site that posts severe weather warnings for your county.

Live Broadcasts

Live connections to many locations can add dimension to the classroom that was never before possible. Such locations could include electronic field trips to museums, special events, breaking news stories, and private links to zoos, theaters, and libraries. During the summer of 1997 my classes watched the live video of the Sojourner robot exploring the Mars landscape. The video feed from NASA was broadcast through the web site of one of the major news networks. Experiences like this, beyond the pure amazement of it, can open doors to further reading and research by fascinated learners.

Exercise 3. Go to the web site of the Smithsonian Institution (http://www.si.edu). Browse the contents there. Name three of the on-line museum collections. Then, visit one of those collections, and name three different facts you learned there.

Reference

There are standard dictionary, thesaurus, and encyclopedia references on the Internet. Typically, these tools are the latest updates of the more traditionally printed materials. Accessing them through the Internet provides a cost-effective way to provide the latest up-to-date materials to students. These reference materials do not require shelf space or desk space and never get out of date. Also, a trip to the library is not required. Browse the following URLs:

- http://www.wordsmyth.net
- http://www.dictionary.com
- http://www.encarta.com
- http://thesaurus.reference.com

Exercise 4. Go to a dictionary site on the web (http://www.dictionary.com). First, notice the resources there in addition to looking up word definitions. Now, look up any word. Scroll through the results when they appear and list the sources of all the reference materials the site used to define your word.

Research

The Internet is an ideal place to do research: Learn about an animal—where it lives, what it eats, how long it lives; research the foods people eat in other parts of the world;

find out where rivers flow, what happens to the rain, or why the sky is blue. Research medical conditions, types of transportation, or what makes a volcano. But be forewarned: Searching on the Internet can sometimes yield misinformation. Seek reliable information sources such as government agencies, reputable organizations, research groups, or educational institutions. Make use of the links that a reliable resource may offer to locate similar or related information.

Exercise 5. Select one of the previously mentioned topics, or pick one of your own. Formulate at least three questions concerning the topic. Using your choice of search engine, answer each question, providing one or more URLs to answer each question. For example, for the topic "The Fish in Lake Superior," the questions might be: (1) Name five species of fish native to Lake Superior, (2) Name three foods that these particular fish eat, and (3) For each of the fish species indicate whether it is a food for people.

Instruction

The Internet offers many and varied exciting opportunities to learn new skills and information. There are tutorials on many different topics that give you step-by-step instructions. You can locate instructions for beginning cooks, directions for how to knit or crochet, tutorials on how to make a web page, and even how to make a *PowerPoint* presentation. Web sites such as *How Stuff Works* (http://www.howstuffworks.com/index.htm) provide clear and entertaining information about a variety of science topics. To learn how to make your own web page, *Web Monkey* and *Web Monkey for Kids* (http://hotwired.lycos.com/webmonkey/kids/) provide carefully crafted and illustrated step-by-step tutorials to get you started.

You can also use the web to present your own instructional modules using WebQuests. A WebQuest is a web-based activity in which learners use information found on the Internet. A learner can explore, but within teacher-defined limits. WebQuests can help learners become more effective researchers and are ideal for classes that contain learners with different ability levels. Learners follow the links on the lesson rather than browsing or searching the web on their own, making more efficient use of their time. Often teachers publish and share WebQuest modules. Visit the original WebQuest site at San Diego State University to see examples (http://webquest.sdsu.edu). Look for other samples by searching for: **webquest.** Wayne K. Mock at Ball State University has designed and published an easy-to-use application that allows teachers to generate their own electronic lessons. *WebQuest Generator* for both Macintosh and Windows computers can be found on the web (http://web.bsu.edu/wmock/wqg/). Another template can be accessed at: http://www.spa3.k12.sc.us/WebQuestTemplate/webquesttemp.htm.

Assessment

An Internet environment is ideally suited to data collection—tests, surveys, rating scales, and checklists. There are companies, systems, and software that specialize in providing the environment for the delivery of electronic assessment materials. Both *BlackBoard* (http://www.blackboard.com) and *Quia* (http://www.quia.com) offer teachers fully integrated delivery of instructional materials, assessment, and class management.

Tools

Teachers can locate various tools on the Internet. There are calculators, conversion tables, graph paper, and other science and mathematics aides. You can locate software add-ons or updates for programs that you own, current printer drivers, plug-ins for browsers, and other free material to enhance the functioning of your computer and its peripheral devices. Look for stable sites that offer downloadable software for your computer platform and provide virus-free downloads.

Shopping

There are countless opportunities for purchasing things over the Internet. Many companies with traditional stores also support web shopping. Companies that previously offered only catalog shopping are now in the online shopping arena. There are also companies that have sprouted on the web and never existed with floor space or paper invoices! Shopping does not necessarily mean buying. In the classroom, learning activities can be structured around budgeting, purchasing necessities with limited budgets, calculating taxes and shipping charges, making change, and making wise decisions.

Entertainment

Last, but certainly not least, is use of the Internet for entertainment. There are sites designated for special interest—authors, storybook characters, historical events, celebrities, and every hobby imaginable. There are places to view movie trailers and preview video games. There are web sites dedicated to video gaming—even sites where you can play games against remote opponents. Many game opportunities feature role-playing adventure opportunities. There is every type of arcade-type game imaginable and many electronic versions of traditional board games. There are card games and dozens of word games including crosswords and word searches. There are educational sites with math and science games. All are free online. A few minutes with a carefully chosen game can be a powerful reinforcer for more challenging work accomplished by struggling learners.

Exercise 6.   Locate and list URLs for the following entertainment sites:

1. A place to play crossword puzzles.
2. A site for a word game that is not a crossword puzzle.
3. Any site offering free play of arcade-type skill games such as mazes, falling blocks or gems, or others.

This has been a brief look into the uses of the Internet within the classroom. Web sites come and go; content of seemingly stable sites changes overnight; features are regularly added or removed. The web is an ever-shifting, elusive assembly of resources. Seek accessible sites that offer opportunities for students to think, to ask questions, and to find answers.

Structuring the Work Environment

How can you structure the classroom environment to encourage learners to remain on task while working on the Internet? One suggestion is to arrange the classroom so that the computer is located where you can view the computer monitor easily. Students are more likely to stay on task when they know you are monitoring their progress. Another suggestion is to structure the activity carefully. A learner should have a specific, detailed assignment before beginning the computer work. If the project is a large one, break it down into smaller one-session segments. Expect the learner to show you the results of each session. Students with specific assignments, a limited time, and an expectation for completed work will be less likely to stray.

Another idea to consider for classrooms is Internet content management software. There are several titles offering different features that filter the Internet content coming into the computer. A teacher or parent can configure filtering software to block specific categories of web sites. These programs have varying degrees of success. If you are interested in software of this type, research the current titles and their effectiveness.

There are several web sites designed just for children. They offer attractive, entertaining, and informative content and provide a safe environment for children to browse. Here are a few sites that may or may not be available as you read this:

- Ask Jeeves for Kids (http://www.ajkids.com)
- Berit's Best Sites for Children (http://www.beritsbest.com)
- KidsClick! (http://sunsite.berkeley.edu/KidsClick!)
- Kid's Tools for Searching the Internet (http://www.rcls.org/ksearch.htm)
- PBS Kids (http://pbskids.org/)
- Yahooligans (http://www.yahooligans.com)

Exercise 7. Identify one additional web site suitable for exploration by young children.

As you begin using the Internet in your classroom, work with your students to help them develop good computer habits. Teach them how to work cooperatively, how to use reference resources, and how to conduct productive searches. Teach them about personal security on the Internet. They should learn not to give their names, addresses, or telephone numbers to anyone. Teach them not to talk to strangers and be cautious of unsolicited e-mail. The better your students understand what you expect of them and how they should perform, the more likely it is that they will stay on task and profit from their experiences on the Internet.

Did you know . . .

- the monitor should be at eye level or slightly below to reduce neck fatigue?
- the upper arm and forearm should form an angle slightly greater than 90°?
- the forearm, hand, and wrist should be in a straight line?
- the shoulders should be relaxed?
- the hips and knees should be at 90° angles with feet flat on the floor?
- the chair back should support the lower back?

Consult an occupational therapist or a physical therapist to help position a learner for efficient, productive computer use free from fatigue, muscle strain, or injury.

What's Next?

At some point you may want to create your own web page. You may want to publish your own class page—a place for you to make announcements, suggest interesting links, and share the creative endeavors of your students. Learners with Internet access at home could share classroom stories with their families, discover homework tips, and visit teacher-recommended web sites together.

There are many easy-to-use software programs designed to help you write your own web pages. In fact, there is even web page software designed for young children to use. An alternative to using page creation software is to write the page yourself with HTML (Hypertext Markup Language), the language of the web. Regardless of how you construct a web page, make it accessible to all learners.

With thoughtful selection of resources, careful planning of student activities, and considerations for special needs, the Internet can add a rich dimension to your daily curriculum. The Internet can literally bring the world to your classroom!

KEY TERMS

browser
fair use
Internet

plagiarism
search engine

URL
web

PART THREE
Making Adaptations for Learners with Special Needs

CHAPTER

9   Making Adaptations with Hardware and Software

As computers take on a greater importance in our business, education, and home environments, they have an even greater importance for persons with disabilities. The computer can be an equalizer, empowering persons with disabilities to achieve results previously possible only to their peers without disabilities. For a person with special needs, the computer can become a means of communication, a tool for independent living, a valuable recreational outlet, and an opportunity for employment. This chapter focuses on empowering learners with special needs to (a) achieve their potentials using computer adaptations to provide computer access, (b) accomplish work in easier and better ways, and (c) enhance the work environment with software aids and adaptations.

An employee of a large company in our community called my office a few years ago. Concerned about being compliant with the Americans with Disabilities Act (ADA), he wanted my advice about how he could set up a computer workstation for potential employees with disabilities. I told him that there was no one-size-fits-all computer station for persons with disabilities. After he hired an employee who needed adaptations, he should then acquire whatever that employee needed to do the work effectively and efficiently.

As you begin to learn about different kinds of computer devices, there is a concept for you to remember: There are no specific devices you should recommend for someone who has a physical disability, a sensory impairment, or cognitive deficits. With computer adaptations, there is no such thing as "one size fits all." Devices should be matched to an individual's needs after considering their strengths, weaknesses, and preferences.

A section later in the chapter addresses some of the issues to consider when selecting appropriate adaptations.

The ideal instructional setting for this chapter is in an adaptive computing lab providing opportunities for hands-on exploration of software and hardware of the types described in the chapter. A second-choice setting is a computer lab with a touch window, several different mouse devices, and assisted keyboard control panels—*Easy Access* or *Universal Access* for Macintosh and *Accessibility Options* for Windows computers. A follow-up visit to an adaptive computer lab, an assistive technology demonstration site, a rehabilitation center, or a school program where students can observe individuals using special devices would be ideal. If hands-on experiences and observations cannot be arranged, the last-choice option would be to invite someone to class with an assortment of devices to demonstrate. In order to fully appreciate computer adaptations it is strongly suggested that some hand-on experiences be available to readers of this chapter.

Although computer technology changes rapidly, the basics of adapting the computer are relatively stable. Newer devices take advantage of newer technology, but the basic principles remain the same—a learner needs (a) alternatives or adaptations made to the standard keyboard and mouse devices for computer input, or (b) output alternatives or adaptations to enhance or supplement the monitor output or (c) both.

This chapter is divided into sections that reflect different types of adaptations. Appendix B contains activities that readers should complete to directly experience some of the most commonly used computer adaptations. The reader will be prompted in the text when a particular activity is appropriate. Use as many of the activities as you can. Modify them as you wish to make the best use of the software and hardware adaptations that are available. The chapter closes with a list of study questions.

Simple Solutions

Persons who are unable to use a computer adequately with the standard keyboard or mouse often can do so with very small, relatively simple adaptations. This section primarily describes some simple modifications and suggests activities to allow the reader, who has no motor coordination difficulties, to simulate a motor impairment.

Keyboard and Mouse Shortcuts

As we develop computer skills, we build ways to accomplish tasks that become habits. Many of us touch type quickly using ten fingers and drive a mouse around like a pro. We often do not even think about clicking and dragging with the mouse—our hands do it automatically. As we become more proficient, we begin using shortcuts or alternative ways of accomplishing tasks that help us become faster and more efficient. One example is in saving a document. The most obvious way to save is to move to the File menu with the mouse, drag down the menu to **Save** . . . and then release the mouse button. An alternate and more efficient way to save, for persons adept at keyboarding, is to use the keyboard equivalent—⌘**s** for Macintosh or **[ctrl]s** for Windows. Look in the menus to see if there are keyboard equivalents for the options there. For Macintosh, keyboard shortcuts are listed along the right side of each menu. For Windows, keyboard shortcuts are identified in the menu text as underlined letters and can be accessed by holding down **[ctrl]** while pressing the letter key. Oftentimes, a proficient typist prefers to use keyboard equivalents for frequently used menu choices to avoid having to move a hand from the keyboard to drive the mouse.

Persons who have difficulty typing or have a motor impairment that prevents them from using a mouse often have to find alternative ways to do their work efficiently. It is critical that a learner who cannot use a mouse well be taught keyboard equivalents for frequently accessed menu choices. A shortcut that is optional for a typist with good motor skills may be the only way a person with a motor impairment can work. You may find a particular shortcut useful or fun, but your students may desperately need it to enable their computer use.

Some persons with motor impairments may prefer using a mouse, even with limited use. For these users any shortcut to reduce mouse movement would increase their efficiency. A helpful mouse shortcut on a Windows computer is **right-click** on the mouse to bring up a contextual menu. The equivalent to the right-click on the Macintosh—there is only one mouse button—is **[ctrl]-click**.

Shortcuts are available for many other purposes. Search for Shortcuts in the computer's help system and also within specific software help files.

Keyguard

A *keyguard* is a Plexiglas, plastic, or metal plate with holes that lies over any standard or *alternative keyboard*. It isolates keys, allowing the user to rest on its surface without striking keys. The purpose is to prevent the depression of unwanted keys by someone with poor fine-motor control. In general, a single-finger typist or someone who is depressing keys with a stick, stylus, or other pointing device uses a keyguard. The illustration in Figure 9.1 is of a keyguard mounted over an Apple Design Keyboard, along with an unmounted keyguard. Some keyguards fit down over the keys and others fasten on with Velcro strips.

Keyguard manufacturers offer the device for virtually any style keyboard. Keyguards are an excellent, portable, low-tech solution for many persons. However, keyguard use is not indicated for someone attempting to touch type or use multiple fingers for keyboarding.

Touch Screen

A *touch screen* is a clear plastic frame with tiny touch-sensitive sensors that attaches to the computer monitor, usually with Velcro making it easy to remove when not in use. The purpose of a touch screen is to provide direct access to choices on the monitor. It can replace all functions of a standard mouse in all software that uses a mouse for both Macintosh and Windows. Unlike the earlier versions of touch screens that only worked with limited early childhood or special education software, the devices today are truly alternative mouse devices. The device requires the installation of utility software to provide various touch options, along with a utility to *calibrate* the touch screen (line up the sensors on the touch screen with the monitor behind it), assuring accuracy when pressing the screen. Figure 9.2 shows an Edmark TouchWindow.

FIGURE 9.1 Transparent keyguard alone and placed atop a standard keyboard.

FIGURE 9.2 A touch screen attached to a monitor.

Touch screens are useful as an input device whenever the learner can benefit from direct input. With a standard mouse, the learner must move a mouse on the desktop to move a pointer on the screen, and then click a mouse button to "touch" that spot. Pointing to the monitor with a finger is a direct action that is desirable for many learners with special needs and less demanding physically and conceptually than standard mouse devices. See the touch screen shown in Figure 9.2. If there is a touch screen available to you, use the Touch Screen Activity in Appendix B to explore its features.

Mouse Devices

There are some features and characteristics of the standard mouse that probably make it the poorest choice for individuals with motor disabilities or cognitive deficits. You will examine some of these characteristics first and then look at the features of a few ***alternative mouse devices.***

- When moving a standard mouse across the screen, you must often pick up the mouse and replace it in another spot on the mouse pad. This is a difficult concept both to understand and to perform.
- When dragging you must hold down a button with one finger, while continuing to coordinate the mouse move—a complex physical task.
- The standard mouse requires whole arm movement to activate efficiently. Just try resting your wrist on the desk and operating the standard mouse without moving your wrist!

Each of the alternative mouse devices described below offers different features. Many of them have programmable options. When attempting to determine the most appropriate mouse alternative for an individual, give that person an adequate trial with each device before making a final decision. Several different kinds of mouse devices are illustrated in Figure 9.3. From left to right are the colorful Kid-TRAC trackball, Penny + Giles Joystick Plus, Alps Glidepoint Trackpad from Alps Electric, Kensington TurboMouse trackball by the Kensington Group, and Macally Micro mouse.

Trackballs. A *trackball* is like an upside-down mouse. On a traditional mouse, the ball is on the bottom—moving the mouse moves the ball. With a trackball having the ball on the top, the device is stationary. The user moves the ball with the finger(s) or hand. The physical demands are reduced. The user can rest a wrist on the table surface and have full access to all mouse features. Some of the trackballs that have multiple buttons also have programmable features. Buttons can be assigned various actions such as opening a menu or initiating printing, among others. Kid-TRAC has a lock button so the user can drag without simultaneously depressing a button and moving the ball. Large trackballs have balls about the size of a golf ball; smaller trackballs have balls about the size of a large marble.

Track Pads. The ***track pad*** is a tiny device with a touch-sensitive area of about two square inches. Moving the finger over the surface moves the cursor on the screen. In fact, it works best with only slight movement and light touch of one finger. It could even

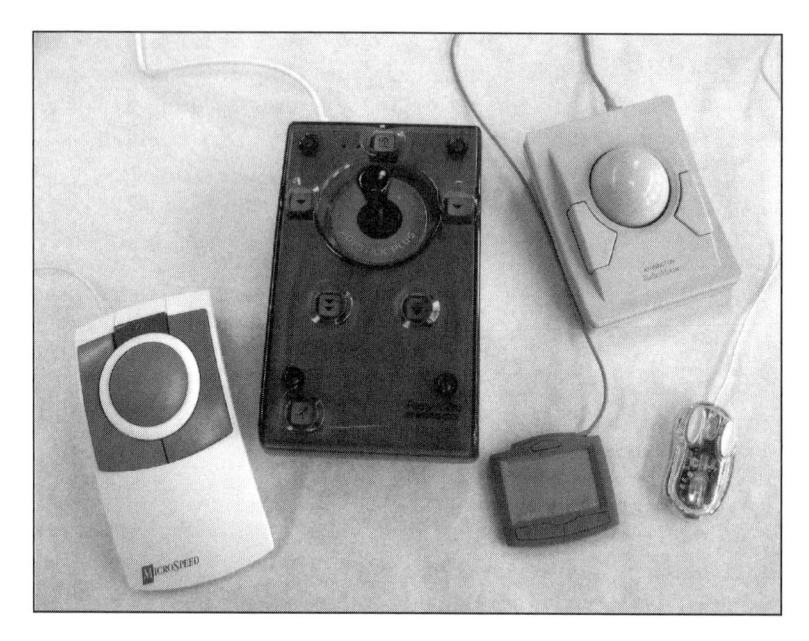

FIGURE 9.3 A variety of mouse devices with differing motor requirements.

be placed in the user's lap. For a computer user with poor large-motor coordination but good fine-motor functioning, a track pad is an ideal mouse device. It takes very little strength or motion to operate effectively. The track pad has become quite popular on powerbook and notebook computers; however, external ones are also available.

Joysticks. The *joystick* is typically viewed as a game device, but it can also serve as an excellent mouse device. There are simple joysticks with a few buttons and far more complex ones with hefty handles, sturdy bases, and many buttons. Many joysticks have been designed to work with various flight simulator programs. Because the programs require different keys to access various features, the joysticks can be programmed for key presses. The programmable buttons can be configured to enter text, select options from menus, or initiate other actions. Because of the versatility, a joystick can be an ideal mouse device for a person who can grip the handle. Most require no movement of the whole arm and can be attached to a surface with Velcro or suction cups.

Head Mouse. A more sophisticated albeit expensive solution for persons unable to use their hands at all is the hands-free alternative mouse devices on the market. One such device is the Track IR Head Mouse from Assistive Technologies. Another is the HeadMouse from Origin Instruments Corporation. Both devices are available for both Macintosh and Windows computers. A **head mouse** is typically composed to two parts—a sensor at the computer and a target attached to the user's forehead or glasses. As the user's head moves, the movements are tracked by the sensor and translated into mouse movements. Clicking is accomplished either by lingering on a spot for a specified time or by clicking a more traditional switch. When a head mouse is combined with an onscreen keyboard, the user has full keyboard and mouse accessibility.

Other Mouse Devices. There are several other mouse devices that are popular in the special education market. The Penny + Giles Joystick and Trackballs by Penny + Giles Computer Products, have small handles and recessed buttons. The SAM (SAM means Switch Activated Mouse) Joystick and Trackball that are made and distributed by R. J. Cooper & Associates combine mouse action with switch activation.

Browse through the input device section of one of the nationwide chains of computer technology stores to see the variety of mouse devices. Stop at each sample, place your hand on it, and move it to simulate actual use. Must you move your whole arm? Can you use it with one finger? Are there multiple programmable buttons? Could you hold it in your lap? If you have several different kinds of mouse devices available, do the Mouse Device Activity in Appendix B.

Other Aids

Moisture Guard. A *moisture guard* is a thin, heat-treated plastic film that fits snugly over many different standard keyboards or alternative keyboards to prevent damage from moisture. Moisture guards are especially useful when working with children who may drool. There is another good use for moisture guards, especially in a classroom for children with special needs. Some educational software requires that users press keys on the keyboard to access features or even run the software. Learners who are not familiar with the keyboard layout are unable to use the software because they cannot locate the keys. Use a moisture guard as a keyboard mask by placing large letters or colored spots of paper under the moisture guard with a glue stick to isolate the important keys the learner needs to press to operate the software. See the illustration of a moisture guard being used as a keyboard mask in Figure 9.4.

Key Stickers. Several different manufacturers make large print key stickers, either black-on-white or white-on-black, to attach to the keyboard to make viewing keys easier for persons with visual disabilities. There is an additional use for these stickers. The standard keyboard can overwhelm young children who are beginning to keyboard. This can also be true of learners with focusing or attention problems. Placing the stickers on just the letter and numeral keys can help the learner to focus on the keys they need. See the illustration of ZoomCaps from Don Johnston Incorporated, in Figure 9.5.

Software Solutions

Software especially designed for learners with special needs is being developed at an incredible pace. This section introduces some of the software categories that enable computer access in addition to modifying the work environment for persons with learning disabilities. These programs have varying applications and often can be combined with some of the previously described simple solutions to provide creative, inexpensive computer access. Software titles named in the following section are by no means the

108   PART THREE / Making Adaptations for Learners with Special Needs

FIGURE 9.4   A moisture guard serving as a keyboard mask.

FIGURE 9.5   White on black key stickers.

only ones available. Check the current catalogs and suppliers for new products, updated versions, and availability for Windows or Macintosh computers.

Assisted Keyboard

The concept of an ***assisted keyboard*** is to modify the functioning of a standard keyboard with software. The software to enable an assisted keyboard is part of the systems of both Macintosh and Windows computers. It is free! On the Macintosh it is called *Universal Access* (*Easy Access* in pre-OS X systems); on Windows it is called *Accessibility Options*. On both computer platforms it is a Control Panel (Macintosh OS X—System Preferences).

Regardless of the computer platform you have available (Macintosh or Windows) the features are the same.

Sticky Keys. One component of an assisted keyboard is **Sticky Keys.** Sticky Keys allow keys to "stick together" to enable a single-finger typist to depress more than one key at a time. For example, to capitalize a letter on a standard keyboard without adaptations, you must depress [SHIFT] and the desired letter at the same time. When Sticky Keys is active, [SHIFT] is pressed and released—but the computer "remembers" that it was pressed. The next key struck appears in upper case.

Slow Keys. Another component of an assisted keyboard is **Slow Keys.** When Slow Keys is activated, the computer's acceptance of a key press can be delayed to block stray touches on the keyboard from being accepted as key strikes. The length of the delay can be adjusted to individual preferences.

Mouse Keys. A third component of an assisted keyboard is **Mouse Keys.** When Mouse Keys is activated, a user who is unable to operate a standard mouse can strike keys on the keyboard to simulate all mouse actions. Mouse Keys turns the numeric keypad—at the right end of standard keyboards—into mouse keys. The *5* in the center becomes a mouse click. The *2, 4, 6,* and *8* keys move the mouse down, left, right, and up, respectively. The *1, 7, 9,* and *3* keys move the mouse diagonally. Pressing the *0* turns on dragging. The *5* or the "." turns off dragging.

Some versions of these utilities include a screen enlarger, a temporary quick fix for users with visual disabilities—"temporary" because often the scrolling motion accompanying the movement is dizzying. However, it is useful occasionally to view small images. Also you may find a menu-blinking alternative to the standard system beep that is especially useful for users who are hearing impaired or deaf. Instead of a beep sound to alert the user to a system error or message, the menu bar blinks.

When used in various combinations, depending on the needs of the learner, these software adaptations provide a functional accommodation for the single-finger typist at no cost. All three features can be turned on and off from the keyboard to create an independent computing environment. Use your computer's help system to learn how to use the keyboard to turn the features on and off. If you are using a Windows or Macintosh computer, you have the assisted keyboard features. Locate (or install) the software, and then do the Assisted Keyboard Activity in Appendix B.

Talking Word Processors

Talking word processors are word processors that actually talk! There are quite a few different titles, many having similar features. With all of the titles, however, the speech capability is the feature that appeals to special educators. The software can speak letters as keys are pressed, words as spaces are placed after words, and sentences as end punctuation is added to a document. Other speech options include speaking any selected text or speaking the entire document. Some of the titles offer simplified menus for young children or learners with special needs. All of the programs also offer custom dictionaries and the ability to edit pronunciation.

Talking word processors can be beneficial for learners who need to hear what they have typed, whether they cannot see it or, for whatever reason, they cannot read it. They are also useful to provide spoken instructions to learners who could "replay" the written instructions. I know of one individual with learning disabilities who uses talking word processors as quick and easy talking books. He downloads text from the Internet and then opens the documents in a talking word processor, listening at his leisure. Two fullfeatured talking word processors are *IntelliTalk* from IntelliTools, Inc. and *Write:Outloud* from Don Johnston Incorporated.

On-Screen Keyboards

An **on-screen keyboard** is a software program that places a keyboard on the monitor, sharing the monitor space with any other software. It functions exactly like a standard keyboard with all software. The user accesses the keys through any input device—mouse, joystick, trackball, or touch screen. Some on-screen keyboards have programmable features, enabling the teacher to configure the keys for everything from running specific software programs to creating talking communication boards. An on-screen keyboard is appropriate for someone who needs to sit close to the screen, someone who would be unable to look back and forth between the screen and the keyboard, or someone who needs an alternative mouse device for input. See the illustration of *Discover:Screen* marketed by Madentec Limited in Figure 9.6.

Examples of on-screen keyboard software include *Discover:Switch* (for activation by switch) and *Discover:Screen* for both Macintosh and Windows. These programs are

FIGURE 9.6 *Discover:Screen*—an on-screen keyboard.

from Madentec Limited and have numerous features to customize the screens for individual needs. There are other on-screen keyboard programs, both shareware and proprietary, with varying features.

Word Prediction Software

Word prediction software is designed to work in conjunction with any text entry program. It cannot be used by itself. The purpose of word prediction is to reduce the number of keystrokes a user must make in order to enter text. The original idea was to make text entry easier for persons with physical disabilities. And it does that quite well. However, more and more persons with learning disabilities are using word prediction software because of the reduced need to spell accurately. It is especially good for very young children who have learned to read but not spell.

When the user presses the first letter of a word, the software predicts what that word will be by placing a list of words in the word prediction window. If the word is there, the user can select it several different ways. If the word is not there, the user presses the second letter. The list changes to include only words that begin with those two letters. For example, the typist who wishes to type the word *Sunday* first strikes the letter *s*. The list that appears in the predictor may contain *some*, *show*, *so*, and *sweet*, among others. Since the desired word is not in the list, the typist presses the *u*. A new list appears with *su-* words. This continues until the desired word appears in the word prediction window. The typist selects the word one of several different ways, depending on how the software has been configured, and the word is placed into the sentence along with a trailing space. When the user reaches the end of a sentence, that sentence is dumped into the word processor (or other text entry program) where it can be formatted, saved, or printed as desired. The typist then returns to the predictor to build another sentence.

The *Co:Writer* software from Don Johnston Incorporated (available for both Windows and Macintosh computers) "learns" the words that you use. The more you use the program, the quicker the words you use most often will pop into the prediction lists. This is a wonderful feature for young writers with smaller vocabularies. Words that are not in the dictionary can be added; however, the first time they are used, they must be spelled out completely. Words can be selected from the list by pressing the number of the desired word and by a single mouse click as the software scans the choices. If you have word prediction software available, do the Word Prediction Software Activity in Appendix B.

Screen Enhancing Software

There are ways to enhance the screen with software—useful for persons who have difficulty seeing the monitor. R. J. Cooper & Associates has a selection of large cursors. In addition to helping a user with a visual impairment to locate the cursor, these cursors are useful for powerbook or notebook computers (those screens are so small!) and also on computers using data projectors.

There are applications and control panels that enlarge the screen—*inLarge* for Macintosh (pre–OS X only) is one. Created by ALVA Access Group, *inLarge* offers screen magnification from one to sixteen times, along with other features that can be customized to meet individual needs. A similar program for Windows computers by NanoPac, Inc. is called *ZoomText*.

Another type of product for persons who cannot see the monitor, also made by ALVA, is *outSPOKEN*, for both Macintosh (pre–OS X only) and Windows computers. *OutSPOKEN* is a talking interface that announces virtually everything on the screen—icons and menus in addition to text. Another screen reader for Windows computers is *Jaws* by Freedom Scientific, Inc. with features similar to those of *outSPOKEN*.

Writing Tools

Writing tools such as spell checkers and grammar checkers are often attached to word processing software. They are invaluable tools for the poor speller and poor typist. There are stand-alone spell checkers and grammar checkers that can serve the user in e-mail programs or any program where text is being entered. Dictionary and thesaurus software are additional software-based writing tools.

Macro Programs

Macros are commands incorporating two or more actions or keystrokes into a single keystroke. For example, typing your name, entering today's date, opening an application, or shutting down the computer can all be accomplished with a macro program. Because they reduce keystrokes and mouse actions, macros are ideal for users whose skill with input devices is reduced by motor limitations. *QuickKeys* from CE Software, Inc. is macro software that is available for both Macintosh and Windows computers.

Specialized Alternative Devices

There are various specialized alternative devices available for the individual whose needs cannot be met by the simple modifications or software solutions described in the previous sections. The devices in this section are available from the manufacturer or through resellers. Be sure to see the list of resources in Appendix D.

Alternative Keyboards—Fixed

There are different keyboards that have features similar to a standard keyboard but vary in shape, size, or both. They offer input alternatives to the user who, for whatever reason, finds using the standard keyboard difficult or impossible.

Tash Mini. The Tash Mini, available for both Macintosh and Windows from Tash, is a tiny full-featured keyboard that includes mouse actions in its keys in addition to the traditional key functions. Its entire key surface is only 3 by 6 inches; whereas, a standard keyboard is approximately 6 by 18 inches. See the illustration in Figure 9.7. Who, do you think, might benefit from the use of such a keyboard?

FIGURE 9.7 The Tash Mini keyboard.

One of my former students had always used a standard keyboard and mouse, but work was laborious because of her physical limitations. She typed with only one finger as she had excellent fine-motor coordination. However, her gross motor control was not good. If she raised her arm, she lost the finger control. To accommodate for this limitation, she would lock her elbow down to her side. With her arm tight to her side the range for her typing finger was reduced to only a few inches. Consequently, to reach back and forth along the length of an eighteen-inch standard keyboard, she moved her entire upper body, making text entry laborious, very tiring, and slow. I asked her if she would like to try a mini keyboard to help speed up her keyboarding. She tried it, eventually acquired one, and to this day still uses it. Using the smaller keyboard, she doubled her typing speed, was less tired, and more satisfied with the quality of her work.

Big Keys (Plus). Big Keys and Big Keys Plus are large keyboards from Greystone Digital that have one-inch keys. Originally intended for use by preschoolers to run educational software, they are popular in special education classrooms and also with adults who have motor impairments. These keyboards are simple to use because they eliminate extra keys, come with QWERTY or ABC layouts, can have colored or black and white keys, and are available for either Macintosh or Windows computers. The key-repeat feature of standard keyboards is not implemented with the Big Key keyboards so users whose fingers linger too long on a key will still strike it only one time. See the illustration of a Big Keys with colored keys in Figure 9.8.

Little Fingers. Little Fingers is a complete standard keyboard with a built-in trackball and ports for connection to both Macintosh and Windows computers. The keyboard area is only about 3 by 9 inches. Each key is approximately $3/8$ inch in diameter, compared to the $1/2$-inch size of a key on a standard keyboard. The built-in wrist rest and

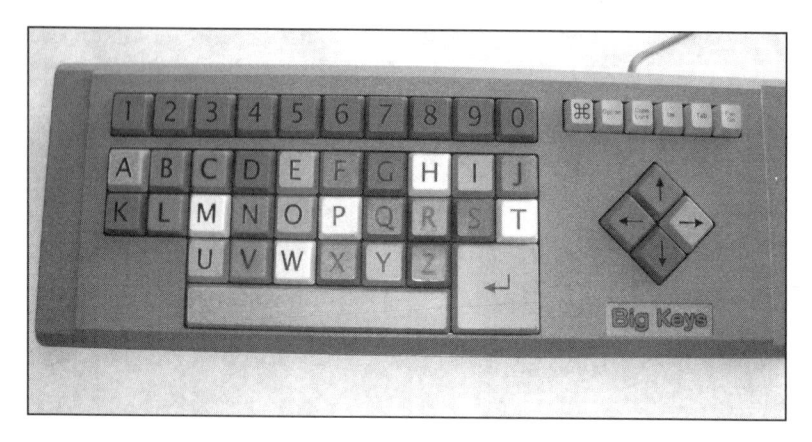

FIGURE 9.8 The Big Keys keyboard.

trackball brings the total footprint of the device to 7 by 12 inches. Designed by DataDesk Technologies for small hands, Little Fingers is the perfect keyboard for young children to use when learning touch keyboarding. It is also a keyboard to consider when the user is a single finger typist, has good fine motor coordination, but has a limited range of motion. The Little Fingers keyboard is pictured in Figure 9.9.

Ergonomic Keyboards. *Ergonomic keyboards* are those that offer the user a more natural hand and finger position to help reduce the stress and injury often associated with frequent keyboarding. Typically these keyboards also offer wrist rests and built-in mouse access. DataDesk Technologies and Adesso, Inc., offer ergonomic keyboards

FIGURE 9.9 The Little Fingers keyboard.

with mouse access provided in various ways. A Tru-Form keyboard by Adesso, Inc. is pictured in Figure 9.10.

One-Handed Typing. For the one-handed typist there are alternate keyboards with modified keyboard layouts to facilitate one-handed typing in addition to software programs that teach touch-typing with only five fingers. When choosing a way to make text entry easier for a one-handed typist, it is important to consider whether or not the condition is temporary, the age of the typist and size of the hand, and any typing experience the typist already has. See the One Hand Typing and Keyboarding web site for more detailed information or search the web for "one hand typing."

Alternative Keyboards—Programmable

For persons unable to use any of the previously mentioned input devices, there are several other keyboards offering customized access capabilities because they can be programmed. Both IntelliKeys from IntelliTools, Inc. and Discover:Board from Madentec Limited offer a selection of standard *overlays* along with the flexibility of creating your own custom keyboard layout with an easy-to-use software program. See illustrations of IntelliKeys in Figure 9.11 and Discover:Board in Figure 9.12, each displaying one of the standard overlays.

The standard overlays include the standard keyboard layout for both Macintosh and Windows computers, a numbers layout for running arithmetic software, mouse overlays for operating mouse-driven software, and basic writing overlays for beginning writers. There are standard overlays for both QWERTY and ABC keyboard layouts. The newer IntelliKeys USB also includes a standard overlay for an Internet browser.

FIGURE 9.10 A Tru-Form ergonomic keyboard.

FIGURE 9.11 An IntelliKeys USB keyboard.
Used courtesy of IntelliTools, Inc.

FIGURE 9.12 A Discover:Board keyboard.

Other features of these two keyboards vary. One of the advantages of the Discover:Board is that the keys can talk. Consequently, customized overlays can include communication overlays to allow a learner to speak by pressing the keys. Also with the Discover:Board, setups can be attached to particular applications so that when the new software opens, a new setup is automatically available to the user. These features are not available with IntelliKeys.

With the IntelliKeys keyboard the standard overlays have magnetic coding strips that enable the keyboard to automatically recognize each unique overlay. Because of this feature, IntelliKeys is quite portable. Connect either a Macintosh or a Windows cable to the original version to the IntelliKeys, and take the keyboard and its standard overlays with you to any computer. With Discover:Board, software is installed on the computer and each overlay setup, even the standard ones, must be sent to the keyboard. The Discover:Board is consequently anchored to the computer where the software is installed. With the newer IntelliKeys USB the keyboard features are accessed through a control panel, so software must be installed to use this keyboard too.

Both keyboards offer features to enable mouse access and change key response time. In addition, the software to customize your own keyboard layouts for both of these keyboards is simple to use. In fact, teachers have begun using the programmable features of these keyboards to offer customized lessons for learners, in addition to using the keyboards to provide computer access, as you will discover in the later chapters.

Switch Input

Persons who are unable to use any keyboard are often able to operate the computer using a *switch*, if they are able to make any voluntary sound or movement. First, a switch creates a single action, similar to that of a single key press. Hitting a large button or a small button, waving an arm or hand, blowing or sipping with a straw, or hitting a wand with chin or cheek or arm can activate a switch. Every imaginable type of single switch can be purchased or constructed to meet the individual's needs. Switches can be activated with as little pressure as the brush of an eyelash or be sturdy enough to withstand the kick of a boot. They can also be activated by breath, sound, or light rays. Several switches that can be activated in different ways are pictured in Figure 9.13.

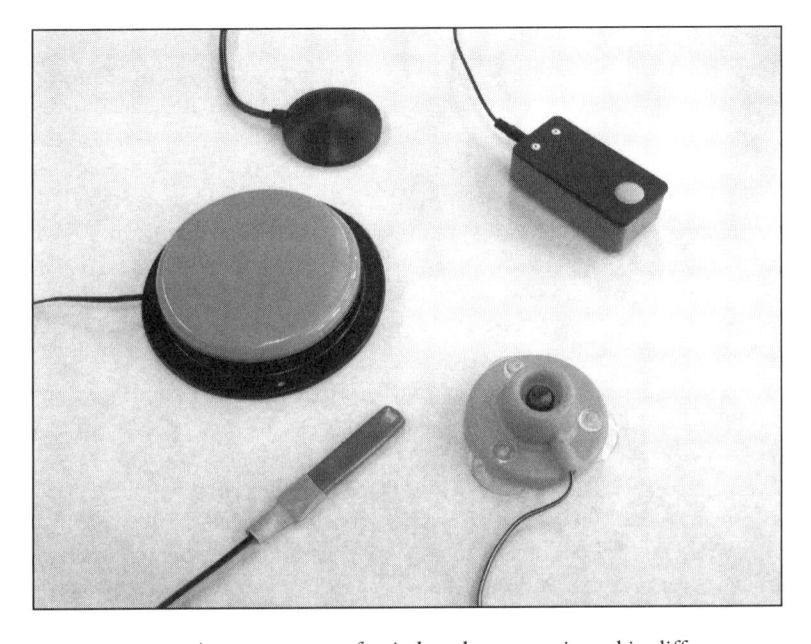

FIGURE 9.13   An assortment of switches that are activated in different ways.

Regardless of the method of activation, switch technology remains the same. The computer requires an *interface* to enable a switch to be plugged in. Switches come with ¼ or ⅛ inch plugs; there is an adaptor if your switch does not plug in to the interface that you have.

You can divide software for switch users three ways. First, there is software specifically designed for use with switches. Typically these programs teach switch use, provide *cause and effect* activities, enable simple arcade-style games, and provide early concepts instruction. Often, even though the programs are intended for switch use, mouse clicks or spacebar presses can substitute for switch clicks. Some of the software in this group include the *SwitchIt!* series from IntelliTools, Inc, *Switch Intro* from Don Johnston Incorporated, and many different switch titles by R. J. Cooper & Associates.

Another group of software for switch users is software designed for multiple input methods. The teacher can choose among keyboard, mouse, switch, and even IntelliKeys (for those titles from IntelliTools, Inc.). Many of the titles from Don Johnston Incorporated, IntelliTools, Inc., MarbleSoft, and Laureate Learning Systems, Inc. supply instructional software designed for multiple input methods. These titles exemplify Universal Design with their versatility and application to a wide range of abilities.

The third group of programs for switch users is the most versatile. Software can substitute for any keyboard or mouse function by placing full-featured *scan arrays* on the screen enabling the user to operate any software, not just special switch programs. Madentec Limited markets Discover:Switch which is similar to Discover:Board in that setups can be customized and modified for different purposes: typing, Internet browsing, playing games, drawing images, and so on. Indeed, a switch, even one activated by a puff of breath or eye gaze, can replace all standard keyboard and mouse functions creating an independent computing environment for a person with even the most severe physical disabilities. Amazing!

How can a person with only one key—a switch—do all of the things other people can do with over one hundred keys and a mouse? The secret is that the software supplies the person with choices, so that when the desired choice is presented on the screen, the user can activate the switch. This process is called *scanning*.

Look back at the sample screen from *Early Learning* shown in Figure 7.5 for a simple example of scanning. In this number sequence activity, a question mark rests between "4" and "6." The voice prompt is "Which one goes here?" One by one, the numerals at the bottom are highlighted. When the "5" is highlighted, the user activates the switch to select the "5." With the *Early Learning* software the user could also press "5" on the keyboard or click the on-screen "5" with a mouse.

More complex scan arrays exist with Discover:Switch setups that provide complete keyboard and mouse access. A full keyboard scan, called Advanced ABC, is shown in Figure 9.14.

For complex scan arrays like a complete keyboard, the software does not scan all choices one-by-one. The process would be too time-consuming. Instead, it first scans rows. When the user clicks the switch on any particular row, the software scans that row in, perhaps, three sections. When the switch is activated on the desired section, the individual keys in that section are scanned.

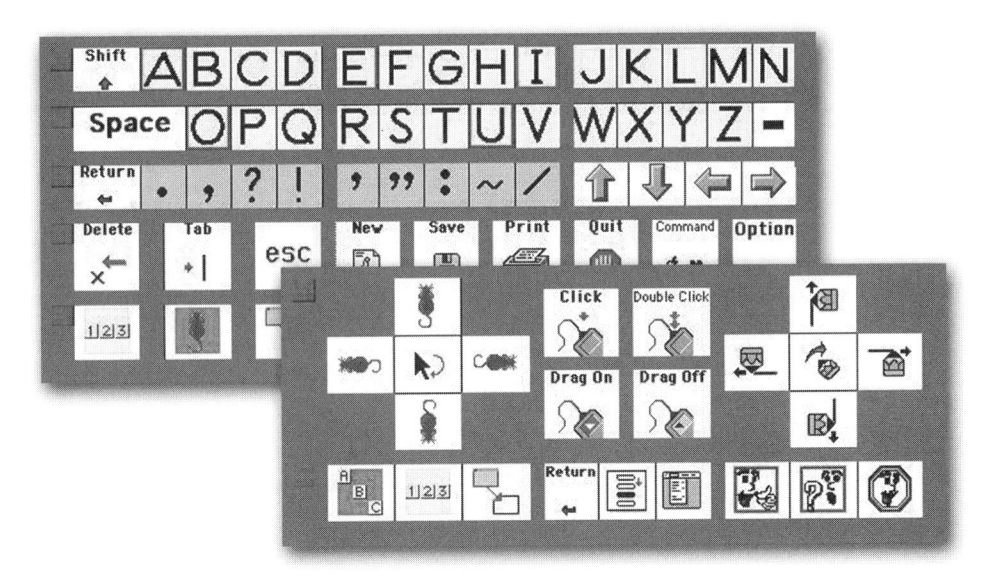

FIGURE 9.14 Discover:Switch Advanced ABC and Mouse setups.

Because every single choice cannot be placed on a single scan, complex scan arrays contain branching scans. On the Advanced ABC setup there are keys on the bottom that branch to a Numbers setup and a Mouse setup. See the Mouse setup in Figure 9.14. Each of those scans includes keys to return to the Advanced ABC setup.

A final dimension for switch users is the scan method and speed. The speed at which the scan moves can be customized for individual needs. Also, there are various scan methods to customize the switch environment. With an ***automatic scan,*** the scan progresses automatically, at a pre-determined speed, with the user clicking the switch to make a selection. In ***inverse scanning,*** while the user is holding down the switch, the scan progresses until the switch is released—just the opposite of automatic. Another variation is called ***step scanning.*** The user must click the switch to advance the scan. There are also various combinations of these scan methods that can be customized for use with two switches.

Scan method and speed adjustments along with customized scan arrays can create the ideal computer environment for the switch user. A popular shareware game, *Snood,* can be played entirely by mouse movements and clicks. Because the game is user activated—there are no increasing speeds or time limits—it is an ideal arcade game to be played with a switch. It is a skill game, offering levels ranging from that for the youngest player to that of the most sophisticated game strategist. Mouse actions needed to play the game are Mouse Left, Mouse Right, and Mouse Click. If you observe the Mouse setup in Figure 9.14, you will see that there are many more options in the full mouse scan. A simplified mouse setup to provide quicker game play is shown in Figure 9.15 along with a screen shot of the *Snood* game. This setup is a trade-off: faster game play with less independence. Playing the game with the full mouse setup

FIGURE 9.15 The *Snood* game with a custom *SnoodPad* mouse setup.
Image provided by Snood, LLC. © 1996–2003 Snood, LLC. Snood is a trademark. All rights reserved.

would slow down game play considerably because of the necessity of scanning each unnecessary mouse movement. However, it would give the player control over other aspects of the game not accessible with the limited mouse control; for example, starting new games, choosing levels, or quitting the software. It should be entirely up to the player to decide on quicker play versus independence.

An additional product by Madentec Limited is Discover:Kenx. Kenx is a small, powered interface that allows for the connection of a Discover:Board in addition to switches. Individually, the *Discover:Screen*, Discover:Switch, and Discover:Board each have their own software interface for the particular input mode. With Kenx, all three input methods are supported. In addition, Kenx supports input with Morse code. Kenx is an appealing choice for a classroom in which children may be using several of these modes of input.

If you have a selection of switches available, do the Switch Activity in Appendix B.

Speech Recognition

Speech recognition is the ability of the computer to recognize the user's voice. This technology has been evolving for a few years now. Although great strides have been made, there is still a long way to go before speech recognition can be the primary means of computer input for many persons with disabilities. There are two aspects to speech recognition to consider as you begin to explore this exciting technology: dictation of text and control of the computer. Each of these areas deserves separate consideration, particularly in the special education scene.

First, however, we must clarify what the needs are for speech recognition. Does the user need a totally hands-free work environment? Does the user wish to dictate text because typing, for whatever reason, is laborious? Does the user need speech recognition for command and control of the computer in all situations?

Beyond the user's needs loom their physical, intellectual, and motivational challenges. Does the user have clear, unaccented speech? Can that speech be consistent? Does the user have the cognitive ability to understand and handle the training, correcting, and consistency issues? What are the user's expectations for speech recognition?

As computer technology becomes better, faster, and cheaper, there is an increased demand for dictation of text into documents—typing by voice—by persons who have no disabilities but prefer to dictate text. However, because only short samples of text need to be read in order for the computer to "learn" the user's voice, the software cannot understand the speech of someone who does not have clear, unaccented speech. Speech-recognition software, which requires clear, consistent, unaccented speech, is not yet a viable solution for persons with articulation problems—a very large group of people who would benefit from speech-recognition accessibility to computers.

What does the speech-recognition software have to offer the computer user with special needs? There are several software programs offering voice input of text into text entry programs. *NaturallySpeaking*, from Dragon Systems for Windows computers, offers continuous speech text dictation and editing of text. Also, *ViaVoice* from IBM, for both Macintosh and Windows computers, provides opportunities for dictation and text editing into word processing or e-mail programs. With both *ViaVoice* and *NaturallySpeaking* the user can speak naturally into a microphone to produce printed text. Either of these programs would be appropriate for the individual who has difficulty keyboarding. *ViaVoice* is not totally hands free when attempting to edit previously entered text.

Choices are limited for software that offers complete computer control with voice commands. *Dragon Dictates* (Windows software from Dragon Systems) has in the past been the only software available for complete command and control of the computer desktop using voice input. Version 6 of *NaturallySpeaking* has added mouse control to its voice commands.

There are issues for persons with special needs with any of these programs. The user needs a strong motivation to develop the skills necessary to make voice input effective. Training, although not extensive, is necessary, and training should be accomplished under the same conditions in which the software will be used. The user must be able to read the training text. Also, the user must be able to speak continuously, with few sprinklings of "Ahh," "Umm," or "You know." The more practice with the software the user gets, the better the text production will be. In part, this is because the user learns to speak in a way that the software is better able to process (i.e., the software trains the speaker to speak its "dialect").

The user must understand that the computer does not listen to their speech as another person might. The computer "hears" the words, locates them in its dictionary, and then produces them on the screen. Consequently, if the user says, "Watcha doin' fer lunch?" the software will not type, "What are you doing for lunch?" More likely the sentence will say, "Watch year doon fur lunch?"—all perfectly acceptable words, but no recognizable meaning!

The environment around the voice-activated computer should be relatively quiet. When we listen to voices in a noisy environment, we can often screen out the sounds that are not speech, but speech-recognition software listens to all sounds that it hears. When the user is ill with a cold, is coughing or sneezing, or has a hoarse voice, the quality of text input will be diminished.

Speech-recognition technology has changed dramatically in a short time. Who knows what kinds of breakthroughs will be forthcoming as new technology is developed? Hopefully, future advances in speech recognition will bring better speech input options for persons with disabilities.

A Functional Assessment

A functional assessment is a process by which you can determine which kind of ***assistive device(s)*** or software may be best to enable computer use for a learner with special needs. You should not expect that the experiences you have had up to this point would prepare you to make those kinds of decisions by yourself. However, at some point, you will find yourself part of a team that is making exactly that decision, because it is a requirement of IDEA that every student with an Individualized Educational Program (IEP) be considered for assistive technology. The information in this section should help you contribute to making the right decision.

You have read about, seen, and explored a wide variety of special hardware devices and software programs. Now it is time to consider how to determine which solution is best for any particular student. Begin by using the following "Watch-Listen-Identify" process described below.

Watch-Listen-Identify

Watch. Begin by observing the student. Watch how the individual is currently doing things. What things are they unable to do? Which things do you believe they could do a better, easier, or faster way with an accommodation of some kind? How does the student appear to be compensating, or trying to compensate, for a disability?

Listen. Talk with your students. Find out what they feel they are unable to do, what things they cannot do but would like to, and what they can do but would like to do in a better or easier way. A conversation of this kind is not always possible with students with severely limited communication abilities. However, whenever possible, you should talk with the students about their needs and preferences.

Identify. First identify goals for the individual. For example, is the goal to produce text documents? Is it to communicate? Is the goal to operate mouse or switch-driven software? Next, list the abilities and strengths of the individual. After talking with the student, if that is possible, you should have some ideas of their interests and preferences. If at all possible, involve the student in the decision for adaptive technology to help assure their acceptance of it. Did you ever know someone who was uncomfortable wearing their new eyeglasses because they thought it made them look odd? This same phenomenon can occur when you deliver some sort of adaptation to a student who, because of a disability, is already different. And, it does not matter at all how much better they can perform when using the device. If they think that it makes them look funny, then they may not use it! Allowing the student to participate in the evaluation and selection of the adaptation will help to assure that they will use it.

At this point you want to identify and eliminate the barriers that prevent the student from achieving their objectives. As you identify barriers, try to identify potential interventions that would be appropriate to meet the objectives for that particular individual.

Select the Least Restrictive Adaptation

As you begin to determine the specific software and hardware solutions for an individual, try to select the least restrictive adaptation. This means to stay as close as possible to the standard computer devices. For example, if a student can use a standard keyboard with a keyguard attached, then a standard keyboard should be the main input device rather than a programmable keyboard or switch input. The simpler and closer to standard the device is, the less expensive it usually is; the easier it is to learn to use, to repair, to replace; and the better it may be accepted by the student.

Locate a Device

Once you have a good idea about the kind of adaptation the students needs, how do you locate it? First, look for devices or software at your local national computer store chain. There are several keyboards and mouse devices that are slightly different from the standard devices—just different enough to provide the access some people need. Look through the catalogs and web sites for the manufacturers and suppliers of assistive devices and software. Visit an adaptive computer lab, a rehabilitation center, or another school to see what others are doing. See the resource list in Appendix D.

Use a Team

Use a team approach both for determining what the adaptation should be and also for implementing it. This team could include parents, other teachers, paraprofessionals, therapists, and even peers. It is important that all team members be aware of the student's needs and of the adaptation and its use.

Try and Train

When approaching the purchase of any particular device, the money issue usually comes up: What if Susie really cannot use this four-hundred-dollar keyboard? Use the phrase "Try before you buy!" Can you borrow one, even for a short time? Can you take Susie to a lab, to another school, or to a resource center to try one first? Can you take pictures of her using the device? You are more likely to get funding for assistive technology if you can demonstrate that with the device the child can do the work that her peers without disabilities in the general education program can do.

After you acquire the device, make a plan for training. Determine who else besides the student needs to be trained in its use. As the child gains proficiency with the adaptations, and you modify its use, keep all members of the team informed of the changes. A computer adaptation is beneficial only if the student is using it effectively!

Go to the activities in Appendix B and complete the final activity—Catalog Activity.

Study Questions

- How can computer use empower a person with disabilities?
- Describe how word prediction works.
- With reference to computer adaptations for persons with special needs, what is scanning? Which adaptive devices require scanning?
- Why is it important to calibrate the touch screen?
- Describe three different computer store mouse devices. Distinguish among the physical requirements necessary to activate each one.
- What is an interface? Name an adaptive device that requires one.
- Describe two writing tools that might assist text production for a person with learning disabilities.
- What is a keyguard? What purpose does it serve?
- How is a QWERTY keyboard layout different from an ABC keyboard layout?
- Describe how both (a) sticky keys and (b) mouse keys modify a standard keyboard.
- Can an individual who is unable to use a mouse, but is competent with an assisted keyboard, be independent at the computer? Explain.
- Can an individual who is unable to use a standard keyboard or mouse, but is competent with a switch, be independent at the computer? Explain.

KEY TERMS

alternative keyboard	inverse scanning	Slow Keys
alternative mouse device	joystick	speech recognition
assisted keyboard	keyguard	step scanning
assistive device	macro	Sticky Keys
automatic scan	moisture guard	switch
calibrate	mouse keys	touch screen
cause and effect	on-screen keyboard	track pad
ergonomic keyboard	overlay	trackball
head mouse	scan array	word prediction software
interface	scanning	

CHAPTER

10 Customizing Curriculum Content

What It's All About

A child with special needs, depending on the nature of those needs, may be served best in a self-contained classroom, or in a resource room, or maybe in a fully inclusive setting. There are countless administrative designations for placement to accommodate the individual needs of each child in the least restrictive manner. Regardless of the placement, however, the child's needs for customized curriculum content remain the same. Teachers, both special education and general education, need to adjust materials to enable the learner with special needs to have access to the general education curriculum.

This means that the curriculum in special education classrooms should be based on the general education curriculum following the academic standards established by individual states for general education students. Oftentimes, commercially available materials intended for general education populations teach too much at a time, provide too little practice, move forward too quickly, or are in a format unable to be accessed by the learner with special needs. Because learners have such diverse needs, sometimes even commercially available special education materials are inadequate. Many learners with special needs learn best when lessons are presented in small steps, provide extra practice, and move forward slowly. This section is designed to assist teachers in developing methods for preparing instructional materials that are customized to enable individual learners to achieve their social and/or academic and/or prevocational objectives.

You already know that the IntelliKeys keyboard, with its easily interchangeable standard overlays, is an incredible device to enable a child, who otherwise would be unable to use a computer, to have easy access to all computer features. Likewise, the Discover products—Discover:Board, *Discover:Screen*, Discover:Switch, and Discover: Kenx—provide computer access for persons whose physical disabilities might have prohibited them from ever using a computer. For users who need keyboard modifications beyond those standard overlays that come with both IntelliKeys and the Discover products, there are easy-to-use software programs (*Overlay Maker* and *Discover:Create—Macintosh*) to create custom keyboard overlays.

The specialized hardware and software combinations that allow students with disabilities to access the computer can be used to customize learning activities for all learners with special needs, not just those with physical disabilities. Custom overlays are appropriate for needs ranging from interacting with a specific software program to a communication overlay enabling a child who does not speak to participate in classroom activities by pressing talking keys. The tutorials in the next chapters provide instructions for both IntelliKeys (Chapter 11) and any of the Discover keyboards (Chapter 12). In addition, *IntelliPics Studio 3*, authoring software from IntelliTools, Inc., is an excellent tool for customizing learning activities. Chapter 13 features *IntelliPics Studio*. To get started let's look at some examples.

Look at Figure 10.1. A student using this overlay is learning to count objects by pressing keys on a custom overlay of an alternative keyboard. When the student presses the key with the picture of two balls, "two balls" is spoken in response. Other keys on that overlay picture three cats, four telephones, and one bus. The student counts the objects, presses the key to hear the correct count, and then tries to find the correct numeral key on the right side of the overlay. Upon pressing any numeral key the student will hear the number word spoken. There are no correct or incorrect responses. The student can freely explore the objects and numerals.

The overlay illustrated in Figure 10.2 is designed with *Overlay Maker* for the IntelliKeys keyboard. Picture a student creating sentences in a word processor by pressing keys which contain whole words, eliminating the motor challenge of keyboarding, the complexity of a standard keyboard, the need to spell accurately, and the fine motor skill of writing with a pencil.

The overlay in Figure 10.3 will enable a child who is unable to speak to participate in the classroom activity "Simon Says." The learner presses a key on a customized

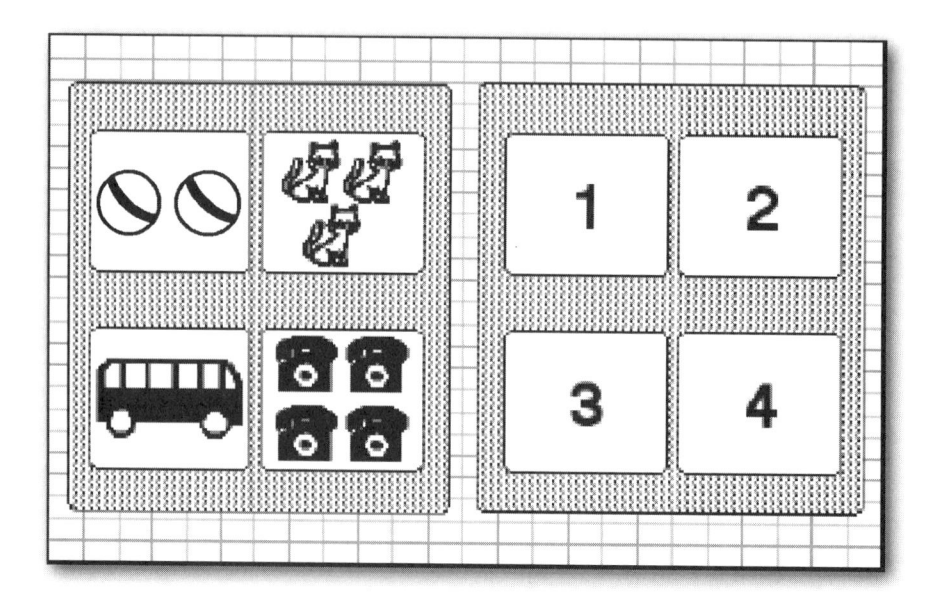

FIGURE 10.1 A custom keyboard overlay to practice counting.

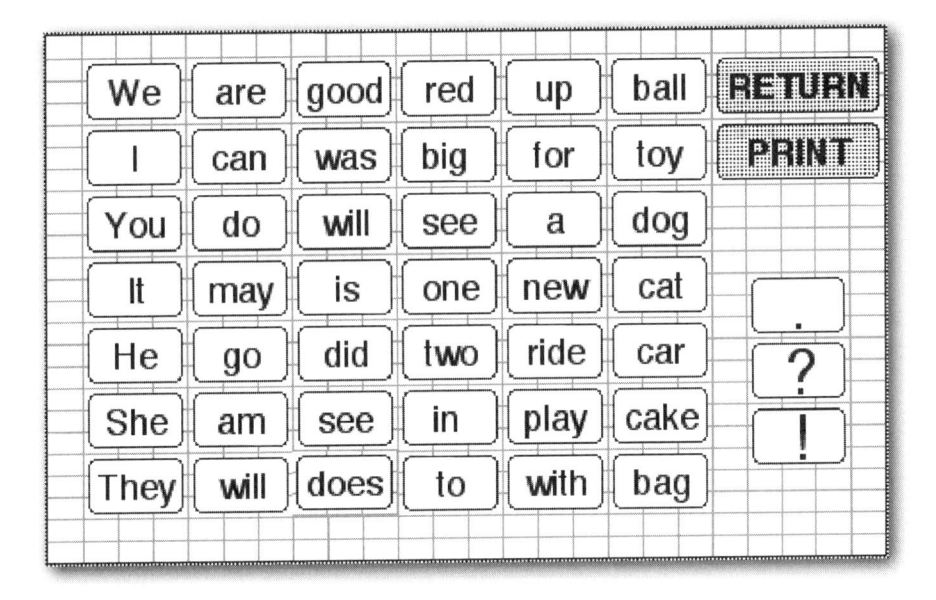

CHAPTER 10 / Customizing Curriculum Content **127**

We	are	good	red	up	ball	RETURN
I	can	was	big	for	toy	PRINT
You	do	will	see	a	dog	
It	may	is	one	new	cat	.
He	go	did	two	ride	car	?
She	am	see	in	play	cake	!
They	will	does	to	with	bag	

FIGURE 10.2 A simple sentence writing overlay.

Simon Says

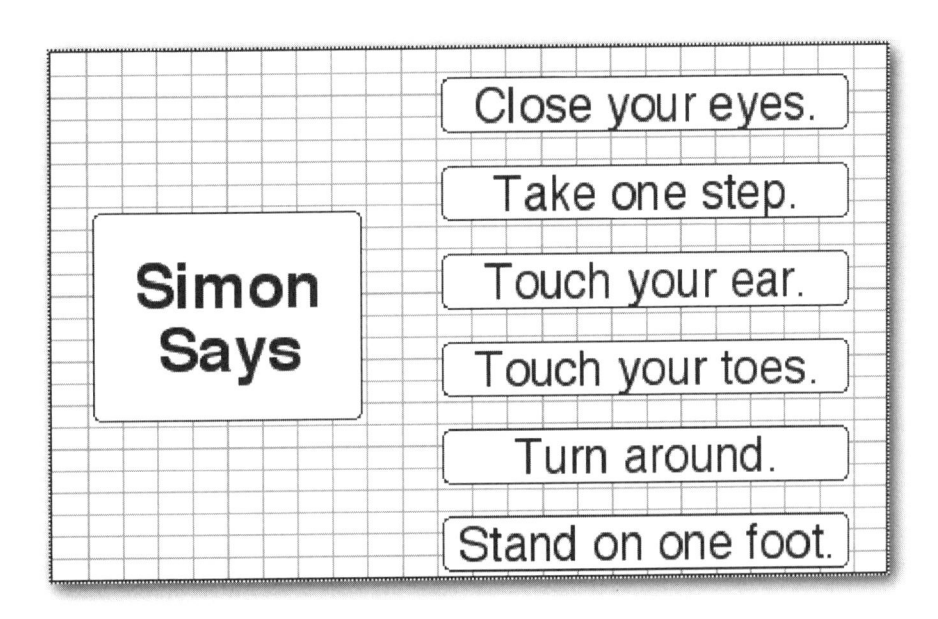

- Close your eyes.
- Take one step.
- Touch your ear.
- Touch your toes.
- Turn around.
- Stand on one foot.

FIGURE 10.3 A "Simon Says" overlay.

overlay for an IntelliKeys keyboard, thereby typing the words "Simon Says" into a talking word processor that speaks the words—because IntelliKeys cannot speak. Then the learner presses one of many commands placed on other keys, such as "Touch your nose" or "Close your eyes." Provide a key to print and that same student can print a list of "Simon Says" commands for a classmate to read, thus orchestrating the entire activity! Because this setup is designed just for speech, the same activity made on a Discover keyboard would not use a talking word processor because the Discover keyboards talk.

The sample overlay in Figure 10.4 is made with *Overlay Maker* for IntelliKeys. Here is an example of a custom lesson that could be prepared to help a student learn states and capitals. The student can press specially designed keys on either an IntelliKeys or Discover keyboard that type out whole words and phrases into a word processor to create sentences. After constructing the sentences, the student could print the exercise for the teacher's appraisal and also use the printout as a study guide. If the word processor were a talking one, the student could hear the sentences spoken by the computer.

A similar sentence-writing activity is illustrated in Figure 10.5. However, the learner presses keys with images on them instead of words. The custom keys type the words into a word processor.

Look at Figure 10.6 for a final example. In this exercise the learner is practicing sentence writing and word usage. The words can be put together many different ways to make accurate sentences, yet in each case the correct verb must be selected.

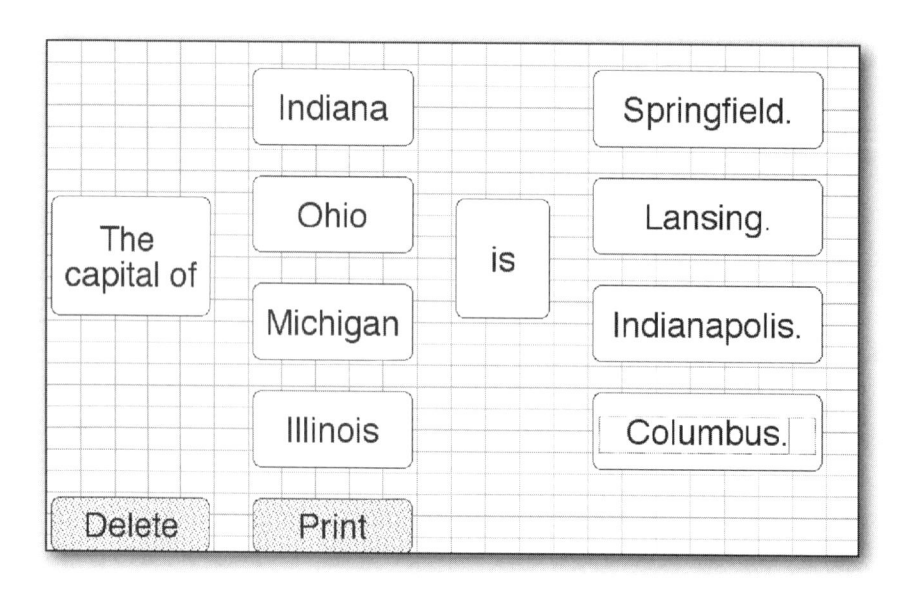

FIGURE 10.4 A states and capitals writing activity.

CHAPTER 10 / Customizing Curriculum Content

FIGURE 10.5 A custom keyboard overlay with picture keys.

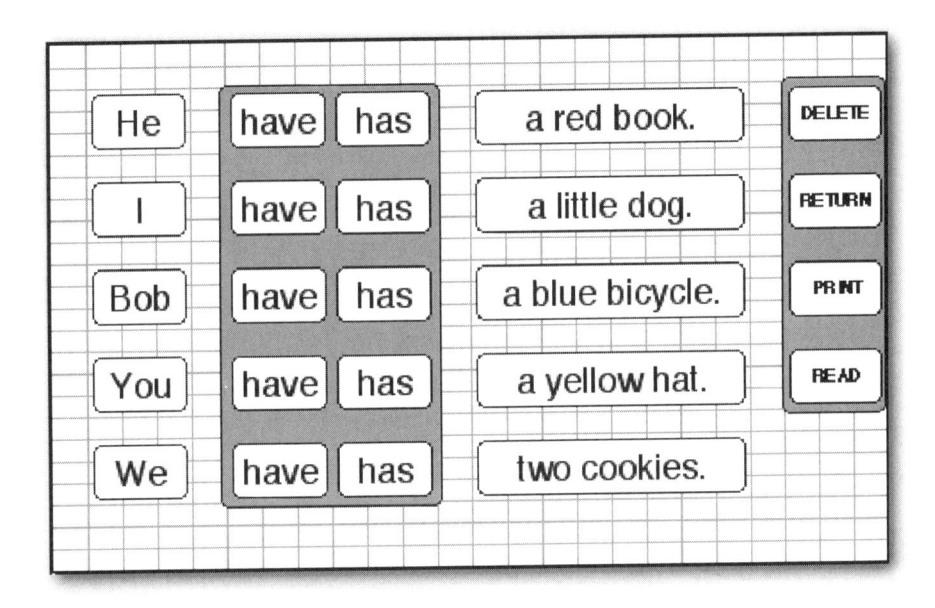

FIGURE 10.6 An activity for selecting correct verb forms.

Student populations that might benefit from working with customized instructional activities include students who:

- cannot use a standard keyboard.
- need extra practice to learn concepts.
- learn in smaller steps.
- need help in writing sentences.
- could benefit from typing sentences by pressing words or pictures instead of letters.

Customized instructional activities such as these are easy to create and implement with a talking word processor and a programmable alternative keyboard. *Overlay Maker* (for IntelliKeys) and *Discover:Create* (for Discover keyboards) are software applications that allow you to design and print custom paper overlays for alternative keyboards. They also allow you to design the key content (what the computer does) for the modified keys and send those instructions to the keyboard. While working on the layout with these design programs, you will use a standard keyboard and mouse and work as you might with a simple graphics program. In order to actually use the overlay/setup you create, you must first save the work and then "send" it so that the alternative keyboard "understands" what to send to the computer when one of the custom keys is pressed. The Discover products for Windows do not have the same *Discover:Create* software that is available for the Macintosh computers. However, Madentec Limited offers an assortment of templates that can be customized.

IntelliPics Studio, for both Windows and Macintosh, is an authoring environment in which you can create tutorials and learning activities. It is an excellent tool for elementary and middle school students to design and implement their own stories, reports, and presentations. For the purpose of customizing curriculum content, the program offers teachers a full-featured platform for designing creative multimedia lessons, making it easy to add spoken text, video clips, and animations. Lessons created with *IntelliPics Studio* can have some features similar to those created with the alternative keyboard creation software, but would not be suitable for text entry into a word processing program. Access to *IntelliPics Studio* activities is through any keyboard, mouse or any alternative mouse device, IntelliKeys keyboard, or switch device. *IntelliPics Studio's* multimedia features, ease of use, and non-linear format make it appropriate for broader lesson presentations than can be accomplished using an alternative keyboard.

Two other applications, *IntelliTalk* and *IntelliMathics* both from IntelliTools, are already well known for their versatility in creating customized instructional content. They have amazing capabilities and well-designed tutorials for developing instructional materials in their manuals to help get you started. If you are interested in these programs, visit the IntelliTools web site and explore the teacher materials shared there. *IntelliTalk* and *IntelliMathics* will not be included in this guide.

To develop your own customized learning activities using the instructions in this text, you need any talking word processor and one of the programmable alternative keyboards—IntelliKeys or one of the Discover boards—along with the software to create custom keyboard overlays for your keyboard. In addition, you can also use *IntelliPics Studio*.

Designing the Custom Overlay

When you create custom keys on any alternative keyboard—IntelliKeys or any of the Discover keyboards—there are two basic elements to each key: first, what the student sees printed on the paper overlay and, second, what the computer does when the key is pressed. On a standard keyboard you see "J" or "A" or "M." When you press one of those keys, the computer receives a message to print that character into your document.

What the Student Sees

On a standard keyboard what you see on the key is what the computer types when you press that key. On a custom overlay this does not have to be true. What the student sees and what the computer does can differ. When you customize keys on an overlay, you can choose to show a single letter, a word, a picture, a phrase, or any combination of these. You can put just about anything on each key of the printed overlay that the student sees.

What the Computer Receives

The second element of a keyboard is what happens when you press the key. Unlike a regular keyboard where usually the computer receives the same character that you see on a key, on an alternative keyboard the computer can receive any letter, word, or phrase when the custom key is pressed. Therefore, when a student presses a key with a picture of a dog on it, the computer could type, "This little dog's name is Spot." into an open word processing document. The computer can also receive commands such as to print or delete and commands to initiate mouse actions.

What the Student Hears

"What the Student Hears" is a third feature available with the Discover products but not with the IntelliKeys keyboard. Because the Discover:Board, *Discover:Screen*, and Discover:Switch are talking keyboards, the key presses can be spoken as they are pressed. If you have a Discover keyboard, you will learn more about "What the Student Hears" in Chapter 12.

Considering Complexity

Look at Figures 10.7 and 10.8. In each example the student is typing two sentences—"The dog barks." and "The dog growls."—each on a separate line. In Figure 10.7 the spaces, periods, and the [RETURN] key press at the end of the sentence are all built-in to the keys. The layout is simple and does not require the student to type spaces or end punctuation.

In Figure 10.8, the student must press a key for each space, period, or [RETURN] key press. Although the same sentences can be printed using the keyboard layout in Figure 10.8 as with the first layout, in the second one the student is required to provide the spaces, punctuation, and the [RETURN] key to begin the second sentence on a new

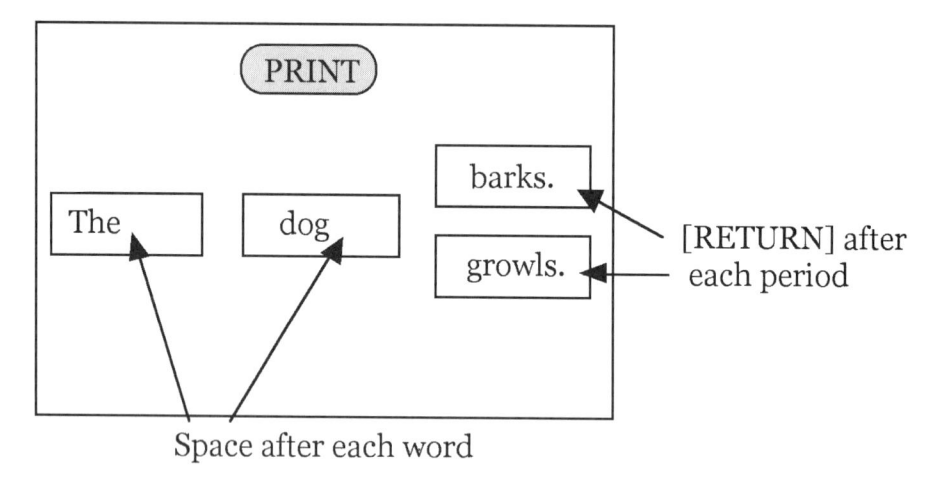

FIGURE 10.7 Sentence activity with spaces and punctuation included in the keys.

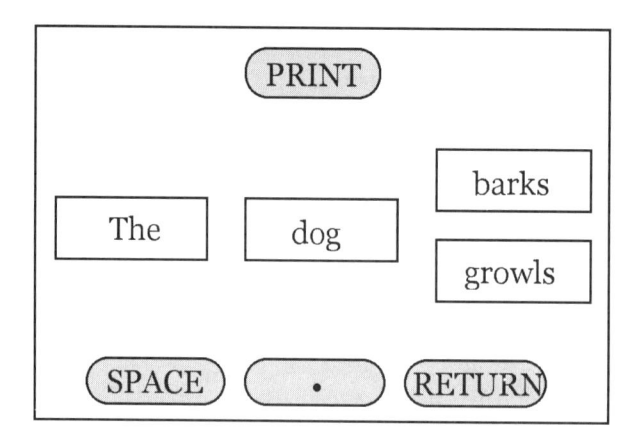

FIGURE 10.8 Sentence activity in which learner must press space and punctuation keys.

line. Thus, the second layout is more difficult. You should consider the complexity of the activity in addition to the lesson content. Structure the exercise to assure the success of the learner and minimize the likelihood of errors.

Planning the Overlay

First, decide on the purpose for the overlay. Is it:

- to assist a student in learning sentence writing?
- to explore sounds?

- to practice counting?
- to write a story?
- to make a science report or book report?
- a worksheet to practice facts?
- a matching game?
- a test?

Decide, generally, what the keys will do. Will a key:

- type a letter, a word, or a phrase?
- speak a word or make a sound?
- be used to delete previously entered text?
- read a word, a sentence, or all of the document text?
- be used to print the document?
- need to include a space or end punctuation along with text?
- be needed to press [RETURN] or [ENTER]?

Decide on the overall look of the printed overlay.

- Is the layout simple and easy to understand?
- Should the student see text only, graphics only, or a combination of both on the keys?
- Do common elements have uniform key size and spacing?
- Are multiple colors and key sizes used purposefully?
- Can the utility keys be distinguished from the content keys by size or location?

Decide *exactly* what is to happen when each key is pressed. Here are some tips to make your keys work perfectly.

- Will the keys type letters, words, or phrases? If so, plan for spaces between words either by adding a space into the key content along with the word(s) being typed or by providing a utility key with which the student can add a space.
- Will a key print the document? Think about what you do when you initiate printing from the keyboard. When you initiate printing with ⌘p or **[ctrl]p**, a Print Dialog Box appears. Pressing [RETURN] or [ENTER] will print one copy of all pages of the document—the default settings. Consequently, a Print button on your layout should activate **⌘p[RETURN]** or **[ctrl]p[ENTER]** to print a single copy of all pages.

Often the details of the overlay design determine whether or not the learner is successful. Little things, such as the availability of a [DELETE] or [BACKSPACE] key, adding spaces after words, and blocking or color coding similar keys, can turn a fair design into a fantastic plan to ensure the learner's success.

With this brief introduction to customizing instruction for learners with special needs you are ready to begin the tutorials. If you have one of the alternative keyboards, work through the appropriate chapter: Chapter 11 (IntelliKeys: if you have *Overlay Maker*) or Chapter 12 (Discover: if you have *Discover:Create* for Macintosh). The chapters have similar content. You should only work through one of them. If you have *IntelliPics Studio 3*, you should also complete Chapter 13. However, it is not necessary to have worked through Chapter 11 or Chapter 12 to work in Chapter 13, *IntelliPics Studio*.

CHAPTER

11 How to Do It—Using IntelliTools *Overlay Maker*

You should have read Chapter 10 before you begin working in this chapter. Use the following instructions to develop customized instructional content if you have an IntelliKeys keyboard available along with the *Overlay Maker* software and any talking word processor for speech feedback.

Simple Talking Activities

This section describes ideas for some of the simplest activities to develop. The skills you will gain learning to make these activities will help you when you begin to develop more complex activities.

The easiest lessons and activities to create are designed so that when the student presses a key a voice speaks a word or phrase. See Figure 10.1 for an example of this kind of lesson. When any one of the eight keys on this layout is pressed, the number word is spoken. The overlay is designed to allow the learner to practice counting and matching objects with the correct numeral. There are no right or wrong answers (that is, the correct matching of pictures and numerals is not required).

Look closely at how this overlay is designed. The object keys are on the left side; the numeral keys are on the right. There are no extra keys to distract the student. The keys are large, for small fingers, and evenly spaced.

Figure 10.3 is a further example of the same kind of activity, actually following the same design. When a key is pressed, words are spoken, enabling the learner who cannot speak to participate in the classroom activity, "Simon Says."

The counting activity and "Simon Says" were created with *Overlay Maker* for use with an IntelliKeys keyboard. The key component, "What the Student Sees," is obvious and could contain pictures of the actions instead of words. "What the Computer Receives" are the words that you wish to have spoken when the key is pressed. The IntelliKeys keyboard is not capable of speech. When the content of a key is "typed" into a talking word processor with the speech feedback turned on, the words are spoken.

Ideas for other talking activities include matching upper case and lower case letters, matching words with pictures, matching numerals with number words, matching colors with color words, matching shapes with their names, picking pairs of rhyming words, and identifying common signs and symbols.

The design for simple talking activities is also appropriate for creating overlays that allow a student who does not speak to participate in group activities, such as the "Simon Says" activity illustrated in Figure 10.3. Keys could display words or pictures, whichever the learner can use confidently. Here are a few other ideas: a morning circle overlay with greetings and weather words, an overlay with number keys to answer arithmetic questions, and a talking overlay with snack choices.

As you embark upon this experience of creating a simple talking activity, you may have already decided exactly what you want to do. In case you have not, here are a few ideas for you to choose from. With all of these activities, the learner should be free to explore; there are no correct or incorrect answers.

- Create an activity to enable a learner who does not speak to participate in a "Simon Says" activity. Use the illustration in Figure 10.3 as an example. Choose commands that all of the participating learners will be able to do. You may place words or images on the keys.

- Create an activity to give a learner practice matching colors with color words. Place several keys on the left side of the overlay—big bright solid-colored keys—that when pressed speak the color name. On the right, place the corresponding color words on keys that when pressed also speak the color name (color printer or colored pencils/markers necessary).

- Create an activity to give a learner practice recognizing matching upper and lower case letters. Place several keys on the left side of the overlay, each with an uppercase letter on it. When one of these keys is pressed, the words "Big A" or "Capital A" or "Uppercase A"—whichever term the learner is accustomed to hearing—are spoken. On the right side of the overlay, make matching keys with lower case letters—again, using the term for lower case letters that the learners are familiar with.

The following instructions should be used as a guideline to get you started. Use the *Overlay Maker Owner's Manual* for more detailed information about the tools or extra options.

Locate the *Overlay Maker* software and open it. Opening the software reveals a new blank overlay and a toolbar, labeled in Figure 11.1.

What the Student Sees

First, create the printed portion of the overlay or "What the Student Sees." Using the **Key Tool** at the top of the toolbox, draw and space the keys, as you would like them to appear on the overlay. Move or resize the keys with the **Pointer Tool.** Do not overlap any keys.

What do you want the student to see on each printed key? If you want the student to see letters or words, choose the **Text Tool** from the toolbox, click on the key, and type whatever letter(s) or word(s) you want the student to see.

To place graphic images on the key, choose **Picture Library** from the Edit Menu. You are not limited to graphics from the built-in Picture Library. Any image that can be

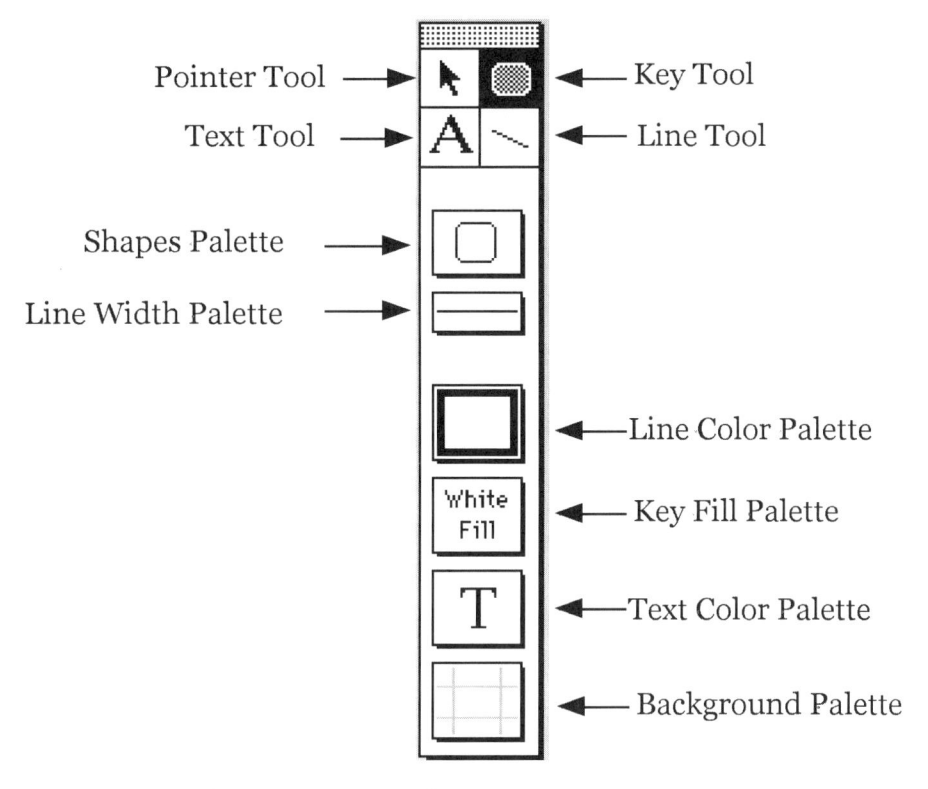

CHAPTER 11 / How to Do It—Using IntelliTools *Overlay Maker* **137**

FIGURE 11.1 The *Overlay Maker* toolbar.
Used courtesy of IntelliTools, Inc.

copied to the computer's clipboard can be pasted to a key. This could include the Mayer-Johnson *BoardMaker* images, photos, and screenshots. If you are at all handy with paint or draw programs, you can create your own images. Because *Overlay Maker* can place only one image on a key, if you wish to place multiple images on a key like the keys on the left side of the overlay illustrated in Figure 10.1, look for instructions in the **Tips and Troubleshooting** section at the end of the chapter.

Explore the additional tools on the toolbox to change key shape and color, line width and color for the key border, text color, and background color or patterns. Free Shapes (Macintosh: ⌘-Key Tool; Windows: **[ctrl]**-Key Tool) allows you to draw non-functional shapes that could be used to unify buttons having a common purpose. Look at the illustration in Figure 11.2. The three large rounded rectangles are Free Shapes while the small white squares represent three different sets of keys, each having a similar purpose.

Now, complete the "What the Student Sees" portion of each of the keys on the overlay. Sometimes when you get busy and involved with a project you forget to save it (a dangerous practice!). If you have not already saved your overlay, save it now.

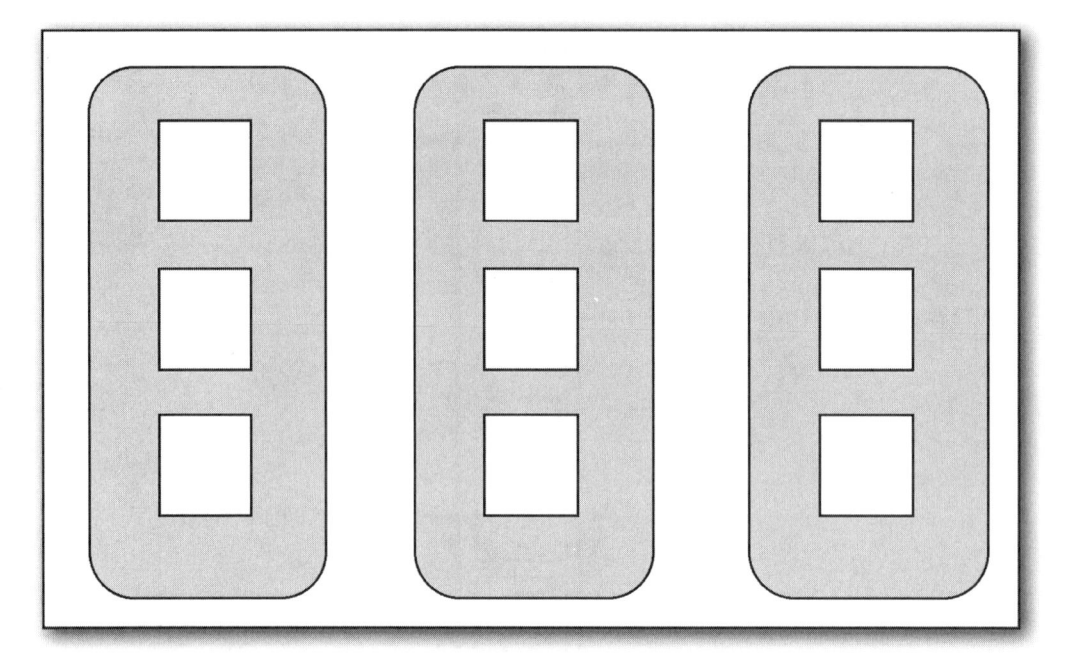

FIGURE 11.2 An example of one way to group keys.

What the Computer Receives

The next step in creating the overlay is to assign the actions that the computer will make when the keys are pressed, called Key Content in *Overlay Maker*. The Key Content can be a single character; a word or phrase; a special keyboard character such as [RETURN], [ENTER], [SPACE], [⌘], [ctrl], [alt]; or a combination of characters, words, phrases, and special keyboard characters. The Key Content can also be mouse actions. To access Key Content, first select the target key with the **Pointer Tool** and then choose **Edit Content** from the Keys menu, or double-click on the target key using the **Pointer Tool.**

Select and "open" one of your buttons to explore the Key Content features. You should see the Key Content dialog box as illustrated in Figure 11.3.

When the Key Content dialog box opens, the Key Content is, by default **[Same as Text Label].** This means that when the key is pressed any letters or characters the learner sees on the key will be typed. For the simple talking activities, the words that you type into the Key Content should be the words that will be typed into the word processor and then spoken. Replace [Same as Text Label] with the actual text you want the student to hear including a [SPACE] after the last word—more about this later.

[Show Special] allows you to access special keyboard characters and mouse actions. You will explore these when you make a more complex activity later.

For each of the keys on your overlay, enter the Key Content now. When you have completed the first draft of your activity, save it again.

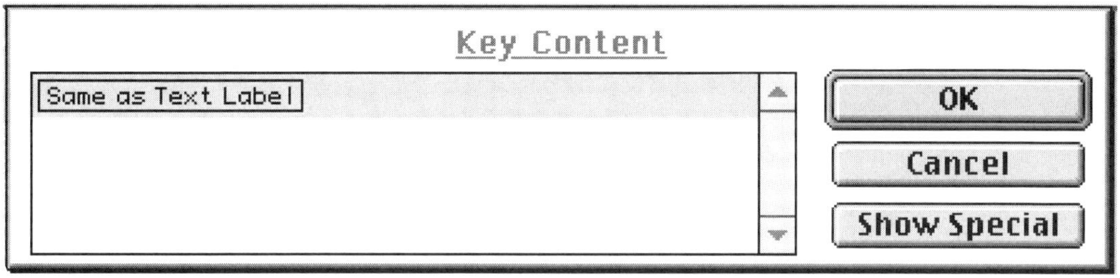

FIGURE 11.3 The Key Content dialog box.
Used courtesy of IntelliTools, Inc.

Print, Send, and Test

To print the paper overlay, first go to **Page Setup** in the File menu and change the page orientation to Landscape. While Page Setup is open, check on paper size. If you have legal-sized paper (preferable for printing overlays) available, change the paper size to Legal (8½ × 14). If the only size paper available is Letter (8½ × 11), make that selection. Overlays printed on letter-sized paper appear on two pages, which you must then trim and tape together. Place the chosen size of paper in the printer's paper tray. As you initiate printing you may wish to use a draft mode, especially if you are using a color printer and expect that you may make changes before your final draft is ready. Go ahead and print a copy. If you have used legal-sized paper, trim the sheet along the dotted line. If you have used letter-sized paper, trim and tape the pages together to fit your IntelliKeys keyboard.

Now for the exciting part—trying it for the first time! First, make sure that there are no magnetically coded overlays installed in the IntelliKeys keyboard. Slip the printout of your new overlay into the keyboard. The next step is to send the information to the keyboard regarding the content of your newly defined keys. While the completed overlay is still open in the *Overlay Maker* program, choose **Send Overlay** from the File Menu. Once the overlay is sent to the IntelliKeys keyboard you can **Quit** (File Menu) the *Overlay Maker* software (Windows: **Close**). However, you may wish to leave it running in case you decide to modify any keys after the first test run.

Open the *IntelliTalk* software (or any talking word processor) to a new blank document and set the Speech options to **Speak Words.** Press the custom keys on the IntelliKeys, just as you might expect the student to. Are the words spoken by the word processor word-by-word? Are all of the words spoken?

Note: *IntelliTalk* "sees" a word as a group of letters followed by a space and then tries to pronounce that word. This is why you must use a space after the last word on a key.

Experiment with different key sequences, trying all possible combinations the student might need to press. Also listen carefully to how the talking word processor pronounces each word that is typed. If any word is not pronounced correctly, edit its pronunciation (Speech menu) in *IntelliTalk*. For example, when pronouncing the word "Chihuahua" the word processor may say "chi-who-a-who-a." If you spell the word "chi wah wah" the pronunciation is more likely to be accurate.

If any keys need to be modified or if you wish to make any design changes, return to *Overlay Maker*, open your saved document, and make the changes. Save the edited overlay, and choose Send Overlay again to send the revised overlay to the IntelliKeys for testing. All changes to the Key Content must be saved and sent to the IntelliKeys keyboard in order to be in effect. Cosmetic changes you make to the paper layout can be made at any time and will not affect the function of any keys.

When all keys work and the layout design is complete, print a final copy. Do not forget to save the final draft! You may wish to laminate an overlay that will get a lot of classroom use. Here is a big *Overlay Maker* tip! If you frequently change the overlays, you do not need to open the software every time you want to send a new overlay. While the overlay is open in *Overlay Maker*, save it as Content Only on the computer desktop (in addition to the original saved document). Simply double-clicking on the Content Only icon sends its contents directly to the keyboard avoiding the steps of opening the software, sending the overlay, and quitting the software.

Simple Talking Activity Checklist

- Printed overlay keys are logically arranged.
- Printed overlay keys have clearly expressed words/images.
- All words are spoken as expected when keys are pressed.
- All words are pronounced correctly.
- The overlay content is presented adequately/logically.

Summary

In this section you have:

- examined design features of simple talking lesson activities.
- created a new overlay.
- drawn custom keys.
- put text, graphic images, or both on custom keys.
- explored toolbox tools to further customize key appearance.
- entered text into Key Content.
- edited previously made custom keys.
- printed the paper overlay.
- sent an overlay to the keyboard.
- adjusted speech features of a talking word processor.
- edited word pronunciation in a talking word processor.

The next section of this chapter will guide you through the more complex key definitions you will need to help students with simple writing activities.

Simple Writing Activities

The lessons and activities that can be created with the simple writing design are probably the most versatile. Figures 10.2 and 10.4 are simple illustrations of this design. The essence of the design is that the learner can press keys on an alternative keyboard causing words to be typed into a word processor. The speech features of a talking word processor would enable the student to have auditory feedback. Many learners, especially those with learning disabilities or visual impairments, can benefit from hearing what they have written. However, a talking word processor is not crucial to the development of these activities. Any word processor will do if the talking software is not available or the learner does not have a need for speech feedback.

In this section you will examine the details of designing simple writing activities, explore ideas for creating lessons, and create your own simple writing activity. With these designs the key component, "What the Computer Receives," has a greater importance than it did in the previous section. In many activities the result becomes a printable document. Keys may function to speak the text, print, delete, or include other "utility" features. Also you may be considering placing spaces, [RETURN] or [ENTER] key presses, mouse actions, or multiple elements in the Key Content.

Look again at the activity illustrated in Figure 10.4. It could be a test or it could be a learning activity in which the student would be referring to reference materials to locate the answers. What elements must be included in its design to assure the learner's success? First, look at the word keys. Because there is no spacebar, it is necessary to include a space after each word when planning "What the Computer Receives" so there will be spaces between the words when they fall together in the word processor. Each of the keys with capital names includes a period and a [RETURN] or [ENTER] key press so that each new sentence can begin on a new line. The [DELETE] or [BACKSPACE] key deletes only one character at a time. If a student makes many errors it might be difficult to delete all of the letters, especially if the student has poor motor skills. The [PRINT] key prints a single copy of all words in the word processing document. The learner has the tools to write the sentences, correct mistakes, and print a copy of the completed work.

Now examine the design of the exercise illustrated in Figure 10.2. The teacher's instructions might be to write and print five complete sentences, ending each with appropriate punctuation. There is little structure with this overlay. It is expected that the pronouns in the first column, capitalized, will be used to begin the sentences. The column of words on the far right contains a list of nouns to be used as sentence objects. In between are four columns of verbs, simple prepositions, a few adjectives, and two articles. All of the words will not fit together. There is no "map" on this overlay to direct a student to choose specific words.

The fact that there is little structure is not necessarily bad. Learners who are ready to choose their own words should have that option. They also need to learn to choose words carefully. However, some learners could find this design confusing.

First, it is not exactly clear which words are meant to begin the sentences. If they were colored differently from other keys, their use would be more easily understood. Extra space could divide the first column of words from the rest for a visual separation. The same idea goes for the object words in the last column. What happens if the student presses a word by mistake? There is no [DELETE] or [BACKSPACE] key! Even a [DELETE] key that backs up one character at a time is necessary for any activity in which the learner could possibly press an unwanted key. A [READ] key would be useful to allow the learner to hear a completed sentence, assuming that the word processor being used had speech capabilities.

Examine the new version of the same activity in Figure 11.4. The revised layout, while still keeping the "open" structure, reduces the likelihood that the student will make a mistake.

A different kind of sentence writing activity can be implemented using numbers as illustrated in the overlay in Figure 11.5. The student is instructed to create and print four related number facts using the three numeral keys on the left side and the three operator keys in the center. An acceptable result might be "4 + 3 = 7," "3 + 4 = 7," "7 – 4 = 3," and "7 – 3 = 4." Each numeral and symbol key includes leading and trailing spaces so the keys can be pressed in any order and still have spaces between them when printed. The "utility" keys on the right provide the learner with tool keys to insure success with the activity. The design is simple and clean and easily modified to use with different sets of numerals.

Take another look at the activity illustrated back in Figure 10.6. Here is a language arts activity with which the learner writes sentences by selecting the correct verb form.

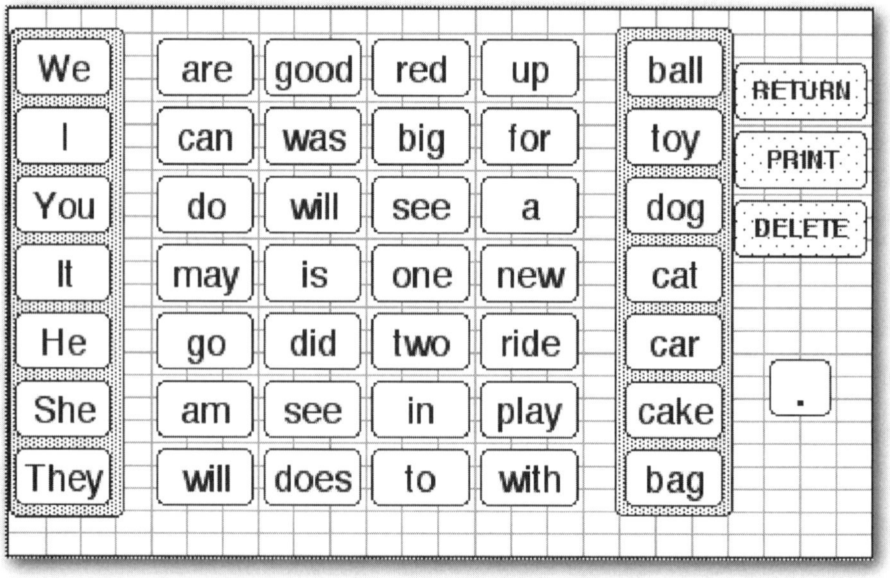

FIGURE 11.4 The revised sentence writing activity.

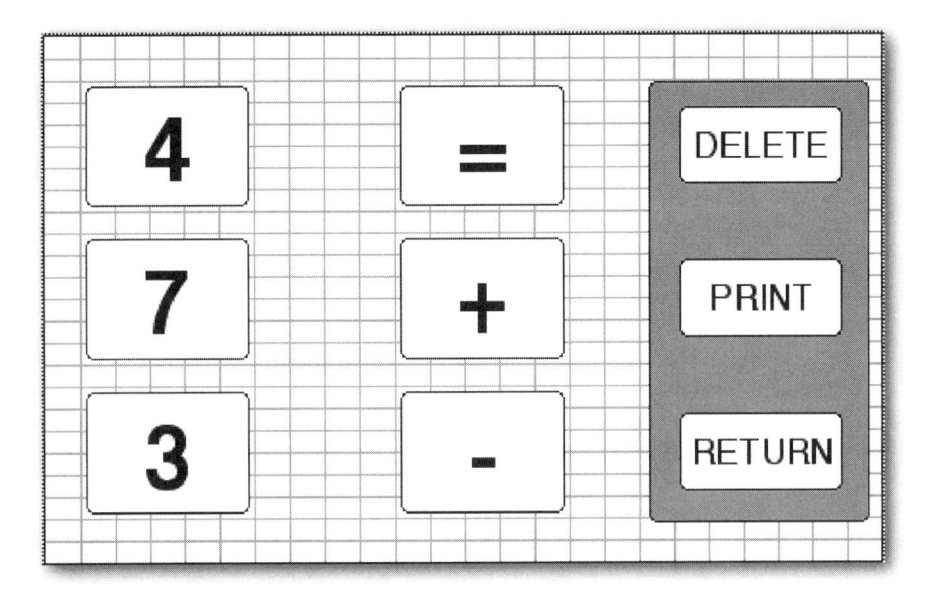

FIGURE 11.5 An overlay for writing number sentences.

The overlay has all the elements to assure learner success. It has a key to delete, a [RETURN] key to start a new line, a key to print, and a key to read all of the text in the document. These utility keys are isolated from the word keys. The "have/has" keys are blocked to isolate them and prompt the learner to press only one.

The sentence elements are mix-and-match so the learner can concentrate on choosing the correct verb form. Because the purpose of this lesson is to choose the correct verb form, making the sentence elements all mix-and-match allows the learner to focus on the correct verb form rather than being required to choose a grammatically correct sentence ending.

As you begin to design your own lesson materials, try to introduce new elements slowly. For example, if there are too many new words in the "have/has" exercise, the original purpose of using "have" and "has" appropriately is lost as the learner struggles to read the words. Do everything that you can to minimize the likelihood of learners errors, thereby assuring that they will progress efficiently and successfully through the lessons.

Inspect Figure 11.6 for an additional variation of the simple writing design. This activity is designed to help a child learn to type and spell simple words. Pressing a picture key on the left side of the overlay will type the word, along with several spaces, into the word processor—preset by the teacher to a large-sized font. The learner's task is to find the letters from the middle of the keyboard to type the same word. The student is instructed to press the "Smiley Face" after completing a word. When the "Smiley Face" key is pressed the computer receives the signal for a [RETURN] or [ENTER] key press, thus creating a new line for the next word. When all of the words are completed, the learner can press the "Stop" key, indicating that work is complete, which will print

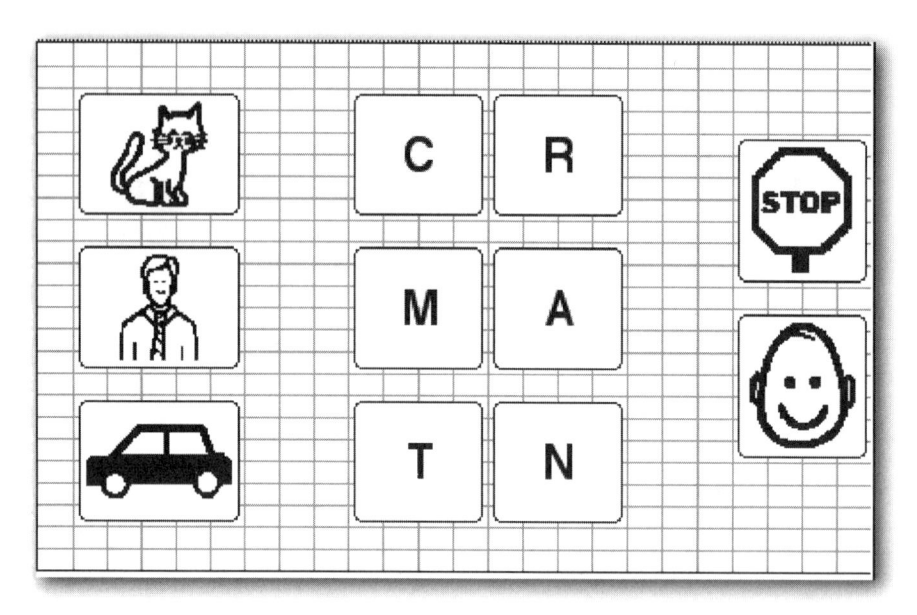

FIGURE 11.6 A spelling overlay.

all text in the word processing document. Both student and teacher will have a permanent product of the activity.

This activity is versatile. First, the learner could press the picture, look at the word in the word processor, and then find the letters in the middle of the overlay to copy the spelling onto the screen. For students who had progressed further, a slightly more difficult implementation would be to look at a picture, press the letters first, and then press the picture to check their spelling. When an overlay can be used several ways, like this one, it is far more valuable in a classroom where children have differing needs.

In the design of this overlay, another variable to consider would be whether the letters are upper case or lower case. For example, if the words typed into the document by the picture keys were in lower case and the letters viewed by the learner on the printed overlay were upper case, the task would be more difficult than if the letters were the same case.

It is time to make your own simple writing activity. You covered a lot of the basics of using *Overlay Maker* to create your own simple talking activity. The second activity deals almost exclusively with defining "What the Computer Receives" to include special characters and commands and actions. With this new capability added to your repertoire of overlay-making skills, you will be able to create just about anything you might need to further enable your students' progress.

As you begin the instructions to create a simple writing activity, you may have already decided exactly what you want to do. In case you have not, here are a few ideas for you to choose from. With all of these activities, the emphasis is on producing text in the word processor.

- Using the activity illustrated in Figure 10.4 as a pattern, create an activity that could be a sentence-writing exercise for which the learner must select the correct answers to complete the sentences. For example, place a single key along the left side of the overlay that will print "A baby" followed by a space. Next, place a vertical group of keys naming animals (e.g., dog, cat, cow, duck) similar to the "states" keys, also followed by spaces. Then make a "is a" key for the third column, with the text followed by a space. Finally, in the last column, make keys for baby animal names corresponding to the animals you chose (e.g., puppy, kitten, calf, duckling) ending each with a period and a [RETURN] or [ENTER] key press. Adjust the difficulty of the exercise by putting the babies in the correct order or scrambling them.

- Create an activity that allows a learner to write sentences that distinguish between fruits and vegetables. On the left side of the overlay, keys could display pictures or words, depending on the learner's needs. The key content for the left keys should say, for example, "A pear" and include a space at the end of the text. Make as many along the left side of the overlay as you could expect the learner to complete. There could be two keys on the right side: The learner would see "is a fruit." and "is a vegetable." The Key Content for the keys on the right should include a [RETURN] or [ENTER] key press so each new sentence begins on a new line. Include the necessary utility keys to enable the student to correct errors and print.

- Create an activity to give the learner practice using singular and plural nouns appropriately. Along the left side of the overlay, plan the beginnings of several sentences that could end with a singular or plural noun (e.g., "Sue had two" or "Please give me a"). On the right side, at the end of each left-side button, place pairs of keys containing choices of a singular or plural noun ("doll" and "dolls"—"pencil" and "pencils"). Include a space after the words for the sentence beginnings and a period and [RETURN] or [ENTER] key press after each of the nouns. Choose all words carefully. The learner should be able to read all of the words.

What the Student Sees

Begin your overlay, as with the last activity, by laying out the keys and what appears on them. Keep the objectives in mind for the particular learner who will use this activity. Use words that you are teaching or that the learner already knows. Consider the difficulty of the task you are requiring the learner to undertake. For example, will the student have to press a [SPACE] key, [RETURN] or [ENTER] key, or end punctuation for sentences? When all the keys appear as you wish, save the overlay.

What the Computer Receives

Next, you must decide exactly what each key will do when it is pressed—"What the Computer Receives." Some of your keys will be just text, possibly including spaces. How do you decide what Key Content to include when you want something more than text, such as to delete, or read the document, or print a copy?

When learners must choose an item from a menu in the word processor (or other software) they are using, that item is unavailable to individuals who cannot, for whatever reason, use a mouse. It is also unavailable to the student who has not learned yet how to open a menu and make choices. When you are developing customized activities for learners with special needs, consider how they are going to be able to access menu features that would enhance their use of the materials you are developing.

First, inspect the menus of the software that the learner will be using. Notice that many options have key equivalents. For most computer users, these options are alternative ways of making the most frequent choices, and simple preference determines whether or not they are used. For persons with special needs these alternatives are often the only way to access those features. Look at the menus in the word processing software that the learner will be using with the custom keyboard overlay, then identify the key equivalents for menu options that the learner may need to use with this setup.

See Appendix C for a group of special keyboard shortcuts you may wish to use with *IntelliTalk* and *Write:OutLoud* to access some of the menu options, such as to print or read portions of the text that is already typed. You can test their function from the standard keyboard before entering them into your setup.

When you have determined precisely what you want each key to do, begin entering the Key Content. Enter the text for the content keys exactly as you did when you made the simple talking activity, taking care in this activity to include the necessary spaces.

If the key is to produce special keyboard characters or mouse actions, click on **[Show Special]**. Scroll through the **Keyboard Keys** and then through **Mouse Actions, Other,** and **Setup Characters** as illustrated in Figure 11.7. Setup Characters are the adjustments you can make to the default settings of the IntelliKeys keyboard. You probably will not need to place Setup Characters on this lesson overlay. Refer to the *IntelliKeys Access Features Guide* for their uses.

You **MUST** enter special characters or mouse actions into the Key Content by selecting them from the lists. First, locate the custom keys that end sentences or where you would like a [RETURN] or [ENTER] key press to be included. "Open" a key that should have a [RETURN] or [ENTER] key press in its Key Content. Click on **[Show Special]** to open the special characters portion of the Key Content dialog box. Click on the **Keyboard Keys** radio button. In the Key Content portion of the dialog box, click at the end of the content you have already entered to indicate where the [RETURN] or [ENTER] key press should be entered. Next, click on the key name and then click the **[Add Special]** button. Notice that [RETURN] or [ENTER] is now part of the Key Content for that button.

Note: Make all utility keys include the commands for their actions and not the text of their names. Consider the following example: The learner needs a key on the overlay to delete text. What will happen if you enter the letters "DELETE" into the Key Content field? If you remember that what is typed into this field is "real text," then you will realize that the letters D-E-L-E-T-E will be typed into the word processing document. If the key is to perform an action—such as to delete, print, or save—then select those special key combinations the appropriate list.

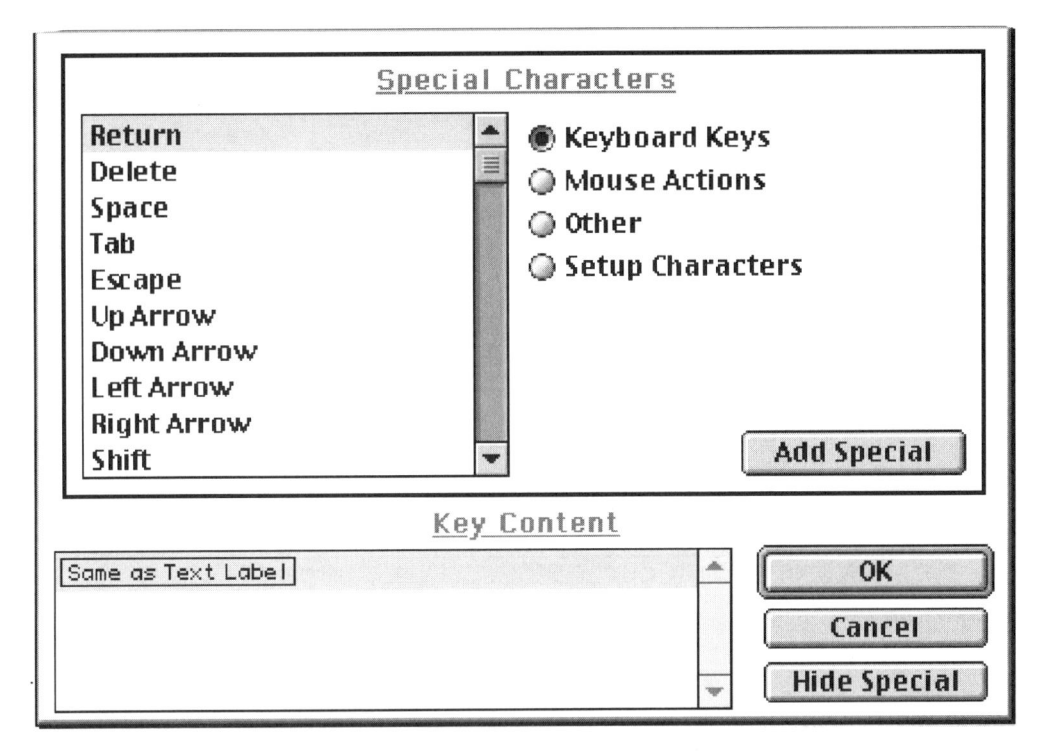

FIGURE 11.7 Special characters dialog box.
Used courtesy of IntelliTools, Inc.

For all of the keys, add the Key Content that is not text. Click the [Add Special] button to add each special key or action to the Key Content. If a key is designed to do multiple things, just keep adding the text or special characters to the Key Content field.

Sometimes students allow their fingers to linger too long on a key, resulting in inadvertent repeated key presses. *Overlay Maker* has a special option to suppress the key repeat, one that is especially useful when students are pressing keys to type longer text strings. In the Key Content dialog box, locate [Non-Repeating] from the **Other** list. Add it to the end of the text you wish the key to type.

For an overlay with which the learner may be creating a lot of text, a simple [DELETE] or [BACKSPACE] key may be inadequate. To allow moving about freely within the text for more efficient editing, add a palette of four small keys (pictured with arrows) that access the arrow keys as provided in the example illustrated in Figure 11.8.

Save, Print, and Test

Save the overlay after the Key Content has been defined for all keys. Print a draft copy of the overlay. Next open the word processor to receive the text when the keys are pressed, and send the overlay to the IntelliKeys keyboard. Adjust the Speech settings in the word processor, if desired.

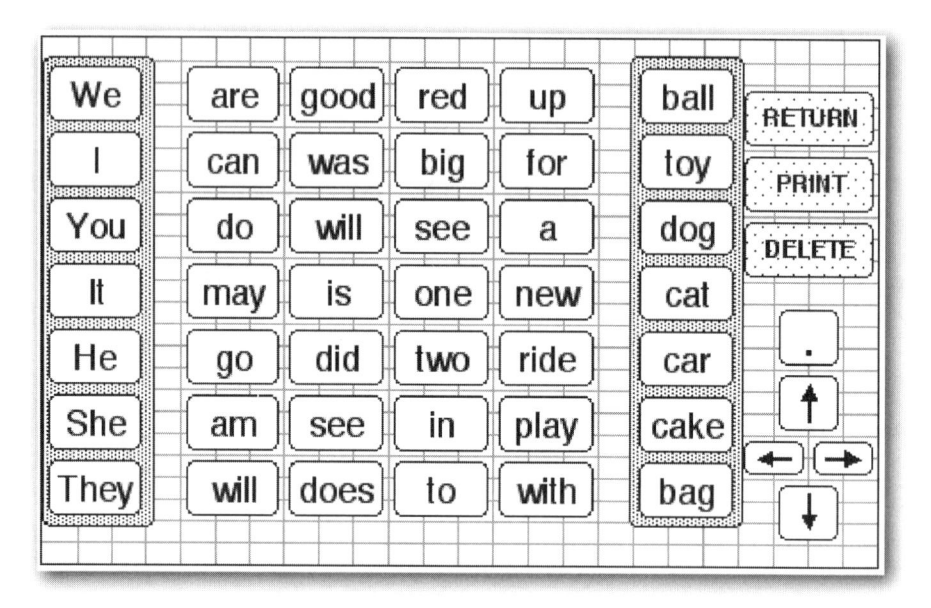

We	are	good	red	up	ball		RETURN
I	can	was	big	for	toy		PRINT
You	do	will	see	a	dog		DELETE
It	may	is	one	new	cat		
He	go	did	two	ride	car		.
She	am	see	in	play	cake		↑
They	will	does	to	with	bag	← →	↓

FIGURE 11.8 An overlay that allows editing.

Test all keys. Try all combinations of keys the learner may press. Do all keys work as you expect? Are all words pronounced correctly? Be sure to check the utility keys, too. For any keys that do not work as you expect, return to *Overlay Maker,* open the overlay again, and edit those keys. Remember, if you make changes in the Key Content, you must save the overlay and send it to IntelliKeys again so that the keyboard will recognize the changes. Continue the "Test-Edit-Save-Send" process until the overlay is perfect. As you test your activity, also be aware of key placement or any design feature that may confuse the learner, such as keys spaced too closely together, utility keys mixed in with content keys, or just too many keys to choose from.

When the overlay is perfect, save the final draft. Print the final overlay using a better quality print and laminate it, if you expect it to receive extensive use.

Simple Writing Activity Checklist

- Printed overlay keys are logically arranged.
- Printed overlay keys have clearly expressed words/images.
- The overlay content is appropriate.
- If speech is used with the word processor, all words are spoken and each word is pronounced correctly.
- Content keys "type" what is expected into a word processor.
- Spacing is built-in to content keys or else utility keys are available for the learner to add spaces or paragraph returns.
- Utility keys function as expected.
- The learner has all keys necessary for successful execution of the activity.

Summary

In this section you have:

- examined design features of more complex activities.
- defined Key Content for actions, such as speak text, print, or delete.

What's Next?

You leave this chapter now with some of the basics necessary to develop customized curriculum content for the learners you are teaching. There are two dimensions to consider as you move beyond what this text has provided.

First, what else can you learn about the physical production of creating overlays for IntelliKeys? Go back to the instructional manual that accompanies your *Overlay Maker* software. Read through it. Experiment with features you have not used before. Visit the IntelliTools web site (see Appendix D for resources) and examine some of the activities that teachers like you have added to the Activity Exchange.

Finally, and most important, how do you get ideas for activities? Examine the state curriculum guidelines for the academic level of the children that you teach. As you scan the guidelines, pick a standard and imagine how you could adapt it for a learner who needs customized lessons. Then do it! The more practice you get customizing lessons, the better you will become at doing it.

Tips and Troubleshooting

The new/edited keys do not work.

> Did you inadvertently leave a standard overlay with magnetic code in the IntelliKeys keyboard?
>
> Did you **Save** first and then **Send Overlay** after you made the changes?

The content keys do not work.

> "Open" a key that does not type what you expect into the word processor. Look at the text that is entered into the Key Content dialog box. Edit the text to reflect what you want the key to type when a student presses it.

The content keys work, but the utility keys do not.

> Edit the utility keys Key Content. Look carefully at what is in the Key Content dialog box. Are special characters used when required? For example, for a utility key intended to print the document, the Key Content should be:
> Macintosh—⌘**p[RETURN]**; Windows—**[ctrl]p[ENTER]** and not the letters P-R-I-N-T.

IntelliTalk is not speaking the word(s) or sentence(s).

> Is the computer's volume up? Adjust the volume control.
>
> Is the **Speak Words** or **Speak Sentences** option turned on in the *IntelliTalk* Speech Menu?
>
> *IntelliTalk* recognizes words only after a space follows a group of letters. Likewise, the software recognizes sentences only after end punctuation—period, question mark, or exclamation point—is typed. Edit the Key Content to include those elements.

I need several similar images on one key. How do I do that?

> You can only paste a single image onto a key. The way to get multiple images on one key is to work outside the *Overlay Maker* program in any graphics program. Copy the image you wish to have multiples of and paste it into the graphics program. Then copy and paste the image to make as many as you need. Arrange the images as you want them to appear on the key. Then select and copy them all. Go back to the key in *Overlay Maker* and paste the revised multiple image.

CHAPTER

12 How to Do It—Using *Discover:Create*

You should have read Chapter 10 before you begin working in this chapter. Use the following instructions to develop customized instructional content if you have one of the Discover keyboards—Discover:Board, *Discover:Screen*, Discover:Switch, or Discover: Kenx along with the *Discover:Create* software for Macintosh computers.

Simple Talking Activities

This section describes ideas for some of the simplest activities to develop. The skills you will gain learning to make these activities will help you when you begin to develop more complex activities.

The easiest lessons and activities to create are designed so that when the student presses a key a voice speaks a word or phrase. See Figure 10.1 for an example of this kind of lesson. When any one of the eight keys on this layout is pressed, the number word is spoken. The overlay is designed to allow the learner to practice counting and matching objects with the correct numeral. There are no right or wrong answers (that is, the correct matching of pictures and numerals is not required).

Look closely at how this overlay is designed. The object keys are on the left side; the numeral keys on the right. There are no extra keys to distract the student. The keys are large, for small fingers, and evenly spaced.

Figure 10.3 is a further example of the same kind of activity, actually following the same design. When a key is pressed, words are spoken enabling the learner who cannot speak to participate in the classroom activity, "Simon Says."

The counting activity and "Simon Says" were created with *Overlay Maker* for use with an IntelliKeys keyboard. The key component, "What the Student Sees," is obvious and could contain pictures of the actions instead of words. "What the Computer Receives" are the words that you wish to have spoken when the key is pressed. The IntelliKeys keyboard is not capable of speech. When the content of a key is "typed" into a talking word processor, that has speech feedback turned on, the words are then spoken.

These same examples can be created with *Discover:Create* for one of the Discover keyboards in a slightly different manner. Because the keys on the Discover products can also talk, for this kind of lesson a talking word processor is not necessary to enable the students to hear the words.

Ideas for other talking activities include matching upper case and lower case letters, matching words with pictures, matching numerals with number words, matching colors with color words, matching shapes with their names, picking pairs of rhyming words, and identifying common signs and symbols.

The design for simple talking activities is also appropriate for creating overlays that allow a student who does not speak to participate in group activities such as the "Simon Says" activity illustrated in Figure 10.3. Keys could display words or pictures, whichever the learner can use confidently. Here are a few ideas: a morning circle overlay with greetings and weather words, an overlay with number keys to answer arithmetic questions, and a talking overlay with snack choices.

Discover:Kenx is a hardware interface and software combination that allows you to connect a single switch or an alternative keyboard to the computer. In addition, it provides an on-screen keyboard. The software programs that accompany all of the Discover products function essentially the same way. Differences are minor and are due to the variations in input mode; any one of the Discover products can be used for these activities. The illustrations in this guide are from Discover:Kenx, which enables an alternative keyboard, an on-screen keyboard, a single switch, or even Morse code.

Although the actual software that "drives" the Discover keyboards is stored on your hard disk (with some components installed in your computer's operating system so that it works automatically), all features of Discover are accessed from the Discover menu on the menu bar at the top of the screen. When you are using a customized Discover keyboard overlay, for whatever purpose, all of the features to select a voice, adjust response time, and choose other preferences are available to you in the Discover menu. If no setup has been opened for use (is active), then the options in the Discover menu for changing features may be unavailable or "grayed out."

Whether or not your Discover menu is "grayed out," take a brief tour of its possibilities. (**Note:** If you do not see the Discover menu on the menu bar, you may need to install the Discover software.) The Discover menu should resemble the illustration in Figure 12.1; these are some of its features:

- **Change Voice & Volume . . .** Select a speaking voice, change volume, and change the speaking rate for the active setup.
- **Change Response Time . . .** Set how long you touch a key before it registers as a key press on an active setup.
- Use the next set of options to **Open** and use a previously saved keyboard setup, **Edit** one that was previously saved, **Create** a brand new setup, or **Print** an active overlay.
- **Smart Markers** are a special feature that allow you to create "hot spots" on a monitor and scan them for easy access. See the manual for details.
- **Choose User . . .** This is a special feature of Discover:Kenx used to tell the software which keyboard you are going to use—an on-screen keyboard, an alternative keyboard (Discover:Board or Key Largo), a Discover switch, or Morse code.
- **Attach Setup . . .** If you are not using the Kenx software, you will see this item instead of **Choose User . . .** It enables an assigned setup to always open when a particular application is opened.

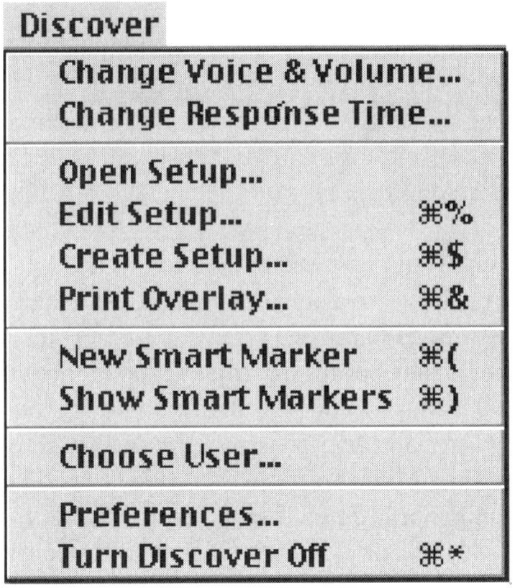

CHAPTER 12 / How to Do It—Using *Discover:Create* 153

FIGURE 12.1 The Discover menu.

- Examine the options available in **Preferences** . . . To enable the Discover keys to speak as they are pressed, activate **Speech Feedback.** The **Click Feedback** is optional. If you want the learner to hear a key click when a key is pressed, put "X" in the selection box. **Note:** If **Preferences** . . . is "grayed out," go to **Open Setup** . . . , locate the folder of Discover (Board, Screen, or Switch) setups on your computer and open any one of them.
- Lastly, notice the final option, **Turn Discover Off.** When the user does not need the alternative input options of the Discover software, Discover should be turned off to prevent it from attempting to attach setups to software the user may open.

As you begin this experience of creating a simple talking activity, you may have already decided exactly what you want to do. In case you have not, here are a few ideas for you to choose from. With all of these activities, the learner should be free to explore; there should be no correct or incorrect answers.

■ Create an activity to enable a learner who does not speak to participate in a "Simon Says" activity. Use the illustration back in Figure 10.3 as an example. Choose commands that each participating student will be able to do. You may place words or images on the keys.

■ Create an activity to give a learner practice matching colors to color words. Place several keys on the left side of the overlay—big, bright, solid-colored keys—that when pressed speak the color name. On the right, place the corresponding color words on keys that when pressed, also speak the color name (color printer or colored pencils/markers are necessary).

- Create an activity to give a learner practice recognizing matching upper and lower case letters. Place several keys on the left side of the overlay, each with an uppercase letter on it. When one of these keys is pressed, the words "Big A" or "Capital A" or "Uppercase A"—whichever term the learner is accustomed to hearing, are spoken. On the right side of the overlay, make matching keys with lower case letters—again using a familiar term for the lower case letters.

Use the following instructions to get you started. Refer to the Discover:Board, *Discover:Screen*, Discover:Switch, or Discover:Kenx manual for further information about the tools, extra options, or advanced features.

Since you are going to create a new setup, **do this:** Choose **Create Setup . . .** from the Discover menu. If you are using Discover:Kenx, first choose the kind of keyboard your students will be using to access the activity—either an on-screen keyboard (*Discover:Screen*), the alternative keyboard (Discover:Board or Key Largo keyboards), or scanning (single switch), and the appropriate new blank setup will appear. If you are using the Discover:Board, *Discover:Screen*, or Discover:Switch software (not Discover:Kenx) a new blank setup will appear.

When you create a new setup you are opening a software application called *Discover:Create*. Look in the Application Menu for Macintosh (last menu on the right) or the Start toolbar for Windows, and see that *Discover:Create* is in the menu, indicating that the program is running. All work you do with the setup you are making or editing should be completed through the menus of *Discover:Create*. The Discover menu remains on the menu bar, but it is only used to set options for the overlays that are already saved and opened for use, called "active" setups by Discover.

What the Student Sees

You should be looking at a new blank keyboard setup. First, create the printed portion of the overlay or "What the Student Sees." There is no toolbar or toolbox. Use your cursor as a drawing tool. With all of the Discover keyboards there are no choices for key shape or color or text font face, size, or color. All keys can be variously sized squares or rectangles that fit the predetermined grid and cannot overlap. There are several differences between creating keys for the on-screen or scanning keyboard and the alternate keyboard.

Creating the Keys for the On-Screen or Scanning Keyboard. Use the cursor to drag key shapes wherever you choose, but they must not overlap. As a key is drawn, it is left with a small selected corner—bottom right. You can drag or push that spot to resize the key.

Creating the Keys for the Alternate Keyboard. The Layout Menu offers you a number of choices for predetermined key layouts. Try some of them. If they are not what you want, then choose **Custom** from the Layout Menu and draw your own. Use the cursor to drag key shapes wherever you choose, but they must not overlap.

CHAPTER 12 / How to Do It—Using *Discover:Create* **155**

Different versions of the Discover software provide various options for modifying the key that has already been drawn. It may have a handle on the bottom right corner, which you can drag or push to resize the key. Some versions also allow you to drag the button by its middle to move it. In another version, once drawn, keys cannot be moved or resized. If a key is not as you want it to be, and you just cannot modify it, click on it once to select it and press [DELETE] or [BACKSPACE] to eliminate it. Then try again.

Draw all of the keys for your simple talking setup. Before you get much further along, save the setup. It may be helpful to name it using your own name. Save it to the setups folder for the particular Discover product you are using. If you save it in another location, it will be more difficult to locate when you want to open it and try it out. When the user attempts to open a setup, Discover first looks in its own folders to locate setups.

In order to define how the key will look and what it will do, double click on the key to open the Key Definition dialog box. Do that now for one of the keys you have drawn. Notice the three distinct sections of the dialog box illustrated in Figure 12.2—**User Sees, User Hears,** and **Computer Receives.**

First, look at the choices in the **User Sees** section. The image on the key can be either a character (a large letter as on a standard keyboard) or a graphic image. The label field is where you type any text you wish the learner to see on the key. The learner could see an image, text, or both on a key. Click on **Set Icon . . .** to choose a graphic image. The hand/stop sign image indicates that there is no image chosen for this key. The DJ Icons extensive collection is accessed through this button. You can browse the images or

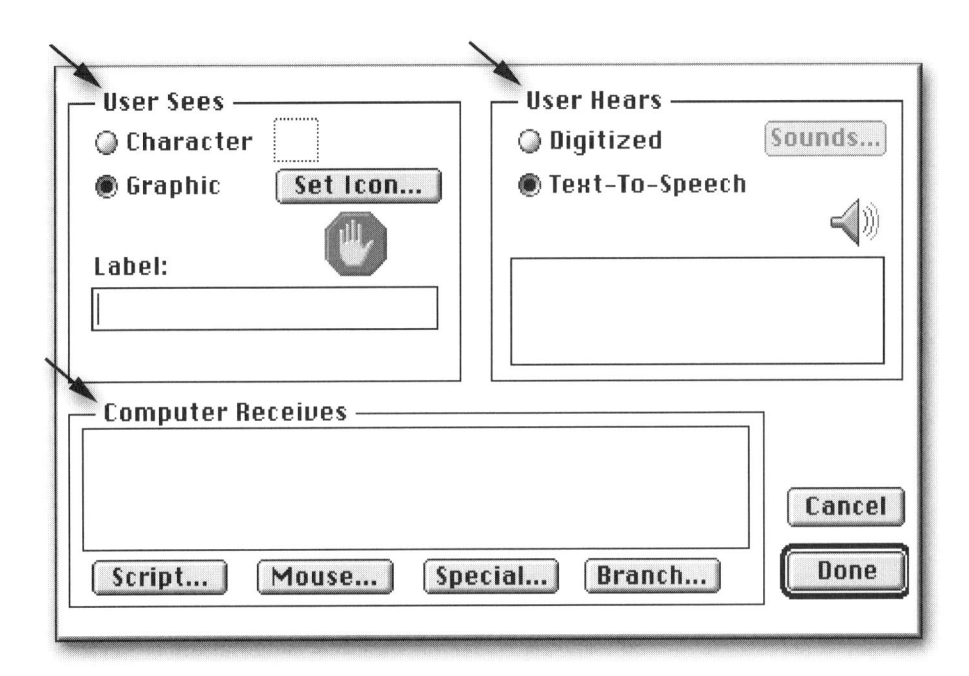

FIGURE 12.2 The Key Definition dialog box.

use **Find . . .** to locate a particular object. You can also edit any of the icons in the library with the **Edit . . .** option. If you wish to use (a) an image not included in the DJ Icons collection, (b) multiples of an image on a single key as in the overlay illustrated in Figure 10.1, or (c) a solid colored icon, look in the **Tips and Troubleshooting** section at the end of this chapter. Do not be afraid to edit icons or add your own images from another source. Added or edited images stay with your setup and will not change the original DJ Icons collection in any way.

Proceed now to define how each of the keys on your setup should look. Save the setup again. As you proceed with defining further features of the keys, if you decide that you want to change the appearance of a key later, you can always edit it.

What the Computer Receives

The portion of the Key Definition dialog box, called Computer Receives in *Discover:Create*, is where you assign the actions that the computer will make when the keys are pressed. When creating these simple talking activities described earlier, the computer does not have to receive any information because the Discover keyboards have their own speech feature. You will explore the Computer Receives features later in another activity.

What the Student Hears

Open one of the keys and look again at the Key Definition dialog box as illustrated in Figure 12.2. There are two sound options to choose from when making a talking lesson. Digitized sounds are "real" sounds, prerecorded and stored in a Discover sound library. First, choose this option and browse the available sounds. If you do not hear anything, check the computer's volume control. Is it turned up? You can also record sounds here, an extremely useful option as students may respond well to your voice (if your computer has sound input capabilities). The second sound option is called Text-to-Speech. Select that choice, type something in the box, and click the speaker icon to hear the text pronounced.

The voices the computer uses to speak with Text-to-Speech are built in to the computer system. The voice that happens to be speaking for you at the moment is the last voice that was chosen for an active setup. To change the voice, if **Change Voice and Volume . . .** is grayed out in the Discover menu, open another setup—any one—and then change the voice.

Because Text-to-Speech uses a limited set of pronunciation rules, words—especially names—are often mispronounced. Correct the pronunciation of any word the learner may not understand. For example, when pronouncing the word "Chihuahua" Text-to-Speech may say "chi-who-a-who-a." If you spell the word "chi wah wah," the pronunciation is more likely to be accurate. Make certain that all words spoken by your setup are pronounced correctly and clearly.

Decide what you want the keys to say when they are pressed and proceed to edit each key. Open the key by double-clicking on it, then click on the **[Done]** button when the key is complete.

Save, Print, and Test

Save the overlay now. It must be saved before the Discover software can open it for use as a keyboard.

To print the overlay, first go to **Page Setup** in the File menu and change the page orientation to Landscape. While Page Setup is open, check on paper size. If you have legal-sized paper (preferable for printing overlays) available, change the paper size to Legal (8½ × 14). If the only size paper available is Letter (8½ × 11), make that selection. Overlays printed on letter-sized paper appear on two pages and you must trim and tape them together. Place the paper in the printer's paper tray.

As you initiate printing you may wish to use a draft mode, especially if you are using a color printer and anticipate that you may make changes before your final draft is ready. Go ahead and print a copy. If you have used letter-sized paper, trim and tape the pages together to fit your Discover keyboard.

Now for the exciting part—trying it for the first time! Place the printout of your new overlay on the Discover keyboard. If the *Discover:Create* software is still open you may want to quit the software to get it out of the way. It is sometimes confusing to see your setup-under-construction on the screen, particularly if you are using the *Discover:Screen* or Discover:Switch keyboards. You need not have any software open on the computer. Choose **Open Setup . . .** from the Discover menu. Locate and open your saved setup so the computer will recognize the new keyboard layout.

Note: Discover:Switch and *Discover:Screen* users do not need to print. If you are using Discover:Switch, there is one additional step you must complete: The scanning. Simply dragging the small blue boxes sets up the areas you want to be divided into scan steps. The top one creates the rows, and the bottom one defines the columns. The one you move first determines the dimension that scans first. Experiment with this as you design your first scanning overlay. See the manual for additional tips on scanning overlays.

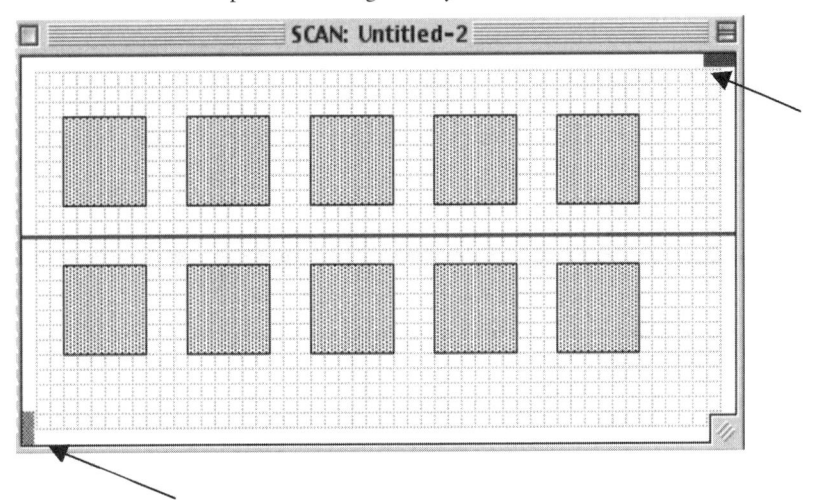

At this time you may wish to adjust some of the Discover features available through the Discover menu: preferences, voice, rate, speech feedback, volume, or others. The most important features for this overlay to be effective with children are the voice, volume, and rate. Select the best possible combination to assure the learner's success with the lesson.

Press the overlay keys just as you expect the student to. Are the words spoken when you press the keys? Test all keys. Listen carefully to how each word is pronounced noting the pronunciation of any word that the learner may have difficulty understanding. See the *Tips and Troubleshooting* section at the end of the chapter for additional help.

If any keys need to be modified, you wish to make any design changes, or you need to edit pronunciation of any words, choose **Edit Setup . . .** from the Discover menu, locate your newly saved setup, and make the modifications. Each time you make changes you must Save, and select **Open Setup . . .** again to test out those changes. Unless you save again and then open the edited setup, the Discover keyboard does not "know" that you made the changes. When all keys work and the layout design is complete, print a final copy. Do not forget to save the final draft! You may wish to laminate a keyboard overlay that will get a lot of classroom use.

Simple Talking Activity Checklist

- Printed overlay keys are logically arranged.
- Printed overlay keys have clearly expressed words/images.
- All words are spoken as expected when keys are pressed.
- All words are pronounced correctly.
- The setup content is presented adequately/logically.

Summary

In this section you have:

- examined design features of simple talking lesson activities.
- created a new setup.
- drawn custom keys.
- put text on custom keys.
- put graphic images on custom keys.
- entered text into "User Hears" section.
- edited word pronunciation.
- edited previously made custom keys.
- printed the paper overlay.
- sent a setup to the keyboard.
- adjusted Discover features such as voice, rate, volume, etc.

The next section of this chapter will guide you through the more complex key definitions you will need to help students with simple writing activities.

Simple Writing Activities

The lessons and activities that can be created with the simple writing design are probably the most versatile. Figures 10.2 and 10.4 are simple illustrations of this design. The essence of the design is that the learner can press keys on an alternative keyboard causing words to be typed into a word processor.

In the last activity, what the learner hears was the most important feature of the setup. For the upcoming activity, the learner could benefit from more sophisticated sound features. The speech features of a talking word processor would enable the student to have auditory feedback of the text they had entered into the word processor. The speech feedback from the Discover keyboard is limited to what is placed on individual keys rather than what is typed into the word processor. Many learners, especially those with learning disabilities or visual impairments, can benefit from hearing what they have written. However, a talking word processor is not crucial to the development of these activities. Any word processor will do if the talking software is not available or if the student does not have a need for speech feedback.

In this section you will examine the details of designing simple writing activities and explore ideas for creating lessons. With these designs the key component "What the Computer Receives" is the most important. In many activities the result becomes a printable document. Keys may function to speak the text, print, delete, or include other "utility" features. Also you may be considering placing spaces, [RETURN] or [ENTER] key presses, mouse actions, or multiple elements in the Key Definition.

Look again at the activity illustrated in Figure 10.4. It could be a test, or it could be a learning activity for which the student would be referring to reference materials to locate the answers. What elements must be included in its design to assure the learner's success? First, look at the word keys. Because there is no spacebar, it is necessary to include a space after each word when planning "What the Computer Receives" so there will be spaces between the words when they fall together in the word processor. Each of the capital keys includes a period and a [RETURN] or [ENTER] key press so that each new sentence can begin on a new line. The [DELETE] or [BACKSPACE] key deletes only one character at a time. If a student makes many errors, it might be difficult to delete all of the letters, especially if the student has poor motor skills. The [PRINT] key prints a single copy of all words in the word processing document. The learner has the tools to write the sentences, correct mistakes, and print a copy of the completed work.

Now examine the design of the exercise illustrated back in Figure 10.2. The teacher's instructions might be to write and print five complete sentences, ending each with appropriate punctuation. There is little structure with this overlay. It is expected that the pronouns in the first column, capitalized, will be used to begin the sentences. The column of words on the far right contains a list of nouns to be used as sentence objects. In between are four columns of verbs, simple prepositions, a few adjectives, and two articles. All words will not fit together. There is no "map" on this overlay to direct a student to choose specific words.

The fact that there is little structure is not necessarily bad. Learners who are ready to choose their own words should have that option. They also need to learn to choose words carefully. However, some students could find this design confusing.

First, it is not exactly clear which words are meant to begin the sentences. If they were colored differently from other keys, their use would be more easily understood. Extra space could divide the first column of words from the rest for a visual separation. The same idea goes for the object words in the last column. What happens if the student presses a word by mistake? There is no [DELETE] or [BACKSPACE] key! Even a [DELETE] key that backs up one character at a time is necessary for any activity for which the learner could accidentally press an unwanted key. A [READ] key would be useful to allow the learner to hear a completed sentence, assuming that the word processor being used had speech capabilities.

Examine the new version of the same activity in Figure 12.3. The revised layout, while still keeping the "open" structure, reduces the likelihood that the learner will make a mistake.

A different kind of sentence writing activity can be implemented using numbers as illustrated in the overlay in Figure 12.4. The student is instructed to create and print four related number facts using the three numeral keys on the left side and the three operator keys in the center. An acceptable result might be "4 + 3 = 7," "3 + 4 = 7," "7 – 3 = 4," and "7 – 4 = 3." Each numeral and symbol key includes leading and trailing spaces so the keys can be pressed in any order and still have spaces between them when printed. The "utility" keys on the right provide the learner with tool keys to insure success with the activity. The design is simple and clean and easily modified to use with different sets of numerals.

Take another look at the activity illustrated in Figure 10.6. Here is a language arts activity with which the learner writes sentences by selecting the correct verb form. The overlay has all the elements to assure learner success. It has a key to delete, a [RETURN] key to start a new line, a key to print, and a key to read all of the text in the document. These utility keys are isolated from the word keys. The "have/has" keys are blocked to isolate them and prompt the learner to press only one.

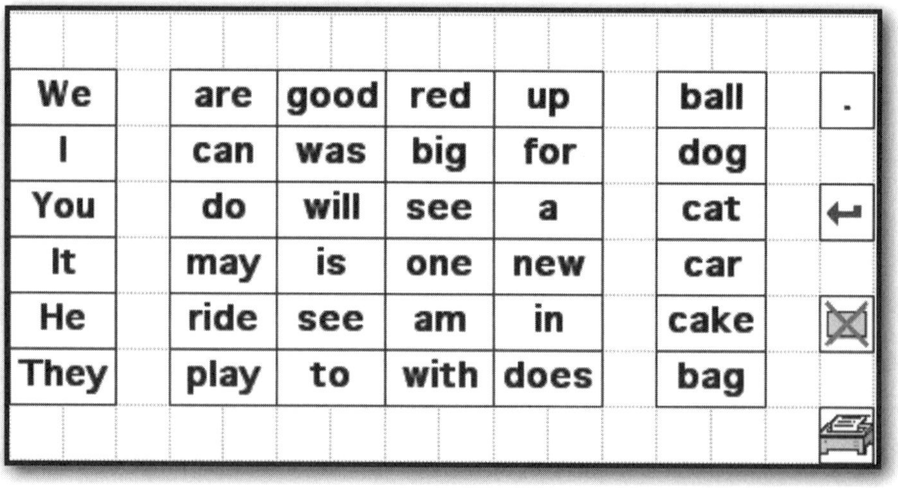

We	are	good	red	up	ball	.
I	can	was	big	for	dog	
You	do	will	see	a	cat	⏎
It	may	is	one	new	car	
He	ride	see	am	in	cake	⌧
They	play	to	with	does	bag	

FIGURE 12.3 The revised sentence writing activity.

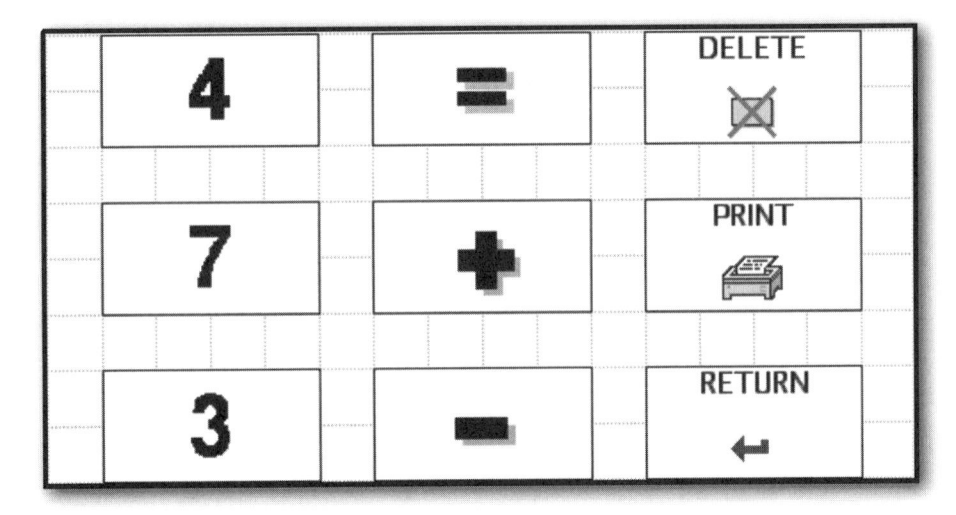

FIGURE 12.4 An overlay for writing number sentences.

The sentence elements are mix-and-match so the learner can concentrate on choosing the correct verb form. Because the purpose of this lesson is to choose the correct verb form, making the sentence elements all mix-and-match allows the learner to focus on the correct verb form rather than being required to choose a grammatically correct sentence ending.

As you begin to design your own lesson materials, try to introduce new elements slowly. For example, if there are too many new words in the "have/has" exercise, the original purpose of using "have" and "has" appropriately is lost as the learner struggles to read the words. Do everything that you can to minimize the likelihood of the learners making errors, thereby assuring that they will progress efficiently and successfully through the lesson.

Inspect Figure 12.5 for an additional variation of the simple writing design. This activity is designed to help a child learn to type and spell simple words. Pressing a picture key on the left side of the keyboard will type the word, along with several spaces, into the word processor—preset by the teacher to a large-sized font. The learner's task is to find the letters from the middle of the keyboard to type the same word and then to press the "Smiley Face" after completing a word. When the "Smiley Face" key is pressed the computer receives the signal for a [RETURN] or [ENTER] key press, thereby creating a new line for the next word. When all of the words are completed, the learner can press the "Stop" key, indicating that work is complete, which will print all text in the word processing document. Both student and teacher will have a permanent product of the activity.

This activity is versatile. First, the learner could press the picture, look at the word in the word processor, and then find the letters in the middle of the overlay to copy the spelling onto the screen. For students who had progressed further, a slightly more difficult implementation would be to look at a picture, press the letters first, and then press the picture to check their spelling. When an overlay can be used several

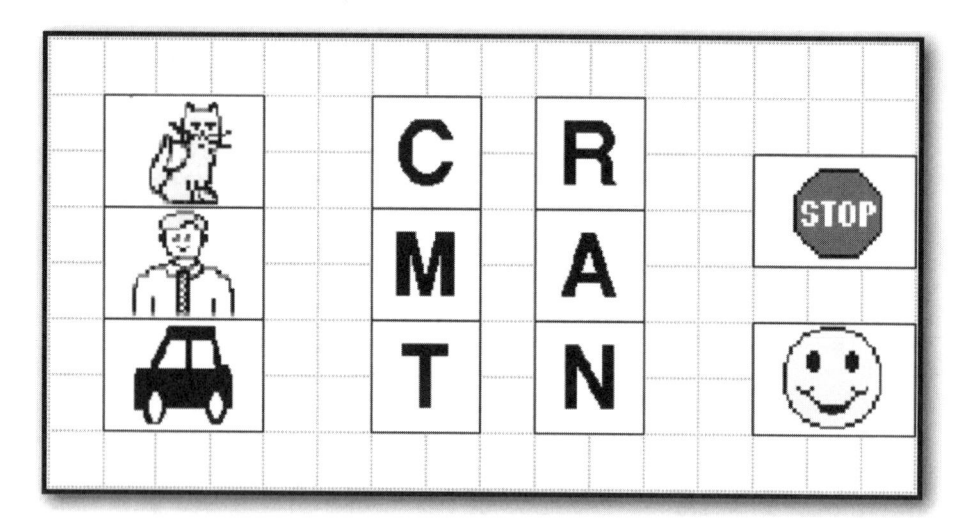

FIGURE 12.5 A spelling keyboard setup.

ways (like Figure 12.5), it is far more valuable in a classroom where children have differing needs.

In the design of this keyboard, another variable to consider would be whether the letters are upper case or lower case. For example, if the words typed into the document by the picture keys were in lower case and the letters viewed by the learner on the printed overlay were upper case, the task would be more difficult than if the letters were the same case.

It is time to make your own simple writing activity. You covered a lot of the basics of using *Discover:Create* to make your own simple talking activity. The second part of this chapter deals almost exclusively with defining "What the Computer Receives," including special characters and commands and mouse actions along with text. With this new capability added to your repertoire of setup-making skills you will be able to create just about anything you might need to further enable your students' progress.

As you begin the steps to create a simple writing activity, you may have already decided exactly what you want to do. In case you have not, here are a few ideas for you to consider. With all of the easy writing activities, the emphasis is on producing text in the word processor. Keep the objectives in mind for the particular learner who will use this activity. Use words that you are teaching or that the learner already knows. Consider the difficulty of the task you are requiring the learner to undertake. For example, will the student have to press a [SPACE] key, [RETURN] or [ENTER] key, or end punctuation for sentences?

- Using the activity illustrated in Figure 10.4 as a pattern, create an activity that could be a sentence-writing exercise in which the learner must select the correct answers to complete the sentences. For example, place a single key along the left side of the keyboard that will print "A baby" followed by a space. Next, place a vertical group of keys naming animals (e.g., dog, cat, cow, duck) similar to the "states" keys, also followed by spaces. Then make an "is a" key for the third column, with the text followed by a space. Finally, in the last column, make keys for baby animal names corresponding with the animals you chose (e.g., puppy, kitten, calf, duckling) ending each with a period and a [RETURN] key press. Adjust the difficulty of the exercise by putting the babies in the correct order or scrambling them.

- Create an activity that allows a learner to write sentences that distinguish between fruits and vegetables. The left side of the setup keys could display pictures or words, depending on the learner's needs. The Computer Receives field for the left keys should say, for example, "A pear" and include a space at the end of the text. Make as many along the left side as you could expect the learner to complete. There could be two keys on the right side: The learner would see "is a fruit." and "is a vegetable." The Computer Receives field for the keys on the right should include a [RETURN] or [ENTER] key press so each new sentence begins on a new line. Include the necessary utility keys to enable the student to correct errors and print.

- Create an activity to give the learner practice using singular and plural nouns appropriately. Along the left side of the keyboard, plan the beginnings of several sentences that could end with a singular or plural noun (e.g., "Sue had two" or "Please give me a"). On the right side, at the end of each left-side button, place pairs of keys containing choices of a singular or plural noun ("doll" and "dolls"—"pencil" and "pencils"). Include a space after the words for the sentence beginnings and a period and [RETURN] or [ENTER] key press after each of the nouns. Choose all words carefully. The learner should be able to read all of the words.

What the Student Sees

With the simple talking activity you created first, you used the talking feature of Discover to speak the words. In the simple writing activities, the student will be pressing keys to enter text into a word processor. If there is a need for spoken text, the word processor should be a talking one, such as *IntelliTalk* or *Write:OutLoud*. The speech features of the Discover product should be turned off for this lesson to avoid confusing the learner with speech from two different sources. You may wish to keep the **Click Feedback** turned on, if the learner needs to hear that a key has been pressed. You will set these features after you have developed the setup and are ready to test it out.

Now, begin your keyboard setup, as you did for the talking activity, by laying out the keys and what appears on them. When all the keys appear as you wish, save it.

What the Computer Receives

The next step in creating the activity is to decide what will happen when each of the keys is pressed. Use the Computer Receives portion of the Key Definition dialog box in *Discover:Create* to assign the actions that the computer will make when the keys are pressed. What the computer receives can be a single character; a word or phrase; a special keyboard character such as [RETURN], [SPACE], [⌘], [CONTROL], or [ENTER]); or a combination of characters, words, phrases, and special keyboard characters. The computer can also receive mouse actions.

Double-click one of your keys to "open" it. Examine the **Computer Receives** section of the Key Definition dialog box. First look at the **Script** . . . choices. Scripts are special actions, useful in many situations. You probably will not need these functions for this activity. (See the Owner's Manual for details). **Mouse** . . . is the way to select mouse actions. **Special** . . . is the list of non-character keys such as [SHIFT], [DELETE], [RETURN], [BACKSPACE], [CTRL], [ENTER], and others. You will probably use many of the special keys along with text. **Branching** . . . gives you options to allow one setup to branch to another in a more complex design than you will be using for this occasion. Again, see the Owner's Manual for more details if you wish to try it. Any or all of these features can be combined in the **Computer Receives** box.

When learners must choose an item from a menu in the word processor (or other software) they are using, that item is unavailable to individuals who cannot, for whatever reason, use a mouse. It is also unavailable to the learner who has not yet learned how to open a menu and make choices. When you are developing customized activities for learners with special needs, consider how they are going to be able to access menu features that would enhance their use of the materials you are developing.

First, inspect the menus of the word processing software that the learner will be using. Notice that many options have key equivalents. For most computer users, these options are alternative ways of making the most frequent choices, and simple preference determines whether or not they are used. For persons with special needs, these alternatives are often the only way to access those features. As you look at the menus in the application software that the learner will be using with the custom keyboard setup, identify the key equivalents for menu options that the student may need to use with this setup.

See Appendix C for a group of special keyboard shortcuts you may wish to use with *IntelliTalk* and *Write:OutLoud* to access some of the menu options, such as to print or read portions of the text that has already been typed. You can test their function from the standard keyboard before entering them into your setup.

For a setup with which the learner may be creating a lot of text, a simple [DELETE] or [BACKSPACE] key may be inadequate. To allow moving about freely within the text for more efficient editing, add a palette of four small keys (pictured with arrows) that access the arrow keys as provided in the example illustrated in Figure 12.6.

Note: Make all utility keys include the commands for their actions and not the text of their names. Consider the following example: The learner needs a key on the overlay to delete text. What will happen if you enter the letters "DELETE" into the Key Content field? If you remember that what is typed into this field is "real text," then you will realize that the letters D-E-L-E-T-E will be typed into the word processing document. If the key is to perform an action, such as to delete, print, or save, then select those special key combinations the appropriate list.

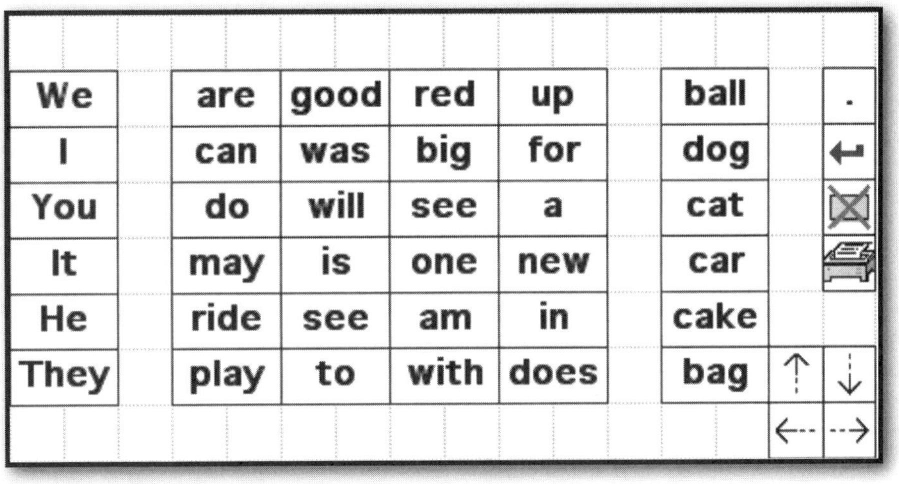

We	are	good	red	up	ball	.
I	can	was	big	for	dog	⏎
You	do	will	see	a	cat	⌧
It	may	is	one	new	car	🖨
He	ride	see	am	in	cake	
They	play	to	with	does	bag	↑ ↓
						← →

FIGURE 12.6 A keyboard setup that enables editing.

Edit your setup now to include what happens when each key is pressed. Select one of your keys to begin. "Open" the key to reveal the Key Definition dialog box. The text that you wish the key to type into the word processor must be typed into the Computer Receives field. Following the text include spaces, a [RETURN] or [ENTER] key press, or any other actions you wish to occur when the key is pressed. Complete defining the remaining keys of the setup and save the completed setup.

Save, Print, and Test

When all of the keys have been completed, save the overlay again. Print a draft copy to test it out. First, open the word processor to receive the text when the keys are pressed. Adjust the speech settings in the Speech menu of the word processor to speak sentences, if desired. Then from the Discover menu choose **Open Overlay . . .** locating your newly saved setup, thereby sending the key definitions to the keyboard.

Discover can "attach" different overlays to software applications so that when a new program is opened on the computer, Discover opens the correct keyboard setup. This is a great feature if the computer user cannot open keyboard setups alone. It is not so useful when a teacher is testing out a new one. Sometimes, if you open the setup to test it before you open the software then another setup is opened when the software opens. Of course, your overlay will not work properly, and you may not realize why. To avoid this potential confusion, **always open the software before you open the overlay.**

Once your setup is the active setup, open the Discover menu and turn off speech feedback. Adjust other features as you choose. Now, test all keys. Try all combinations of keys the learner may press. Do all keys work as you expect? Are all words pronounced correctly? Be sure to check the utility keys, too. For any keys that failed to work as you expected, return to *Discover:Create*, open the setup again, and edit those keys. Refer to *Tips and Troubleshooting* at the end of the chapter, if needed. Remember, if you make changes in the Computer Receives content, you must save the setup and send it to the Discover keyboard again so that the keyboard will recognize the changes. Continue the "Test-Edit-Save-Send" process until the setup is perfect. As you test your activity, also be aware of key placement or any design feature that may confuse the learner, such as keys spaced too closely together, utility keys mixed in with content keys, or just too many keys to choose from.

When the overlay is perfect, save the final draft. Print the final overlay using a better quality print. If you expect it to receive much use, laminate it.

Simple Writing Activity Checklist

- Printed custom keys are logically arranged.
- Printed custom keys have clearly expressed words/images.
- The keyboard setup content is appropriate.
- If speech is used with the word processor, all words are spoken and each word is pronounced correctly.
- Discover speech options are turned off.
- Content keys "type" what is expected into a word processor.
- Spacing is built in to content keys or else utility keys are available for the learner to add spaces or paragraph returns.
- Utility keys function as expected.
- The learner has all keys necessary for successful execution of the activity.

Summary

In this section you have:

- examined design features of more complex activities.
- defined "What the Computer Receives" to enter text into a word processing document.
- defined "What the Computer Receives" for actions, such as speak text, print, or delete.

What's Next?

You leave this chapter now with some of the basics necessary to develop customized curriculum content for the learners you are teaching. There are two dimensions to consider as you move beyond what this text has provided.

First, what else can you learn about the physical production of creating setups for Discover keyboards? Go back to the instructional manual that accompanies your Discover keyboard. Read through it. Experiment with features you have not used before.

Finally, and most important, how do you get ideas for activities? Examine the state curriculum guidelines for the academic level of the children that you teach. As you scan the guidelines, pick a standard and imagine how you could adapt it for a learner who needs customized lessons. Then do it! The more practice you get customizing lessons, the better you will become at doing it.

Tips and Troubleshooting

The new/edited keys do not work.

Did you **Save** and **Open Setup** . . . again, after you made the changes?

The content keys do not work.

"Open" a key that does not type what you expect into the word processor. Look at the text that is entered into the Computer Receives box. Edit the text to reflect what you want the key to type when a student presses it.

The content keys work, but the utility keys do not.

Edit the utility keys Computer Receives box. Look carefully at what is in the Computer Receives dialog box. Are special characters used when required? For example, for a utility key intended to print the document, the Computer Receives content should be: Macintosh—[⌘] p [RETURN]; Windows—[ctrl] p [ENTER], and not the letters P-R-I-N-T.

IntelliTalk or *Write:OutLoud* is not speaking the word(s) or sentence(s).

Is the computer's volume up? Adjust the volume control.

Is **Speak Words** or **Speak Sentences** option turned on in the *IntelliTalk* or *Write:OutLoud* Speech Menu?

IntelliTalk recognizes words only after a space follows a group of letters. Likewise, the software recognizes sentences only after end punctuation—period, question mark, or exclamation point—is typed. Edit the Computer Receives to include those elements.

I would like to use an image that is not part of the icon library.

Locate an image or create one in a graphics program and copy it to the computer's clipboard. Return to the **Set Icon** . . . in *Discover:Create* and choose

Add . . . The editing window appears and you can paste the image you found into the window, edit it as you wish, name it, and click **Done** when the image is complete. The new icon will remain with your setup and will not change the built-in library.

I need several similar images on one key. How can I do that?

You can only paste a single image onto a key. The way to get multiple images on one key is to work outside the *Discover:Create* program in any graphics program. Locate and copy the image you wish to have multiples of and paste it into the graphics program. Then copy and paste the image to make as many as you need. Arrange the images, as you want them to appear on the key. Then select and copy them all. Go back to the key in *Discover:Create*, choose **Set Icon . . .**, then **Add . . .**, and paste the revised multiple image. Give it a name and click **Done**. The modified icon will remain with your setup and will not change the built-in icon library.

I want a key to display a solid colored icon.

If you want a key to display a solid colored square (as an icon), choose **Add . . .** to open the icon-editing window. Choose a color from the color palette, then click on the paint can tool. Upon clicking in the empty icon grid with the paint can tool, the icon square will fill with color. Give the icon a name. Click **Done** and then **OK** to place your new icon on the button.

You could also place a colored stripe along the bottom of a key by using the pencil tool to draw a few lines of color across the bottom of the icon. This colored stripe would replace any other icon but could share the key space with text.

An alternative method for placing color on an overlay is to use colored pencils or markers after printing the overlay in black and white or gray scale.

CHAPTER

13 *IntelliPics Studio*

IntelliPics Studio 3, from IntelliTools, Inc., is a software program especially designed for learners from preschool through middle school. It fits into the software category called authoring—software that enables you to develop activities without knowing a programming language. With *IntelliPics Studio* you can create multimedia instructional activities using painting, drawing, sound, and animations. You can create buttons with actions, text boxes that speak text, and toolbars. *IntelliPics Studio* can be a wonderful tool for teachers to design learning materials for learners with many different academic levels using interactive presentations, quizzes, storybooks, and coloring books.

IntelliPics Studio is designed to be fully accessible to learners with physical or cognitive disabilities. Because all activities can be accessed through use of a standard keyboard and mouse, an IntelliKeys keyboard (USB or classic), or switches, the software is ideal for use in classrooms where students have a variety of learning styles and physical abilities. With its various input methods and opportunities for structuring learning activities, *IntelliPics Studio* exemplifies the concept of universal design. In an inclusive classroom, *IntelliPics Studio* can play an important role by promoting an environment in which all learners, regardless of their abilities, can participate in the same classroom activities.

IntelliPics Studio 3 is available for both Macintosh and Windows computers. Documents created with the software on either computer platform can be viewed on the other platform. In addition, documents created on either platform can be used with *IntelliPics Studio 3 Player*, which can be downloaded free from the IntelliTools, Inc. web site (http://www.intellitools.com). With *IntelliPics Studio 3 Player* activities can be played; however, the full program is necessary for any authoring activities.

To work successfully in this chapter you should have *IntelliPics Studio 3* (or IntelliTools *Classroom Suite*) installed on either a Macintosh or Windows computer. Chapter illustrations were made with the Macintosh OS X version of *IntelliPics Studio 3*, one component of the *Classroom Suite*.

This chapter begins by exploring several activities that are installed with the software. These activities are ready for learners to use and demonstrate the incredible versatility of the software. Next you will learn how *IntelliPics Studio* activities are structured by exploring the different modes that *IntelliPics Studio* has. Finally, you will develop two activities of your own. Let's begin!

Exploring Activities

Locate the *IntelliPics Studio* software on your computer and open it. You should see a screen similar to the Sign In screen from *Classroom Suite* illustrated in Figure 13.1. If you are using the stand-alone version of *IntelliPics Studio 3* the Sign In screen may be slightly different.

IntelliPics Studio expects that multiple users will be using the same software, as would be the case where all children in a classroom might be using the same computer. It also accommodates use by multiple classes in the case where classes visit a computer lab for their work. The software offers user levels for Administrator/Teacher users and for student users. By default, when new software opens for the first time, the only level available (since no individuals have had opportunities to sign in) is Guest, a level without administrator or teacher privileges. The Guest level is fine for exploring activities, creating activities from templates, and even creating activities from scratch. The features necessary for designing and creating exciting learning activities for learners can be accessed with guest access privileges. However, teacher options such as enrolling new users and classes, configuring accessibility options, determining menu access, and showing Talking Tool Tips, among others, are not available at the Guest level. Consult your product documentation for access to the Administrator/Teacher name and password.

After you sign in, either as a registered user or a guest, you will be on the **Navigation Screen,** something like a "home base" for opening previously saved documents, making new activities, or using previously made activities. Figures 13.2 and 13.3 illustrate Navigation Screens for Guest users and Administrator/Teacher users, respectively.

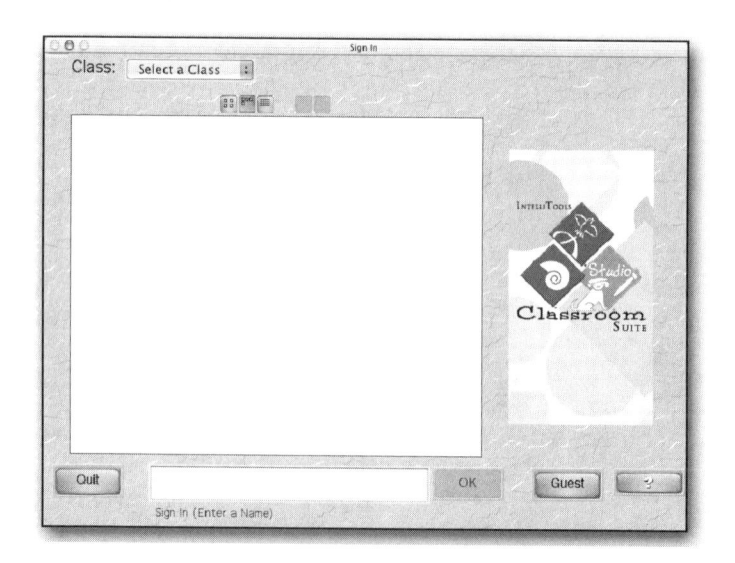

FIGURE 13.1 The Sign In page from *Classroom Suite*.
Used courtesy of IntelliTools, Inc.

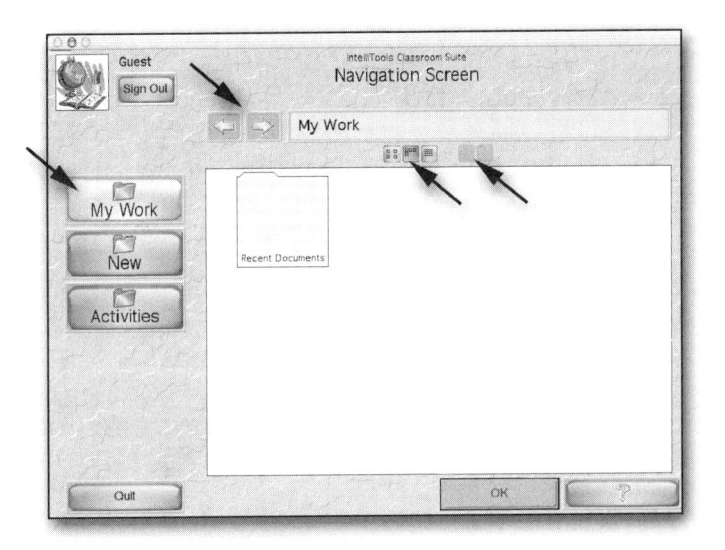

FIGURE 13.2 Navigation Screen for a Guest user.
Used courtesy of IntelliTools, Inc.

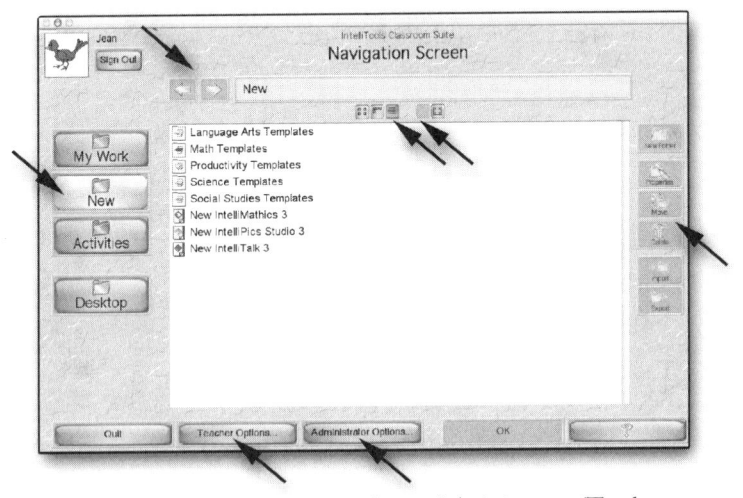

FIGURE 13.3 Navigation Screen for an Administrator/Teacher user.
Used courtesy of IntelliTools, Inc.

The Navigation Screen is where all users have choices to open the particular kind of document they wish to work with: **My Work**—the user's previously saved documents; **New**—a new template or new from-scratch document; or **Activity**—a completed activity that is ready to use. Figure 13.2 shows a Guest Navigation Screen with the **New** button pressed. Notice in this illustration the small buttons above the document window that offer display options. In Figure 13.3, the Administrator Navigation Screen, see the choices for a **New** document, displayed as a list. Also notice the **Teacher Options . . . , Administrator Options, Desktop,** and other utility buttons on this screen.

Figure 13.4 shows one view of **Teacher Options.** Notice the user panel on the left side where the teacher can enroll new users and determine their access privileges. Along the top are tabs to access all features to customize the work environment to meet the needs of individual users.

Explore your Navigation Screen now to become familiar with it. Click each button on the left, exploring its contents. Above the window of files at the top, notice the forward and back buttons that allow you to move through the enclosed folders. Also, try out the small buttons directly over the documents window that modify how files are displayed in the window. Refer back to Figures 13.2 or 13.3 to see arrows pointing to these buttons. When you feel comfortable with the Navigation Screen, click on the **Activities** button to continue.

It is time now for you to explore some of the ready-made activities that were installed with your *IntelliPics Studio* software. After you open the Activities folder, click first on the **Science** folder and then on **Mars Activity.** Notice first the animations (called IntelliMations). Then click the blue button to move on. As you work your way through the activity, as a learner might, note that you are actually exploring or browsing. There are no opportunities for you to add material, change colors, or make any changes in the activity. You can click on any text to have that text spoken. If you do not

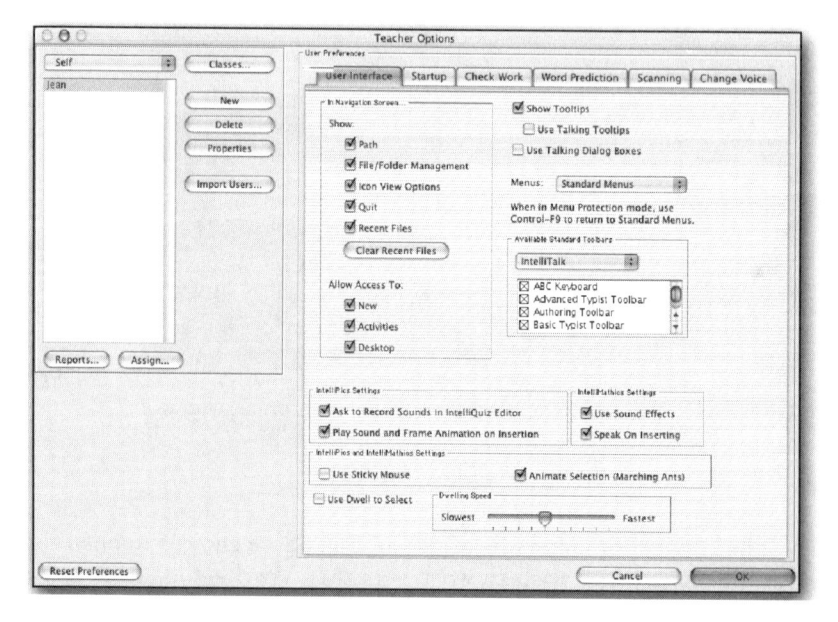

FIGURE 13.4   A view of the Teacher Options screen.
Used courtesy of IntelliTools, Inc.

hear the sound, check the sound volume on your computer. If you wish to end the speech output for any text box you have clicked on, press **[esc]**. Also notice that there are buttons to link to supplemental information on the Internet—for example, the Mars button on the planets page.

When you have finished exploring the Mars activity, close it by choosing Close from the File menu or by clicking the Close Box at the top of the document window. Do not save any changes. You should be back on the Navigation Screen. As you learn to navigate through the different folders in *IntelliPics Studio*, you can always get back to the Navigation Screen by closing a document or choosing **Open . . .** from the File menu. You could also use the appropriate keyboard equivalent for opening a file.

Return now to the Navigation Screen. This time, from the Activities button, choose the **Productivity** folder and click on the **Coloring Book** button. Look at the Color and Play activity. Using the **Next Page** arrow button, click through the pages of the document. Watch the Status Bar at the bottom of the window to follow which numbered page you are on. (If the Status Bar is not visible, choose **Show Status Bar** from the View menu.) Now, explore the different tools; play on the pages. Move the pointer over the tool items to view Tool Tips to identify the various tools. If you do not see the tool name after lingering on a tool for a second or so, go to the Options menu and choose **User Preferences . . .** to turn on Tool Tips. You must have Administrator/Teacher access to open the user preferences.

Navigate to all of the pages; note the differences in the complexities of the instructions. Also note that this activity is strictly linear: You can only move back and forth between the pages much like you do with a book. Next, from the **IntelliPics Studio** menu choose **Play Slide Show;** press **[esc]** to exit a slide show before it is finished. The Slide Show mode is a good choice for material that is linear—that is, it moves from page to page but offers no opportunity for exploring. For learners who have difficulties navigating buttons, the Slide Show mode may be one to consider, along with a linear document design. Additionally, the Slide Show mode offers opportunities for making presentations with *IntelliPics Studio*. Close this activity when you are finished; as before, do not save any changes.

Return to the **Navigation Screen.** This time you will be taking a brief look at the activity called Volcanoes. The Volcanoes activity is located in the Activities/Science folder. When it opens, go to the View menu and choose **Show Status Bar;** also choose **Hide Standard Toolbars** if authoring toolbars are present. As you click the blue buttons across the top to learn about different parts of a volcano, you may see a Paint button appear on the left. Watch the page numbers in the Status Bar as you explore this activity. See how it is structured differently from either of the two previous activities you have explored. The Volcano page (page #2) functions as a menu page. All content pages can be accessed from this page. The Paint button directs the user to other pages, beginning with Page 9, where the learner is encouraged to color the individual features. Activities, such as Volcanoes, where the learner is encouraged to explore or use tools, are not suitable for use in the Slide Show mode. Also note the quiz activity. Try the IntelliQuiz; you can exit from the quiz at any time by pressing the [esc] key.

When you have finished exploring Volcanoes, close that activity. Again, do not save changes, and return to the **Navigation Screen.** This time locate **Explore**

Dinosaurs from the Activities/Math folder. Explore Dinosaurs is an excellent single-page example of how free the learner can be in exploring an activity. Explore it as you might expect a learner to. Explore the on-screen toolbars. Notice the Author Mode button at the top. Click on it and it will toggle to the Student Mode. Experiment with these two modes, and observe how Student Mode limits the features to which the learner has access. The Author Mode enables the teacher to customize the activity for learners with differing skill levels. Close the Explore Dinosaurs activity when you have finished exploring it, without saving any changes.

After returning to the **Navigation Screen,** explore the other activities. As before, when you close each document do not save any changes. After you have finished exploring the remaining sample activities, continue with the text.

Exploring Modes

When the learner is interacting with a prepared activity, such as a cause and effect activity or an IntelliQuiz, the software is functioning in the **Explore** mode. The Explore mode allows actions such as clicking buttons, selecting from toolbars, and using tools determined by the author of the activity. The Explore Dinosaurs Activity uses the Explore mode, as do IntelliQuizzes.

Two authoring modes are the **Paint** mode (the background), and the **Design** mode (objects with attributes such as sounds, actions, or animations that float above the background). As you gain skill with the tools and attributes of these two very different modes, you can begin to understand the incredible power you have within the *IntelliPics Studio* environment to author materials that enhance the learning environment of all learners in your classroom.

The Paint Mode

First, you will examine the Paint mode. If you have an activity open now, close it and return to the Navigation Screen without saving any changes. This time, click on the **New** button.

The illustration in Figure 13.5 shows the contents of the **New** folder. Your view may be slightly different depending on how you have chosen to display the folder contents. Now choose a **New IntelliPics Studio 3** document.

When the new blank document opens, explore the various options in the View menu. The different toolbars offer tools for different purposes. After looking at the different toolbars, choose the **Basic Paint Toolbar.** The Paint Brush icon on the upper left opens the standard paint toolbars. Now, play in the paint environment to become comfortable using the tools. As you explore the paint tools, allow your pointer to linger on the tool items to see Tool Tips. Be sure to try the eraser and rubber stamp tools. After you have explored the paint environment, continue reading.

The concept of **Paint** is analogous to writing on a chalkboard with colored chalk. New chalk covers old chalk; the eraser tool erases as you might erase a real chalkboard. The Paint mode offers learners with disabilities the opportunity to explore color and

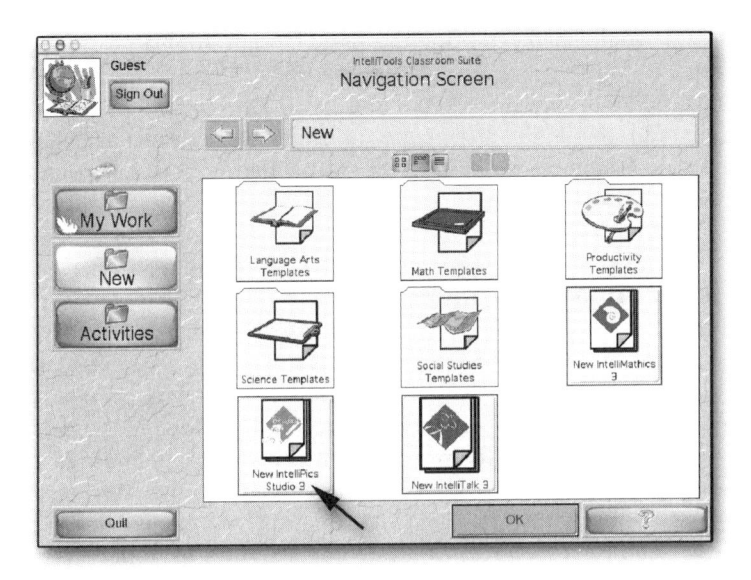

FIGURE 13.5 How to open a New IntelliPics Studio 3 document.
Used courtesy of IntelliTools, Inc.

design, producing graphic art that may never before have been possible. However, the Paint mode by itself is limited if you wish learners to click on buttons, choose items from toolbars, hear sounds, see animations, and move objects around on the screen.

The Design Mode

The Design mode can make all of those things lacking in Paint mode possible. Design objects are placed on layers above the background paint layer. Objects can have attributes such as resizing, playing sounds, navigating to another page, and animating. If working in Paint is analogous to working with paper and colored markers, then working with Design is analogous to creating a collage with words and images that can be layered and freely moved.

To briefly explore Design, return to the View menu and select **Basic Design Toolbar.** Each of these basic toolbars, in their simplicity, offers learners a canvas for creative expression. As before, linger on the tools (Tool Tips) to discern the names of the tool items. The backgrounds scenes on the toolbar at the right side of the page place a painted background you can use as a starting point for your activity. As you select different backgrounds, notice that the choices for graphic items at the bottom of the screen change. Different toolbars of graphic items have been matched to each background scene. However, since there are no paint tools available to the user, the individual backgrounds cannot be erased or modified in any way. Create as many pages as you wish to explore design features. Be sure to explore the Picture Library—use the Picture Library tool or choose **Show Picture Library** from the View menu.

After you have finished exploring the Basic Design Toolbar, close the document without saving and return to the Navigation Screen. You have now freely explored the paint and draw modes of *IntelliPics Studio*. You are ready to learn how to create buttons and animations, add sounds and text, create and edit toolbars, and make your own activities with the built-in templates. With these next activities you will be creating documents that you will save.

Making an Activity from a Template

For your first experience with authoring activities in *IntelliPics Studio* you will create an activity from a template. Typically, when you do an activity, the document you use has a name. Multiple users can open it, interact with it, and then close it leaving it ready to be used again. A template has a different format: It is saved like a tablet of stationery—when you open it, you get a new untitled document with all the attributes of the template. Each time you open a new template document, you are opening an untitled copy of the original. Templates are great for designing activities for different users, who, if using the actual activity document, could inadvertently overwrite or delete elements that you had created. The activity you develop will be similar to the Explore Dinosaurs activity you looked at earlier. Go back now to **Explore Dinosaurs** and examine the attributes of that activity. If you did not try the Dinosaur quiz (Author Mode) before, do it now, before you continue.

Now, return to the Navigation Screen, if you are not already there. Click the **New** button. From the New folder contents, select the **Math Templates** folder, and then **Explore.** Then click on **Explore Template.** Finally, choose the green **My Pictures** button to exit the pre-made Explore tutorial. A new untitled Explore Template document should appear on the screen similar to the one illustrated in Figure 13.6. The Explore Template is a document structured to assist you in creating your own exploring activity.

Look at the toolbars and buttons available to the user of this template. Clicking on any of the six green buttons across the top reveals or hides the standard toolbars—Try it! Notice in the title bar at the top of the window that this is an untitled document. The original template remains untouched. Each new document you create with the template opens with its original features. Also notice buttons for Authoring Instructions, Student Mode, and Finish Activity. If you press Finish Activity, click **Cancel** to exit the Save dialog box. Especially notice the **Picture Toolbar** and the **Backgrounds Toolbar** on the left and right sides of the page. These are the toolbars you will edit to customize the template for an activity of your own.

Using the Explore Template you will create an activity similar to Explore Dinosaurs. See an example in Figure 13.7. In the illustration, notice the Picture and Background toolbars, including the Erase Background button. Also notice that the learner has no access to the authoring capabilities as the Author Mode button has been hidden. Finally, see the Play IntelliQuiz button, enabling the learners to engage in the quiz. The pictures in Figure 13.7 represent a common theme of transportation with outdoor background scenes.

CHAPTER 13 / *IntelliPics Studio*   **177**

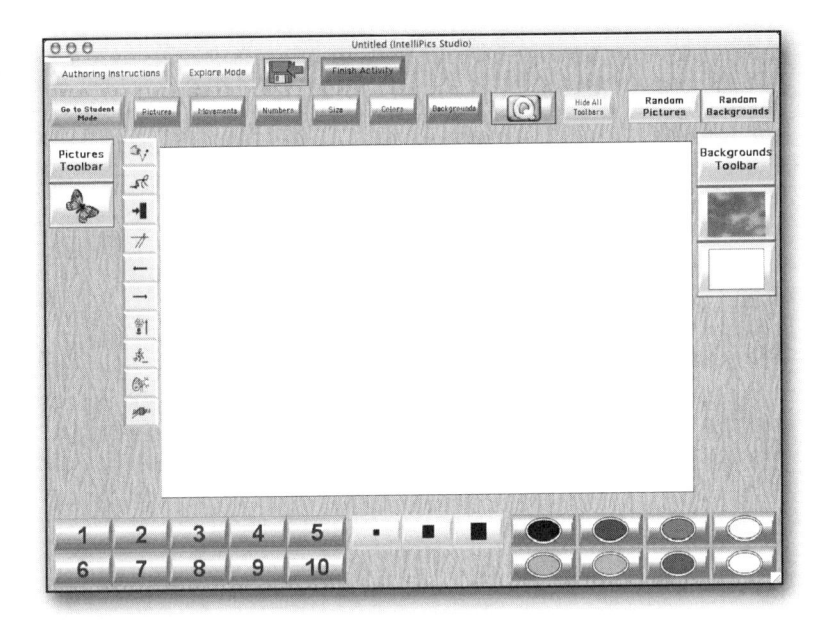

FIGURE 13.6 A new untitled Explore Template document.
Used courtesy of IntelliTools, Inc.

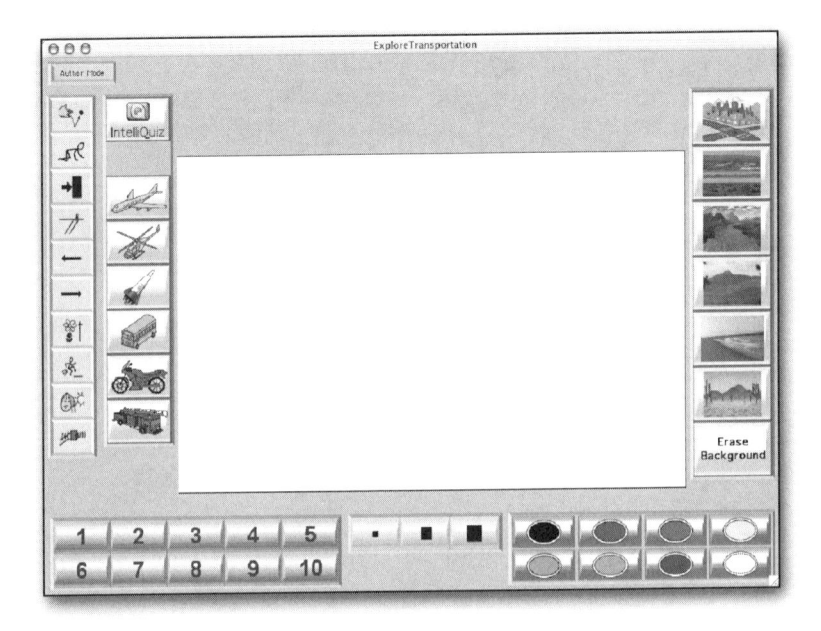

FIGURE 13.7 A sample Explore Template activity on transportation.
Used courtesy of IntelliTools, Inc.

In the upcoming pages you will create the activity in the following sequence:

- Plan a category of images for the Picture and Background toolbars.
- Edit the Picture and Background toolbars.
- Add a button to offer an IntelliQuiz for the activity.
- Hide the Author Mode toolbar.
- Save the document.

Plan the Activity

From the View menu, choose **Show Picture Library.** Browse the different categories of possible images for your Picture Toolbar. Then browse the Background category of images to locate six possible backgrounds to accompany the category of images you chose for the Picture Toolbar. For example, if you selected modes of transportation for the Picture toolbar, you should choose streets, roads, or other outdoor backgrounds. After deciding on the topic for your activity, close the Picture Library (View menu).

Edit Buttons on Toolbars

Use the following instructions to edit the images on the Picture Toolbar and the Backgrounds Toolbar. First, from the Edit menu, select **Custom Toolbars and Buttons. . . .** New controls appear along the top of the screen along with two small colored windows—**Selected Toolbars** and **Selected Buttons**—shown in Figure 13.8.

You will see two buttons at the top left—**Create Toolbar . . .** and **Add Toolbar.** There are some instructions in the top center, and finally, **Help (?)** and **Done** buttons

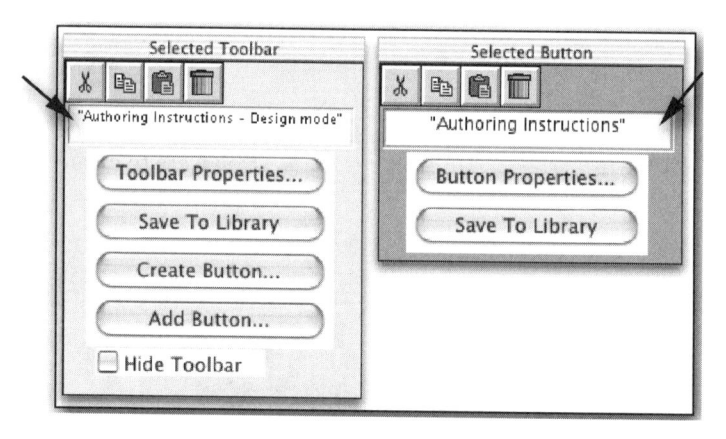

FIGURE 13.8   A view of the **Selected Toolbar** and **Selected Button** windows.

Used courtesy of IntelliTools, Inc.

at the top left side. As you edit toolbars, you will first click on a toolbar to select it. Try this now: Click on the **Pictures Toolbar.** Notice the blinking effect on the Picture Toolbar indicating that the toolbar and a particular button are selected. See the name of the toolbar in the **Selected Toolbar** window and the name of the button in the **Selected Button** window. As you move around to different buttons on the various toolbars, you can see their names appear at the top of the windows.

Click now to select the Picture Toolbar if it is not already selected. The tools available on the **Selected Toolbar** window enable a wide variety of options for customizing toolbars. For this exercise, at this point, you will only be editing buttons on already established toolbars.

Click on the first picture button. When you see the button name on the **Selected Button** window, click on **Button Properties. . . .** From the **Picture** tab, click on the **Picture Library** button. You will see all items in the Picture Library. Use the categories from the drop-down menu at the top to locate the images you want to place on your Picture Toolbar. First select an image; from the **Appearance** tab choose to display Picture only. Continue editing the remaining buttons on the Picture Toolbar. Now edit the Backgrounds Toolbar in a similar manner to complement the pictures on the Pictures Toolbar. Choose the background scenes from the Background category of the Pictures Library. When you are editing the backgrounds buttons, edit only five of them, leaving the Erase Background button. For some learners you might not want the busy background scene. Maybe a learner with a focusing difficulty or a visual disability would have more success with the activity if the objects appeared on a clear screen.

Now, look carefully at the Pictures and Backgrounds Toolbars. Are there six images on each? Will the pictures coordinate with the backgrounds? Make any changes necessary.

There is one more element you should add; but first, some comments are in order regarding templates. A template is a document that simplifies the creation of activities. It is much easier to make this explore activity from the Explore Template than it would be to make it from one of the blank documents with just an authoring toolbar. However, templates may have some features that you do not want and other features that you need. For example, you really do not need an IntelliQuiz button while in the Authoring Mode, but it would be desirable to have one in the Student Mode. This template does not have one in the Student Mode. The button to Go To Student Mode defines which toolbars remain for the Student Mode. Thus, even if you were to create a new toolbar and place an IntelliQuiz button on it, it would disappear when you clicked on the Go To Student Mode button. So, how can you get around this limitation? You could place a Play IntelliQuiz button on an existing toolbar that the Go To Student Mode button leaves on the screen. This is exactly what you are going to do. Read on.

Add and Edit an IntelliQuiz Button

In order to put an IntelliQuiz button on the Student Mode screen, you will put one on the Picture Toolbar, at the top, and modify it slightly to distinguish it from the images that are already on that toolbar. To begin, first click on the Picture Toolbar and choose **Add Button . . .** from the **Selected Toolbar** window. You will copy the image (and function) from the IntelliQuiz button in the Explore Template document. It is possible to add the button from the Standard Library, but since it already exists in the document it is easier to copy it. From the **Add From Open Document** list, carefully select the IntelliQuiz button. It is a large yellow capital "Q" on a green background. See the illustration in Figure 13.9.

The next step will be to move and edit the IntelliQuiz button to prevent learners using the activity from confusing the quiz button with the picture buttons. First, move the new button up the Picture Toolbar to the top by holding down [Shift] while dragging it up. But, be careful not to move it off the Picture Toolbar. Do that now. If you accidentally drop if off the Picture Toolbar, grab it again while holding down [Shift] and try again. Next, while the button is still selected, click on the Button Properties button on the **Selected Button** window as shown in Figure 13.10. Then, click on the **Appearance** tab as shown in Figure 13.11. You will change the IntelliQuiz button two ways. First, change what is displayed to **Picture and Button Name**. Then, add a small amount of **Space after Button** to separate the quiz button from the picture buttons—two or three units. When the two toolbars are complete, click on the **Done** button at the top right. The activity is almost complete.

Hide Author Mode and Save

Because you are working with a template, many of the small, time-consuming tasks you might have to do to prepare your document for use by learners is already accomplished. For example, now you need to hide all of the authoring toolbars, leaving only those the learners will use to interact with the activity. In this template, a single button—Go To Student Mode—does just that. Click that button now. Does the activity look like you want it to look when children will use it? If not, make any changes now.

It is time to save your Explore activity. There will be times when you will want to save your documents in a template format. An activity that you prepare where individuals can make changes to it, like a book report format, should be saved as a template. The template format, like a tablet of paper, opens a new untitled document every time it opens, leaving the original undisturbed. In the case of your Explore document, learners who use the document make no changes. Thus, you can save it in a standard document format. Choose **Save** from the File menu. Keep reading!

The default Save location is into the My Work folder of the currently signed-in user. If you are signed in as a Guest, that is your only option. If you are signed in as a Teacher or Administrator, then you have access to a Desktop button and could save the document on the computer desktop, any other place on the computer, or on an external disk. Keep on reading!

If you have signed in as a Guest user and other users sign in as Guests, then similar documents will be saved in the Guest's folder. How will you distinguish your work from theirs? Give your document a distinctive name, such as adding your initials. I might give the sample transportation activity the name **ExploreTrans-jgu.**

Finally, name your document, decide where you will save it, and **Save** it.

CHAPTER 13 / *IntelliPics Studio* **181**

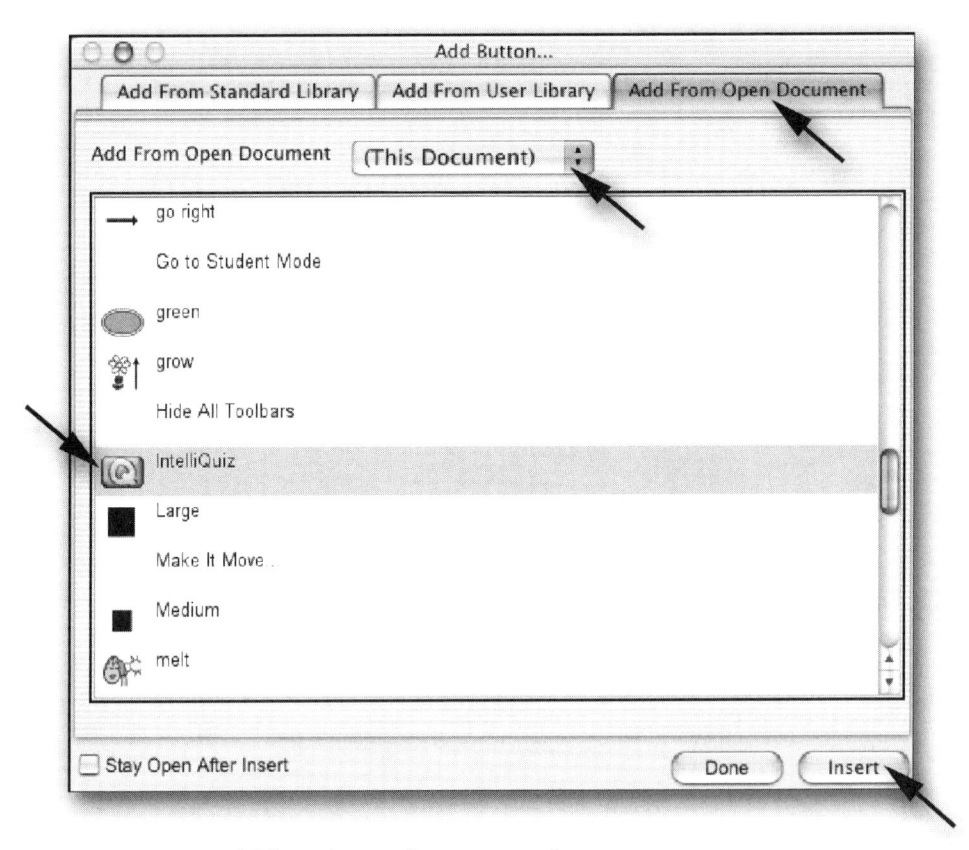

FIGURE 13.9 Adding a button from an open document.
Used courtesy of IntelliTools, Inc.

FIGURE 13.10 Opening the Button Properties for the IntelliQuiz button.
Used courtesy of IntelliTools, Inc.

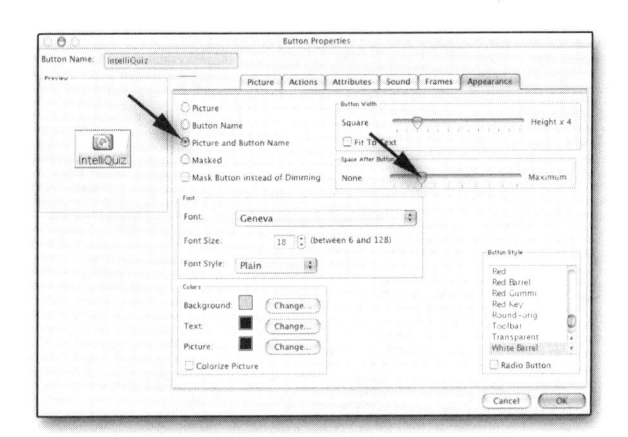

FIGURE 13.11 The Appearance tab of Button Properties.
Used courtesy of IntelliTools, Inc.

Explore Activity Checklist

- Activity is in Student Mode
- Standard template Student Mode toolbars are present.
- There are six images in a similar category on the Picture Toolbar.
- There are six images on the Backgrounds Toolbar.
- Backgrounds Toolbar includes the Erase Background button.
- An IntelliQuiz button is on the Picture Toolbar.
- The IntelliQuiz button is positioned, with extra space, above the pictures and displays its name and icon.

Summary

In this section you have:

- explored a template.
- explored the Picture Library.
- edited picture buttons on toolbars.
- created and edited a toolbar button.
- saved an activity as a document.

Making a Non-Linear Activity

As you begin to plan and design instructional activities using *IntelliPics Studio*, you should consider how the learners might be using the document. Will they be going from page to page, as with the coloring activity you explored earlier? Will they be working on a single page, as with the Explore activity you just completed? Or, will they be accessing different pages as desired, like the Volcanoes or Landforms activities? Look back at those activities now and review the structure of the activity.

The diagram in Figure 13.12 illustrates the layout for a linear activity. Linear designs are like a book; the user can freely move back and forth through the pages, but always in a fixed order.

Non-linear activities could be structured similar to the design illustrated in Figure 13.13. In this design the learner sees an opening page with four buttons on it. Each button leads to an information page. From the information page the learner has a button to return to the menu page. Access to the information pages is through the menu page only. There are no buttons to navigate to the next or previous pages.

For your second *IntelliPics Studio* authoring experience, you will create a non-linear activity with a menu page. Figure 13.14 illustrates an instructional activity about the Food Pyramid. The first page contains a picture of the food pyramid and six buttons

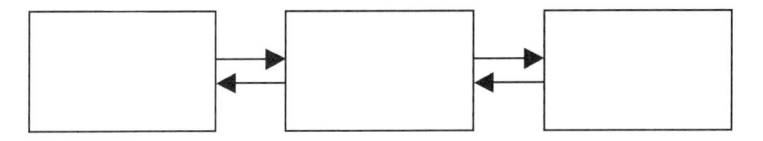

FIGURE 13.12 A simple linear design.

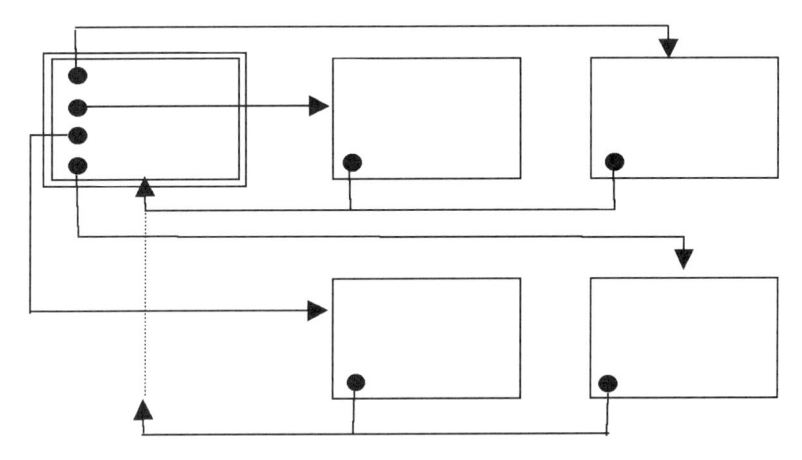

FIGURE 13.13 Diagram of a non-linear activity.

linking the learner to six additional pages where information about each of the six groups can be viewed. Notice on the Milk Group page that there is a button on the bottom left to allow the learner to navigate back to the menu page.

Pause here to decide the content of the non-linear activity you will make. Here are a few ideas to help you get started. You can use one of these, or you can pick your own topic. Your plan should include a minimum of one menu page and three content pages.

- Farm animals
- Neighboring states
- Seasons
- Solar system
- Zoo animals
- Structure of a single cell
- Pond creatures
- Geometry concepts
- Holidays
- Countries or continents
- Plant life
- Tools

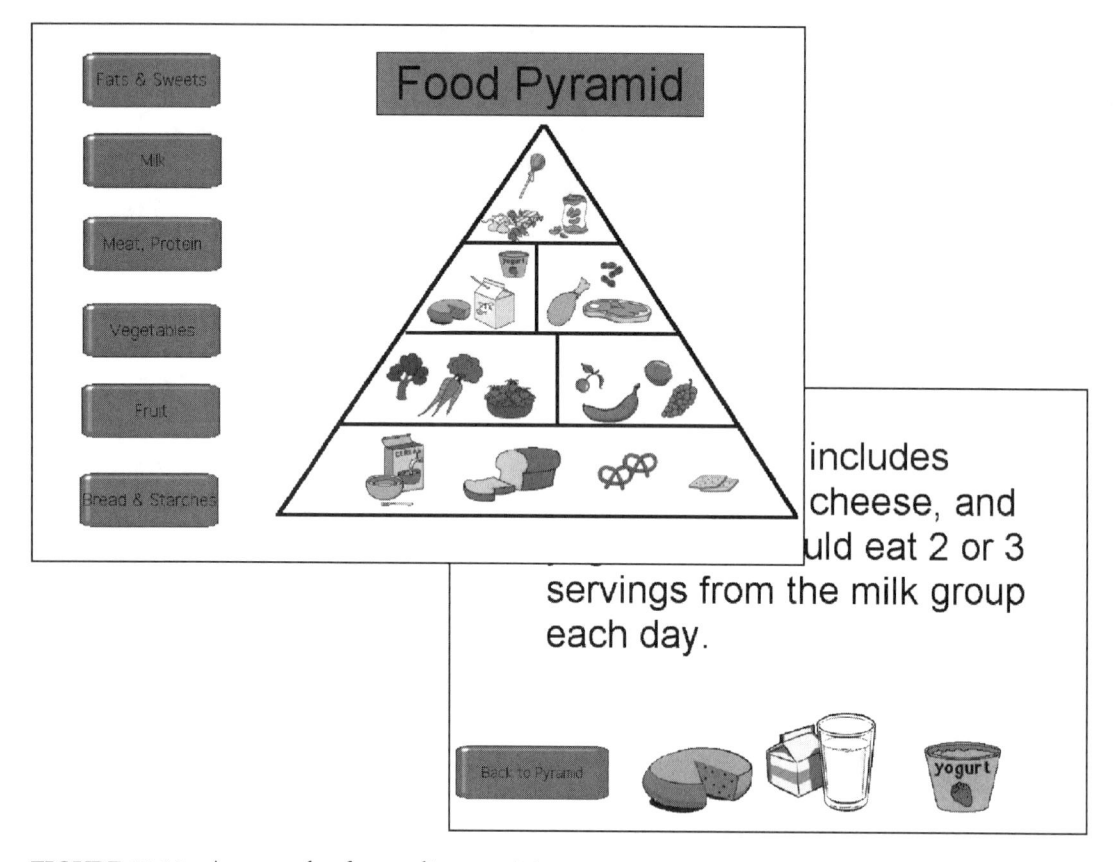

FIGURE 13.14 An example of a non-linear activity.

With your topic now selected, it is a good idea to plan the activity on paper. Take a blank sheet of paper and sketch the pages and their content. Draw arrows to show how the pages will link, as in Figure 13.13. Write brief notes on each page to indicate the content. In the upcoming pages you will create the activity in the following sequence:

1. create and name all pages.
2. design and place image(s) for menu page.
3. create buttons for menu page.
4. link menu page buttons to the content pages.
5. create buttons for content pages to return to the menu page.
6. create talking text boxes to deliver text on content pages.
7. add images to content pages.
8. hide toolbars used for authoring the activity.

Create a New Document

You will be using one of the most versatile environments *IntelliPics Studio 3* has to offer—the **Authoring Toolbar.** If you are not already on the Navigation Screen, choose **Open . . .** from the File menu to get there. First choose the **New** button, and then click on **New IntelliPics Studio 3.** Previously, you explored the View menu and played with the Basic Paint and Basic Design toolbars. This time select the **Authoring Toolbar** as shown in Figure 13.15.

Across the top of the document are sets of standard toolbar buttons. Notice the Basic Paint and Basic Design buttons within the top row of tools. Underneath those basic tools, you can find gray buttons that offer you sets of tools that you will periodically need while creating your new activity. Experiment with these buttons. Open and close the different toolbar sets. Allow your pointer to linger on various tools to discern their names.

Look at the Status Bar at the bottom of the window (View menu—Show Status Bar, if it is not showing). Your new document has only one page. For this activity each page will be named. The reason for doing so will soon be evident. To name this first page, first press and hold **[ctrl]** while clicking anywhere on the blank page. This action brings up the **Page Properties** dialog as shown in Figure 13.16.

At the top of the **Page Properties** dialog box is a text field for Page Name. By default, *IntelliPics Studio* numbers each page. When you begin moving back and forth through pages and making linking buttons, pages with only numbers for names can

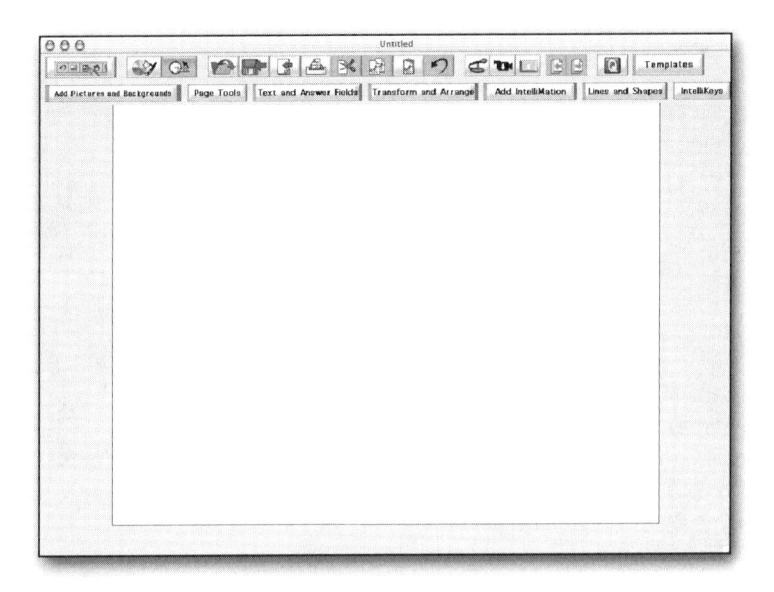

FIGURE 13.15   A new blank document displaying the Authoring Toolbar.

Used courtesy of IntelliTools, Inc.

Big Tip: [ctrl] click on any object will open the properties dialog box for that object.

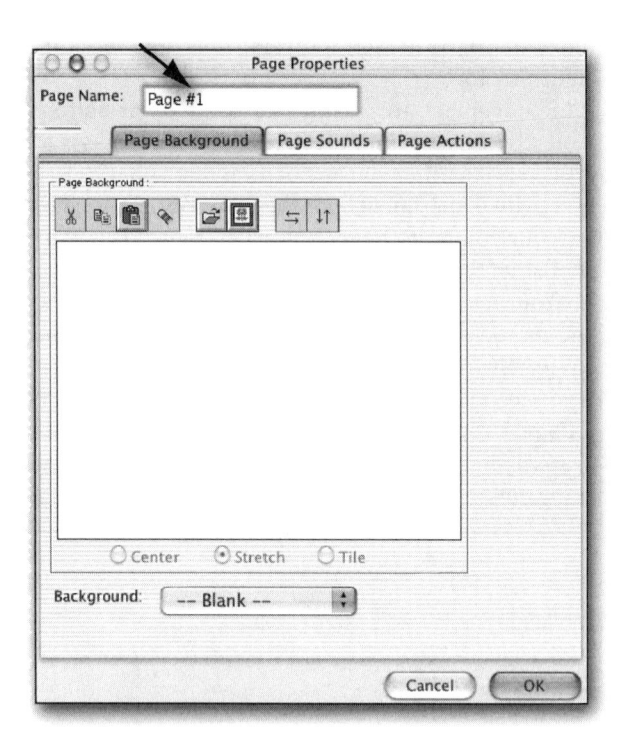

FIGURE 13.16   The Page Properties dialog box.
Used courtesy of IntelliTools, Inc.

become confusing. Name this first page, *Menu* or *Pyramid* (for Food Pyramid) or any name that represents the content of the activity. Before you press **OK** to leave this dialog box, notice the three tabs—Page Background, Page Sounds, and Page Actions. Examine each of these to see what attributes or actions pages can have. An attribute either appears on the page or will be executed (in case of sound or an IntelliMation) when the page is opened. For now, naming the page is the only task at hand, so click **OK** to dismiss the **Page Properties** dialog box. Remember, you only named one page, not the document. Your document remains untitled until you save it.

Add a Title with a Text Box

Next, you will place an appropriate title along the top of this page. Click on the gray **Text and Answer Fields** button to open the text toolbars. Locate the **Text** tool (a large capital "T") and click on it to select it. Click near where you want to begin the title text and drag to the right. A text box with selection handles appears. Choose any text attributes you wish at this time. Later, if you want to change any attributes of the text box or its contents, it is easy to do so. Type your title into the text box. The size of the text box can be modified later, if necessary.

Text boxes are objects, like pages, that can have many attributes. One natural attribute of a text box is its capacity for speech. Any text in any text box can be read aloud by *IntelliPics Studio* simply by clicking in the box. First, however, you need to lock the box and make the text read-only. Use **[ctrl] click** to open the Properties dialog for this text box as illustrated in Figure 13.17.

Use this dialog to access additional features of text boxes. Especially notice the **Read-Only Text** and **Lock** boxes. Read Only means that once checked, the text cannot be changed; it can only be read and consequently spoken. Lock means that the attributes and location of the box cannot be changed. Click in these two boxes now to both lock the box position on the page and prevent the text from being edited, thereby enabling it to be spoken. Later, if you want to make any changes in the content or appearance of the text box, return to the properties dialog, uncheck these boxes, edit, then secure the content by again checking both boxes. Notice also that **Respond to Mouse Clicks** box is

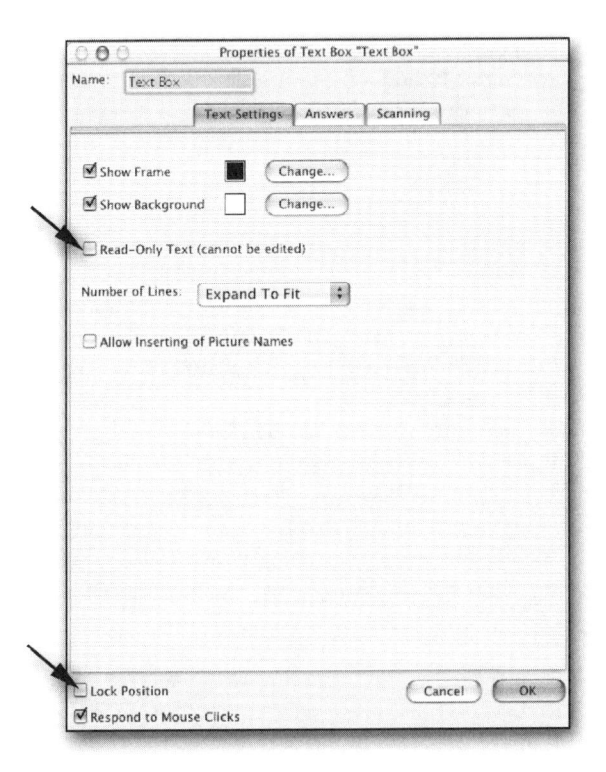

FIGURE 13.17 The Properties dialog box for the title text box.

Used courtesy of IntelliTools, Inc.

checked. Leaving the check here means that when the user clicks on the text, the software will respond by reading it, assuming it is also read-only and locked.

After dismissing the dialog, try clicking in the text box to hear the title spoken. If any word is not pronounced correctly, use **Edit Pronunciation . . .** from the same text toolbar to correct the pronunciation. Another useful tool on that toolbar is the Lock/Unlock button. Use this tool if you want to move (unlock) or modify the size of the text box. Just be sure to lock it again after any adjustments.

Create, Name, and Label Additional Pages

The next step will be to create all additional pages, naming them as you go. Unless you take notes, it will be difficult to determine page identities until some feature has been placed on the pages. To work around this problem, as you make and name each new page, use the **Text Tool** and place the page name, temporarily, on a corner of the page. Later, when you have entered the page content, you can delete the temporary label.

Now click on the gray **Page Tools** button to open the Page Toolbar. Use the **New Page** button to create all additional pages you will need to complete the activity. Each new page you create is placed immediately after the one you are viewing. However, the order of pages does not matter because this activity is not linear. As each page is created, use **[ctrl] click** to name it and then place a temporary label on it using the Text Tool. When you have created, named, and labeled all necessary pages, you can continue with the next section. If you decide later to add a page or delete a page, it is easy to do. Save the document now, in your space or on your disk. Later, when it is complete, you may want to save it as a template.

Design the Menu Page

As you begin work on the various pages of your new document you will be moving between them frequently. Use the **Next Page** and **Previous Page** buttons from the top row of toolbars. Return to the first page using the Previous Page arrow. You should be on the page where you previously placed the title. Use the Status Bar information to assure that you are on the first page.

The layout of the first page is important. You will be placing buttons on this page that will link to the content pages. Buttons will reside within the page space. Unlike the items on toolbars that surround the page as you work, buttons take up space on the page. One advantage of this arrangement is that buttons are more accessible to learners as they browse and work. Now place an image or images that represent the content of the activity on the page, leaving space for the buttons. At this point, do not be concerned about spacing. Once all elements are on the page you can adjust sizes and spacing.

Create Buttons

In this step you will create the buttons that access the content pages. First, you will create a button, decide on its appearance, and finally, assign the action to access the appropriate page.

From the **IntelliPics Studio** menu, choose the **Page Button Tool.** Drag a button shape on the page. The exact size and position on the page does not matter. It can be easily changed later. For new buttons, the Button Properties dialog box, as illustrated in Figure 13.18, automatically opens.

In deciding upon button appearance, consider that the set of buttons you are designing should have a uniform size and appearance. If using text on these buttons, create the longest one first. When one button is complete you can copy that button, pasting it as many times as necessary to complete the set. Then, instead of creating each new button from scratch, you can simply edit their names and links.

Because buttons have such versatility, options abound. Look at button appearance (click on the **Appearance** tab) shown in Figure 13.19. You can choose Picture, Button Name, or Picture and Button Name. If using the button name, be sure to give it a meaningful name that the learners can read. If you wish to display a picture, use the **Picture Library** button at the top of the Picture tab to access the Picture Library. After you have decided on button appearance click **OK** to dismiss that box. You are left with the original properties box.

Make Buttons Link to Another Page

Buttons are powerful because of their actions. Click on the Actions tab and browse the possible actions. See the illustration in Figure 13.20.

When you are ready, click on the ***Go To Page*** . . . item in the scrolling list, and then click the button: **Add: Go To Page** . . . as illustrated in Figure 13.20. Clicking the

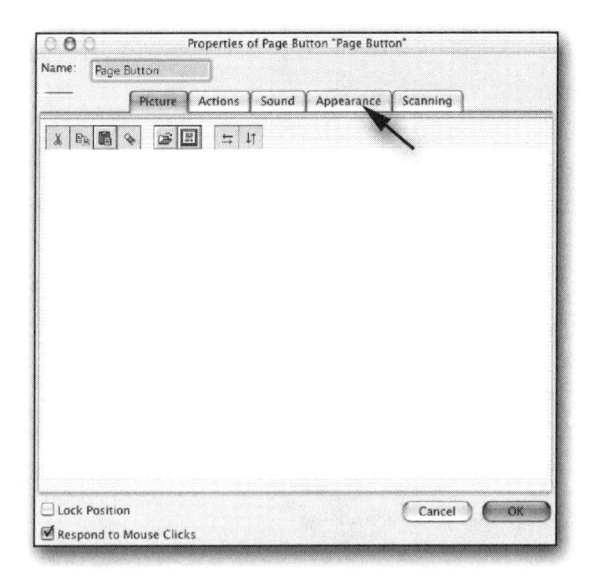

FIGURE 13.18 The Button Properties dialog box.
Used courtesy of IntelliTools, Inc.

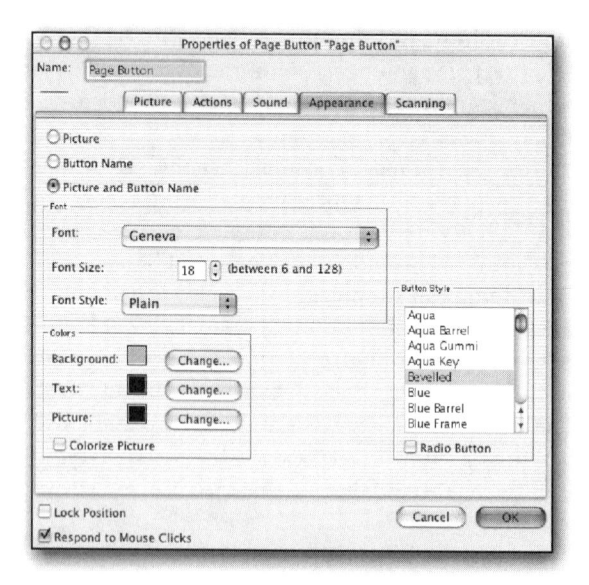

FIGURE 13.19 Appearance tab of Button Properties.

Used courtesy of IntelliTools, Inc.

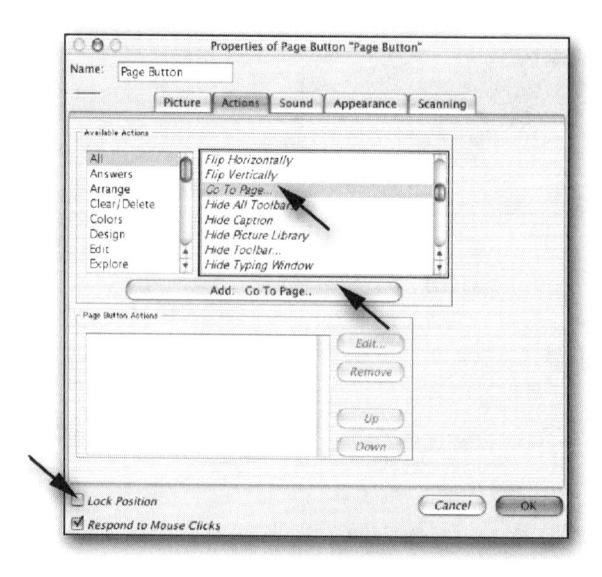

FIGURE 13.20 The Actions tab of the Button Properties dialog box.

Used courtesy of IntelliTools, Inc.

Add: button brings up another dialog that asks you which page you wish to go to. You should see the names of all the pages you previously created and named. Do you see the reason for naming pages as you create them? See Figure 13.21 for an example from the Food Pyramid activity.

Select the appropriate page to link to this button, and click on **OK**. There is one final step to take in completing this first button. Click to **Lock** the button so you can test it out. Then click **OK** to dismiss the Button Properties dialog box. When you click on the button using the **Select Tool,** the correct page should open. If the button worked as expected, you are ready to continue. If not, or if there are any button attributes you wish to change, you can **[ctrl] click** on it to edit it. Voila! You have just completed one perfect button. Your next steps will be to duplicate it as many times as is necessary to create links to the other content pages, and then to edit those copied buttons.

Here are some general rules for working with buttons, text boxes, and images to which you can refer as necessary:

- **Create** objects with the appropriate tool from the toolbar.
- **Use** objects by first checking **Lock** and **Read-Only** (Text Boxes) in the properties dialog.
- **Edit** previously locked objects by **[ctrl] click**ing to open the properties dialog box and unchecking **Lock.**
- **Move** objects by **[ctrl] click**ing to open the properties dialog box and unchecking **Lock.**
- Remember, always return to the properties dialog to check **Lock** before using the object (and **Read-Only** for Text Boxes).

Copy Buttons

With one perfect button prepared, you are ready to learn how to copy that button as many times as is necessary to make links to all of the content pages in the activity. You already know that clicking on that button will activate the button, not let you select it.

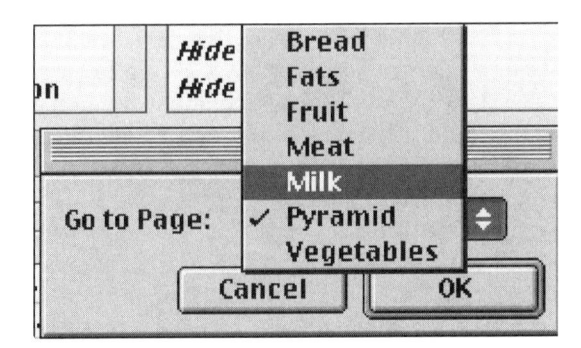

FIGURE 13.21   Selecting the *Milk* page in the Go To Page dialog box.

Used courtesy of IntelliTools, Inc.

So again, **[ctrl] click** the button and unlock it. Return to the page and click on the button. This time, instead of activating the button, you have selected it. You could resize it (by dragging a corner) or move it (dragging the middle).

You can also copy it! While the button is selected (has handles) choose **Copy** from the Edit menu. Since you want to paste it back on the same page, the next step is to choose **Paste** from the Edit menu. The pasted button may appear directly on top of the original. Grab it and move it. **Paste** and move as many times as you need to get buttons that link to each content page.

Behold that you have a beautiful set of identical buttons! Your next step will be to edit the names and links of the copied buttons. But first, adjust their spacing or layout on the page. Then, one by one, **[ctrl] click** on the button. In the properties dialog edit the button name or add the appropriate picture, depending on how you decided to design your buttons. Next, open the Actions tab and edit the **Go To Page . . .** action to the correct page. Lock each button as you complete it. Then, after choosing the **Select Tool,** test all buttons. Edit any that do not work as expected. Save again.

Add Text to the Content Pages

You have learned most of the skills necessary to complete the basics of this activity. As you continue the steps to finish it, you will add text material—that can be read aloud— to each of the content pages. Just as you made the talking text for the title on the first page, you will move to each of the content pages and add text boxes with content appropriate for that page. Do this now.

Check spelling, grammar, and facts carefully! As you complete each box, make it **Read Only, Lock** it, choose the **Select Tool,** and then click on it to listen to the text being read. If any words are pronounced unclearly or incorrectly, use **Edit Pronunciation . . .** from the Speech menu to correct pronunciation. When all text is entered and tested on all of the pages, continue with the next step.

Add Return Buttons to the Content Pages

You have made buttons for the menu page. Each button moves the learner to one of the content pages. However, the learner cannot leave without a button that links back to the menu or title page. Make one new button whose action is to return to the menu page— on any one of the content pages. See the previous instructions if you have forgotten how. When the button is finished, lock it and test it. Once the button works as you expect, read on to learn how to copy it to the other content pages.

As before, unlock the button to select and copy it. This time, however, you must move to a page that needs the button before you can paste it. Do that now. All of the buttons will be identical so you will not have to do any editing. However, you will have to lock each one before you can test it. Paste buttons on all content pages. Then test all buttons before you continue. Save the document.

Add Images to the Content Pages

What you do with these pages depends on how much text you have used. Place at least one image on each of the content pages that enhances the content. Save the document again.

Hide Toolbars and Save

When the document is complete, as with the previous document you created, hide the toolbars you used for authoring the activity. Because all learner actions are made with buttons, hide all toolbars by choosing **Hide Standard Toolbars** from the View menu. All of the toolbars should magically disappear. Also, delete any temporary labels you may have placed on the pages at the beginning. Save the document again.

Menu Activity Document Checklist

- Document opens to a menu page.
- There are no extra pages in the document.
- All toolbars are hidden.
- Title on the menu page is read aloud when clicked.
- Image(s) on title page are appropriate to the content.
- Buttons (names and/or images) on title page link to matching content pages.

Each content page contains:

- an image(s) appropriate to the content.
- text that is read when clicked.
- text that is accurate in spelling, grammar, and content.
- a button to return to the menu page.

Summary

In this section you have:

- created and named new pages.
- created and edited text boxes.
- made text boxes speak.
- created buttons to go to specific pages.
- copied buttons.
- edited buttons.

Create an IntelliMation

The final exercise for this chapter will be for you to create an animation for the opening page of the menu activity you just completed. You will learn to:

- create an IntelliMation for the first page.
- assign an action to a page.
- save the document as a template.

Open your document to the first page. Open the **Authoring Toolbar** again. You will create a frame animation called an **IntelliMation** for this page using picture items you may already have placed on the page or related ones. Click on the gray **Add IntelliMation** button to show the quiz buttons. Then choose the **Create IntelliMation** button. You should see an IntelliMation timeline for five seconds as illustrated in Figure 13.22.

Click on several of the half-second numbers and notice the small blue indicator that marks your position. Move back to "0." First you will make a short sample animation to explore the options. Then you will design an animation to serve as an opening page that is specific to the activity you have designed.

Do this: Place an image on the page (or use one already there). Place it at the top and center of the page. Click the gray **Transform and Arrange** button to reveal those tools. Use a transform tool—**Make Smaller**—to make the image very small. This is the starting place for your sample animation. Click into the "0.5" spot on the time line. Now drag the image down slightly and click on the **Make Bigger** button on the transform toolbar. Next, click on the "1" position on the timeline. Again, drag the image a little and enlarge it. For each half-second segment up to five seconds, continue moving the image down some and enlarging it. At any time you can click on the **Play IntelliMation** triangle, to the right of the 5 on the timeline, to see the IntelliMation; or click on the **Remove IntelliMation Timeline** button next to **Play IntelliMation** to remove segments. Experiment with the different selection tools to flip, rotate, or make smaller. The possibilities for interesting effects using IntelliMation are endless. Imagine characters for a story walking into a scene, cars moving along a roadway, or letters flying in and circling before forming into a word.

Using the **Remove IntelliMation Timeline** button, delete any samples you have been playing with. Decide how you want the opening page to look. Now, design an IntelliMation to match some aspect of the menu activity. Continue with these instructions after the animation is exactly as you want the learner to see it when the document opens. Be careful to end the animation so that a button or text is not obstructed. To remove the IntelliMation timeline from the page, click the **Create IntelliMation** button again.

The next step is to attach that animation sequence to the page so that it plays automatically when the page opens. **Do this:** Open **Page Properties** by [ctrl] clicking on the page. You should see page action options as illustrated in Figure 13.23.

From the scrolling field of page actions, select *Play IntelliMation.* Then click the button **Add: Play IntelliMation.** Notice that **Play IntelliMation** appears at the bottom in the Page Actions window. Finally, click **OK**. You have just told *IntelliPics Studio* to automatically play the animation when that particular page opens.

You are almost finished with the exercise. The final step is to hide the toolbars as you did before you began the IntelliMation. And, lastly, save one more time.

FIGURE 13.22 A five-second IntelliMation timeline.
Used courtesy of IntelliTools, Inc.

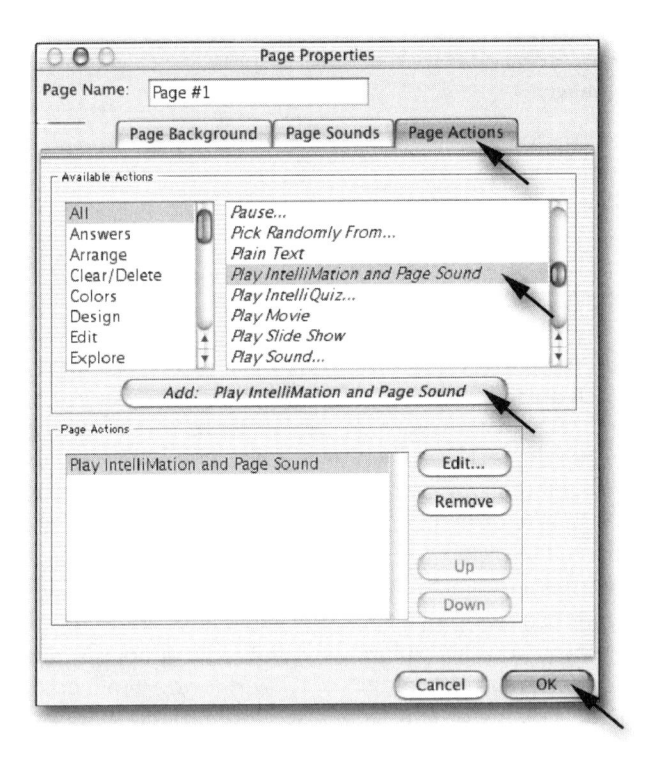

FIGURE 13.23 Page Actions options from the Page Properties dialog.

Used courtesy of IntelliTools, Inc.

Now save the document using **Save As . . .** in template format (Template tab), putting the word *template* in its new name (you must have Admin/Teacher access to save as a template). Even though the document does not require learners to use tools, some learners may access tools through menus and make changes in the activity. For activities that will be used by multiple learners, it is good practice to make a template for learner use after saving the activity in document form. If you decide to make changes, you can throw the template away, open the document version, edit and save, and then create a new template version.

IntelliMation Checklist

- All toolbars are hidden.
- IntelliMation plays when first page opens.
- Animated features are appropriate for the topic.
- When animation is complete, all text and buttons are unobstructed.
- Document is saved as a template.

Summary

In this section you have:

- created an IntelliMation.
- assigned an action to a page.
- saved a document as a template.

Learning About IntelliQuizzes

You had opportunities to view IntelliQuizzes when you explored both the Volcanoes and Early Concepts activities. IntelliQuizzes are activities that you can attach to any *IntelliPics Studio* document that operate in the **Explore** mode—like the Explore Dinosaurs activity when "things happen automatically" when you click something on the page. One use for IntelliQuizzes is to provide an evaluation for the activity content. An IntelliQuiz can ask questions such as: Find the apple. Which one flies? How many can you see? Learners can then reply to the question by clicking on the page, clicking on a toolbar button, selecting an item from the Picture Library, or spelling the answer. *IntelliPics Studio* can automatically provide text and audio feedback for both correct and incorrect learner responses. You can explore the IntelliQuiz options by clicking on the **Create IntelliQuiz** button near the top right of the Authoring Toolbar.

For the specifics in creating IntelliQuizzes, see your product's user guide. You can find a free tutorial with step-by-step instructions for making IntelliQuizzes on the IntelliTools, Inc. web site. The tutorial is called: *Creating an IntelliQuiz Tutorial* and can be downloaded free from the *Fun, Two, Three!* page.

Providing Alternative Access

IntelliPics Studio is designed to be accessible to learners who use a variety of input devices—a standard keyboard and mouse, IntelliKeys or IntelliKeys USB keyboards, or single switches. The software can automatically generate overlays to be used with IntelliKeys keyboards. With *Overlay Maker* software for IntelliKeys you can customize these overlays or create your own. Even without *Overlay Maker* you can use *Overlay Printer*, available on the *IntelliPics Studio* CD, to print the automatically generated overlays. In addition, the software can function in scanning modes, enabling a single switch user access to all activities. Switch options include using a mouse or keyboard as a switch, attaching a switch to an IntelliKeys keyboard, or using any switch connected with a switch interface. If you are working with learners who could benefit from using *IntelliPics Studio* with alternative access, see the *IntelliPics Studio* user's guide. You can also download an excellent free step-by-step tutorial from the IntelliTools, Inc. web site. The tutorial is called *Tutorial: Alternative Access* and can be downloaded from the *Fun, Two, Three!* page.

What's Next?

The experiences you have had with *IntelliPics Studio 3* in this chapter have, hopefully, given you a good start in using a powerful software program. Continue to make activities for the learners you teach. Explore other options like adding sound, movies, and web links. Include your own pictures in your documents. Use the built-in templates and then branch out to making your own. Visit IntelliTools on the web (http://www.intellitools.com) to see activities that other teachers are sharing in the Activity Exchange area.

Manuals and tutorials are also available from the company web site. Browse the manuals and work through additional tutorials to learn new skills and enhance your basic understanding of *IntelliPics Studio*. A must-have for teachers of elementary-aged children are the *Fun, Two, Three!* activities—a free set of early learning activities and tutorials useable with both the *IntelliPics Studio* software and *IntelliPics Studio Player*. So, even if a teacher does not have *IntelliPics Studio*, the free *IntelliPics Studio Player* can be downloaded and used to play the activities. However, the player allows only use of activities, no authoring or editing.

Continue building your skills to enrich the classroom environment for the children that you teach.

APPENDIX A

Special Character Codes

Special Character Codes for Windows

Use the charts below to locate special characters for inclusion in text documents on Windows computers. When you work in *Word*, these characters can be accessed from the Insert menu. One way to include them in other applications is to copy them from the Character Map utility. Another way is to use the codes below to type them directly into your text.

To type these characters into text, do this: First, turn on Num Lock. All numerals you type **must** be entered from the numeric keypad portion of the keyboard. To create any character, **hold down the [ALT] key and then press a zero followed by the numeric code.** For example to make the é in **José** or **résumé**:

[ALT]0233 (upon releasing the [ALT] key the character will be produced)

Code	Char	Name	Code	Char	Name
128	€	Euro	150	–	en dash
129		unused	151	—	em dash
130	‚	baseline single quote	152	~	tilde
131	ƒ	florin	153	™	unregis. trademark
132	„	baseline double quote	154	š	s caron
133	…	ellipsis	155	›	right single guillemet
134	†	single dagger	156	œ	oe ligature
135	‡	double dagger	157		unused
136	ˆ	circumflex	158		unused
137	‰	per mil	159	Ÿ	Y diaeresis
138	Š	S caron	160		non-breaking space
139	‹	left single guillemet	161	¡	Spanish inverted !
140	Œ	OE ligature	162	¢	cents
141		unused	163	£	pounds
142		unused	164	¤	ICU (replaced by Euro)
143		unused	165	¥	yen
144		unused	166	¦	broken bar
145	'	single open quote	167	§	section symbol
146	'	close single quote	168	¨	diaeresis
147	"	open double quote	169	©	copyright
148	"	close double quote	170	ª	feminine ordinal
149	•	bullet (large)	171	«	left double guillemet

199

APPENDIX A / Special Character Codes

Code	Char	Name	Code	Char	Name
172	¬	not sign	214	Ö	O diaeresis
173	-	soft hyphen	215	×	multiply symbol
174	®	registered trademark	216	Ø	O with oblique stroke
175	—	macron	217	Ù	U grave
176	°	ring (degrees)	218	Ú	U acute
177	±	plus/minus	219	Û	U circumflex
178	²	superscript 2	220	Ü	U diaeresis
179	³	superscript 3	221	Ý	Y acute
180	´	acute	222	Þ	Icelandic Thorn
181	µ	micro (mu)	223	ß	German sharp s
182	¶	pilchow	224	à	a grave
183	·	bullet (small)	225	á	a acute
184	¸	cedilla	226	â	a circumflex
185	¹	superscript 1	227	ã	a tilde
186	º	masculine ordinal	228	ä	a diaeresis
187	»	right double guillemet	229	å	a ring
188	¼	one-fourth	230	æ	ae ligature
189	½	one half	231	ç	c cedilla
190	¾	three-fourths	232	è	e grave
191	¿	Spanish inverted ?	233	é	e acute
192	À	A grave	234	ê	e circumflex
193	Á	A acute	235	ë	e diaeresis
194	Â	A circumflex	236	ì	i grave
195	Ã	A tilde	237	í	i acute
196	Ä	A diaeresis	238	î	i circumflex
197	Å	A ring	239	ï	i diaeresis
198	Æ	AE ligature	240	ð	Icelandic eth
199	Ç	C cedilla	241	ñ	n tilde
200	È	E grave	242	ò	o grave
201	É	E acute	243	ó	o acute
202	Ê	E circumflex	244	ô	o circumflex
203	Ë	E diaeresis	245	õ	o tilde
204	Ì	I grave	246	ö	o diaeresis
205	Í	I acute	247	÷	divide symbol
206	Î	I circumflex	248	ø	o with oblique stroke
207	Ï	I diaeresis	249	ù	u grave
208	Ð	Icelandic Eth	250	ú	u acute
209	Ñ	N tilde	251	û	u circumflex
210	Ò	O grave	252	ü	u diaeresis
211	Ó	O acute	253	ý	y acute
212	Ô	O circumflex	254	þ	Icelandic thorn
213	Õ	O tilde	255	ÿ	y diaeresis

APPENDIX A / Special Character Codes

Special Characters for Macintosh

Use the charts below to locate special characters and symbols to place into any text document on a Macintosh computer. You can also copy and paste these characters into documents from the Key Caps utility. All font faces do not support these special characters. When you need to use special characters select a font that will display them.

In the first chart, the characters are produced by combination key presses of [OPTION][KEY CHAR] or [SHIFT][OPTION][KEY CHAR].

Key Char	Option Char	Shift Option Char	Key Char	Option Char	Shift Option Char
A	å	Å	Y	¥	Á
B	∫	ı	Z	Ω	.
C	ç	Ç	1	¡	⁄
D	∂	Î	2	™	∉
E	´	´	3	£	<
F	ƒ	Ï	4	¢	>
G	©	"	5	∞	fi
H	•	Ó	6	§	fl
I	ˆ	ˆ	7	¶	‡
J	∆	Ô	8	•	°
K	˚	▢	9	ª	.
L	¬	Ò	0	º	,
M	µ	Â	-	–	—
N	~	~	=	≠	±
O	ø	Ø	[	"	"
P	π	∏	]	'	'
Q	æ	Œ	\	«	»
R	®	‰	;	…	Ú
S	ß	Í	'	æ	Æ
T	†	ˇ	,	≤	–
U	¨	¨	.	≥	∪
V	√	◊	/	÷	¿
W	∑	„	`	`	`
X	≈	.			

APPENDIX A / Special Character Codes

The Macintosh characters on this page are standard letters with diacritical marks. These characters are considered "composite." This means you must strike the keyboard twice to create the character. Here is an example of how to do it.

To make the **e acute (é)** character first strike [OPTION]e—the [OPTION]key along with the "e" key—and then strike a lower case "e." You would make an **a acute (á)** in a similar way—first strike [OPTION]e and then strike the lower case "a." The [OPTION]e sets up the keyboard to receive the next character as one modified by the acute sign.

The following characters can be created with the acute sign:
Á á É é Í í Ó ó Ú ú

Press to initiate the acute sign: **[OPTION] e**

Lift your fingers and press the lower or upper case character you wish to receive the acute sign.

The following characters can be created with the grave sign:
À à È è Ì ì Ò ò Ù ù

Press to initiate the grave sign: **[OPTION]** \

Lift your fingers and press the lower or upper case character you wish to receive the grave sign.

The following characters can be created with the diaeresis sign:
Ä ä Ë ë Ï ï Ö ö Ü ü Ÿ ÿ

Press to initiate the diaeresis sign: **[OPTION] u**

Lift your fingers and press the lower or upper case character you wish to receive the diaeresis sign.

The following characters can be created with the circumflex sign:
Â â Ê ê Î î Ô ô Û û

Press to initiate the circumflex sign: **[OPTION] i**

Lift your fingers and press the lower or upper case character you wish to receive the circumflex sign.

The following characters can be created with the tilde sign:
Ã ã Õ õ Ñ ñ

Press to initiate the tilde sign: **[OPTION] n**

Lift your fingers and press the lower or upper case character you wish to receive the tilde sign.

APPENDIX B

Activities to Accompany Chapter 9

The activities in Appendix B are provided to give students some guided experiences with computer adaptations, both hardware and software. Each activity is designed to follow a specific portion of the text in Chapter 9—*Making Adaptations with Hardware and Software*. Instructions in the text will direct you to each of the activities at the appropriate time. It is recommended that students complete as many of the activities as possible. Modify the activities, if necessary, to include all adaptations that are available in your particular setting.

Touch Screen Activity

Objectives:

- To experience the direct input enabled by the touch screen.
- To understand the effect of accurate and inaccurate calibration on the operation of the touch screen.

Setup:

- One computer with touch screen attached for each student or pair of students.
- Any graphics program or any game that is mouse driven (e.g., card game, tile-matching game).

Activity:

- Calibrate the touch screen carefully (touch screen control panel)
- Using only the touch screen (with finger or plastic pointer only—no pencil tips or erasers or pen points), play with the software. Draw a city scene if using graphics software. Otherwise, play the game.
- Open the control panel again and recalibrate the touch screen—this time do it incorrectly—at least an inch off!
- Return to the software you were using and continue.
- Again, calibrate the touch screen, correctly this time.
- Quit the software.

Evaluation:

- Why is it important to calibrate the touch screen carefully?
- What position should the person calibrating the device be in, in relation to the person using the computer? Why?

Mouse Device Activity

Objectives:

- To illustrate how different mouse devices have varying motor requirements.

Setup:

- Computers with all available mouse devices connected; e.g., trackball (large and small), standard mouse, joystick(s), trackpad.
- Any mouse-driven software, such as a tile-matching program or card game.

Activity:

- Play the game with each of the mouse devices. Compare the physical demands on the user for each of the devices.

Evaluation:

- Describe the physical movements necessary to activate each mouse device. Consider both fine-motor and large-motor skills.

Assisted Keyboard Activity

Objectives:

- To experience how Sticky Keys and Slow Keys enable full keyboard use for the single-finger (stylus) typist.
- To experience how Mouse Keys enables full mouse functioning from the keyboard.

Setup:

- One computer for each student or pair of students. Control panels should already installed (if necessary)—Windows: Accessibility Options; Macintosh: Easy Access or Universal Access. Each component of the assisted keyboard software should be turned off to begin.

Activity—Part 1:

- Using the mouse, open the control panel and examine the options.
- If there are auditory feedback options, turn all on—Assure computer volume is up.
- Turn on the Sticky Keys and Mouse Keys options. Do not turn on the Slow Keys option at this time.
- Close the control panel.

Activity—Part 2:

- Each participant should place the mouse out of reach.
- Each participant should hold a pencil or pen (blunt end down) in the fist of their non-dominant hand.
- From this point on, all interaction with the computer will be accomplished with this pointer. No fingers or mouse devices allowed!

Activity—Part 3:

- First, experiment with Mouse Keys while on the desktop of the computer. Use the 2, 4, 6, and 8 keys from the numeric keypad of the keyboard to move the mouse down, left, right, and up. Use the 1, 3, 7, and 9 keys to move the mouse diagonally. The 5 key is a mouse click. The zero key turns on the drag action.
- Select an icon on the screen and move it a short distance. To do this you must move to it, turn the drag on, move a short distance, and then turn the drag off (with the 5 key or the decimal key).
- Next, using only the stylus, locate a word processing program and open a new, blank document.
- Type the following text: Mr. Wilson bought six boxes of cookies.
- Place the insertion point just before cookies and insert the text: Girl Scout (be sure you are capitalizing the proper nouns!).
- Select the entire sentence and display it in a larger font face.

Activity—Part 4:

- Using the mouse, return to the control panel and turn on the Slow Keys option. Close the control panel.
- Remove the mouse and return to your stylus.
- Add the words *from Cindy* to the end of the sentence. (Remember, because Slow Keys is on now you must hold down the key for a longer time in order for the computer to recognize the key press.)

Activity—Part 5:

- The simulation is over. Using your mouse, open the control panel.
- Turn off all components of the assisted keyboard. If auditory feedback was an option, leave that on. In the event that one of the components is inadvertently turned on from the keyboard, the sound will alert the user to that so it can be turned off.

Evaluation:

- Was this confusing? Was it frustrating? Was it easy? Was it slow?
- Did you ever realize how many steps were actually involved when you used the mouse to select text or choose from a menu?

- Do you ever use keyboard shortcuts for selecting text, saving, or printing?
- Can you see how key presses that substituted for mouse actions would greatly simplify and speed up work for someone who could not use a mouse?
- Can an individual—a single-finger or stylus typist—who is unable to use a mouse, be completely independent at the computer?

Switch Activity

Objectives:

- To connect and disconnect switch devices.
- To compare physical requirements for activating various switches.
- To experience scanning.

Setup:

- A computer with a switch interface and as many switches, activated different ways, as are available.
- Any switch-activated software, preferably offering choices with scanning.

Activity:

- Operate the software, using each of the switches, one-by-one.
- Evaluate the physical demands placed on the user for each switch.
- Notice that since the user has essentially only one key, that when choices must be made, the software scans the choices allowing the user the choose by activating the switch at the appropriate time.

Evaluation:

- Under what conditions would each of the switches you tried be the single best input device for an individual with physical disabilities?

Word Prediction Software Activity

Objectives:

- To experience the advantages of software that reduces the key strokes necessary to enter text.

Setup:

- One computer with *Co:Writer* or another word prediction program in addition to a familiar word processor.

Activity:

- With the word processor alone, using only one pinky finger, type the following sentence:

    The quick brown fox jumped over the lazy dog.

- Activate the word prediction software. Type the same sentence again, still using only the pinky finger.
- Browse the menus of the word prediction software and observe the features that allow customizing the software to meet individual needs.

Evaluation:

- Did you press fewer keys using the word prediction software?
- Would the use of this software speed up text entry for persons who have difficulty typing?
- Would the use of word prediction software make text entry less physically demanding?
- Would persons who have difficulty spelling benefit from this software?
- In addition to persons with physical limitations, who could benefit from using word prediction software for text entry?

Catalog Activity

Objectives:

- To explore a variety of sources for locating adaptive software and hardware.
- To illustrate the variety of software and hardware devices available.
- To see the availability of products for different computer systems.
- To compare prices between different products and from different manufacturers and suppliers.

Setup:

- Compile a list of manufacturers' web sites from the list of resources in Appendix D or from other sources, or order a set of print catalogs (possibly 6–10) for each student or pair of students.
- Provide each student with a list of questions similar to those on the following Catalog Activity Worksheet. Customize the list to match the items offered in the available catalogs.

Activity:

- Browse some of the catalogs (web sites). Look at pictures, read descriptions, find computer system availability, and cost. Spend enough time browsing to become familiar with the catalog and its layout.

- Using the Catalog Activity Worksheet, or a similar one, browse the catalogs and locate the devices.
- Write or type answers to each of the questions.

If you conduct a web search, you may find other sources for these products. You should be able to find answers to the suggested questions at the following web sites:

Ability Hub: http://www.abilityhub.com
AbleNet, Inc.: http://www.ablenetinc.com
Access First: http://www.accessfirst.net
AlphaSmart, Inc.: http://www.alphasmart.com
Don Johnston, Inc.: http://www.donjohnston.com
IntelliTools, Inc.: http://www.intellitools.com
Riverdeep Interactive Learning: http://www.riverdeep.net
R. J. Cooper & Associates: http://www.rjcooper.com
Tash, Inc.: http://www.tashinc.com

Catalog Activity Worksheet

Name the software or hardware products, the manufacturer or reseller, cost, and computer platform availability.

1. Find software for word prediction.
2. Locate a switch for small children with poor motor control.
3. Find a switch that can be activated by a squeeze or pinch action.
4. Locate a switch that could be used by someone who has limited movement of only one finger and very little strength.
5. Find a software program that places a keyboard on the monitor to allow text input by switch.
6. Name the smallest keyboard you can find. Include its dimensions in your answer.
7. Find two different software programs that enable text entry by voice.
8. Find one software program that enables complete computer control by voice.
9. Locate two alternative keyboards that are larger than the standard keyboard.
10. Find three different mouse devices that differ in motor requirements from each other and from the standard mouse.
11. Locate two different alternative keyboards whose keyboard surfaces can be programmed.
12. Find a portable keyboard that can be carried to different classes for note taking.

APPENDIX C

Keyboard Shortcuts

Keyboard Shortcuts for *IntelliTalk*—Macintosh

Listed below are a group of special key combinations to use with *IntelliTalk* to access some of the menu options. You can test their function from the standard keyboard before entering them into your setup. [⌘] is [COMMAND]. When testing the key combinations from the keyboard, press those written together—[COMMAND]r—at the same time, release them, and then press the letter after the "+." When typing them into your custom keys, do not include the "+."

Read:

all	[COMMAND]r+a
word closest to the insertion point	[COMMAND]r+w
sentence closest to the insertion point	[COMMAND]r+s
paragraph closest to the insertion point	[COMMAND]r+p
word closest to insertion point and advances to next word	[CONTROL][SHIFT]w
sentence closest to insertion point and advances to next sentence	[CONTROL][SHIFT]s
paragraph closest to insertion point and advances to next paragraph	[CONTROL][SHIFT]p

Stop reading   [ESC] or [COMMAND].

Delete:

all	[COMMAND]d+a
character left of the insertion point	[DELETE]
word closest to the insertion point	[COMMAND]d+w
sentence closest to the insertion point	[COMMAND]d+s
paragraph closest to the insertion point	[COMMAND]d+p

Print one copy of all document pages   [COMMAND]p+[RETURN]

Keyboard Shortcuts for *IntelliTalk*—Windows

Listed below are a group of special key combinations to use with *IntelliTalk* to access some of the menu options. You can test their function from the standard keyboard before entering them into your setup. When testing the key combinations from the keyboard, press those written together—[CTRL]r—at the same time, release them, and then press the letter after the "+." When typing them into your custom keys, do not include the "+."

Read:

all	[CTRL]r+a
word closest to the insertion point	[CTRL]r+w
sentence closest to the insertion point	[CTRL]r+s
paragraph closest to the insertion point	[CTRL]r+p
word closest to insertion point and advances to next word	[CTRL][SHIFT]w
sentence closest to insertion point and advanees to next sentence	[CTRL][SHIFT]s
paragraph closest to insertion point and advances to next paragraph	[CTRL][SHIFT]p

Stop reading   [ESC]

Delete:

all	[CTRL]d+a
character left of the insertion point	[BACKSPACE]
word closest to the insertion point	[CTRL]d+w
sentence closest to the insertion point	[CTRL]d+s
paragraph closest to the insertion point	[CTRL]d+p

Print one copy of all document pages   [CTRL]p+[ENTER]

APPENDIX C / Keyboard Shortcuts **211**

Keyboard Shortcuts for *Write:OutLoud*—Macintosh

Listed below are a group of special key combinations to use with *Write:OutLoud* to access some of the menu options. You can test their function from the standard keyboard before entering them into your setup. [⌘] is [COMMAND].

Speak:

Speak all (first select all text then speak the highlighted text)	[⌘]a then [⌘]t
Speak last spoken text	[⌘]r
Speak last word (first select one word back then speak the highlighted text)	[⌘][SHIFT]j then [⌘]t
Speak last sentence (first select one sentence back then speak the highlighted text)	[⌘][SHIFT]i then [⌘]t
Stop speaking	[⌘]. (period)

Delete:

Delete last character	[DELETE]
Delete all (first select all text then delete the highlighted text	[⌘]a [DELETE]
Delete last word (first select one word back then delete the highlighted text	[⌘][SHIFT]j [DELETE]
Delete last sentence (first select one sentence back then delete the highlighted text	[⌘][SHIFT]i [DELETE]

Print one copy of all document pages: [⌘]p[RETURN]

Keyboard Shortcuts for *Write:OutLoud*—Windows

Listed below are a group of special key combinations to use with *Write:OutLoud* to access some of the menu options. You can test their function from the standard keyboard before entering them into your setup.

Speaks:

Speaks all (first select all text then speak the highlighted text)	[CTRL]a then [CTRL]t
Speak last spoken text	[CTRL]r
Speak last word (first select one word back then speak the highlighted text)	[CTRL][SHIFT]j then [CTRL]t
Speak last sentence (first select one sentence back then speak the highlighted text)	[CTRL][SHIFT]i then [CTRL]t
Stop speaking	[CTRL]. (period)

Delete:

Delete last character	[BACKSPACE]
Delete all (first select all text then delete the highlighted text	[CTRL]a [BACKSPACE]
Delete last word (first select one word back then delete the highlighted text	[CTRL][SHIFT]j [BACKSPACE]
Delete last sentence (first select one sentence back then delete the highlighted text	[CTRL][SHIFT]i [BACKSPACE]

Print one copy of all document pages: [CTRL]p[ENTER]

APPENDIX D

Resources

Ability Hub
c/o The Gilman Group, L.L.C.
P.O. Box 6356
Rutland, VT 05702-6356
Telephone: 802.775.1993
URL: http://www.abilityhub.com

AbleNet, Inc.
1081 Tenth Ave., S.E.
Minneapolis, MN 55414
Telephone: 800.322.0956
Fax: 612.379.9143
URL: http://www.ablenetinc.com

Access First, Inc.
P.O. Box 3990
Glen Allen, VA 23058–3990
Telephone: 888.606.6769
Fax: 804.935.6739
URL: http://www.accessfirst.net

Adesso, Inc.:
URL: http://www.adessoinc.com

AlphaSmart, Inc.
973 University Avenue
Los Gatos, CA 95032
Telephone: 408.355.1000
Fax: 408.355.1055
URL: http://www.alphasmart.com

ALVA Access Group, Inc.
436 14th Street Suite 700
Oakland, CA 94612
Telephone: 888.318.2582
URL: http://www.aagi.com

Alps Electric, Inc.
Telephone: 408.432.6000
URL:http://www.alps.com

Apple Computer, Inc
URL http://www.apple.com

Broderbund
See: Riverdeep Interactive Learning Limited

Center for Applied Special Technology (CAST)
URL: http://www.cast.org

CE Software, Inc
1801 Industrial Circle
P.O. Box 65580
West Des Moines, IA 50265
Telephone: 515.221.1801
Fax: 515.221.1806
URL: http://www.cesoft.com

DataDesk Technologies
10598 NE Valley Road, #100
Bainbridge Island, WA 98110
Telephone: 206.842.5480 ext. 103
Fax: 206.842.9219
URL: http://www.datadesktech.com

Don Johnston, Incorporated
26799 West Commerce Drive
Volo, IL 60073
Telephone: 800.999.4660
Fax: 847.740.7326
URL: http://www.donjohnston.com

Edmark Learning
See: Riverdeep Interactive Learning Limited

Freedom Scientific, Inc.
11800 31st Court North
St. Petersburg, FL 33716-1805
Telephone: 800.444.4443
Fax: 727.803.8001
URL: http://www.freedomscientific.com

Greystone Digital Inc.
P.O. Box 1888
Huntersville, NC 28078
Telephone: 800.249.5397
Fax: 704.875.8936
URL: http://www.bigkeys.com

Houghton Mifflin
222 Berkeley Street
Boston, MA 02116
Telephone: 617.351.5000
URL: http://www.houghtonmifflin.com

IBM Corporation
1133 Westchester Avenue
White Plains, New York 10604
Telephone (general inquiries): 800.IBM.4YOU
URL: http://www-3.ibm.com/software/speech/index.shtml

Inspiration Software, Inc.
7412 SW Beaverton Hillsdale Hwy, Suite 102
Portland, OR 97225-2167
Telephone: 800.877.4292
Fax: 503.297.4676
URL: http://www.inspiration.com

IntelliTools, Inc.
1720 Corporate Circle
Petaluma, CA 94954
Telephone: 800.899.6687
Fax: 707.773.2001
URL: http://www.intellitools.com

Kensington Group
2000 Alameda de las Pulgas
Second Floor
San Mateo, California 94403–1289
Telephone: 650.572.2700
Fax: 650.572.9675
URL: http://www.Kensington.com

KidSmart, LLC
3101 North Hemlock Circle
Broken Arrow, OK 74012
Telephone: 800.285.3475
Fax: 800.285.4018
URL: http://www.heartsoft.com

Laureate Learning Systems, Inc.
110 East Spring Street
Winooski, VT 05404
Telephone: 800.562.6801
Fax: 802.655.4757
URL: http://www.laureatelearning.com

Macally
15861 Tapia Street
Irwindale, CA 91706
Telephone: 626.338.8787
Fax: 626.338.3585
URL: http://www.macally.com

Madentec Limited
9935-29A Avenue
Edmonton, Alberta
Canada T6N 1A9
Telephone: 780.450.8926
Fax: 780.988.6182
URL: http://www.madentec.com

Marblesoft
12301 Central Ave NE, Suite 205
Blaine, MN 55434
Telephone: 763.755.1402
Fax: 763.862.2920
URL: http://www.marblesoft.com

Maxis/Electronic Arts
2121 North California Blvd. Suite 600
Walnut Creek, CA 94596–3572
Telephone: 510.933.5630
Fax: 510.927.3736
URL: http://www.maxis.com

Mayer-Johnson. Inc.
P.O. Box 1579
Solana Beach, CA 92075
Telephone: 800.588.4548
Fax: 858.550.0449
URL: http://www.mayerjohnson.com

Microsoft Corporation
URL: http://www.microsoft.com

MicroSpeed Inc.
11489 Woodside Ave.
Santee, CA 92071–4724
Telephone: 619.448.2888
Fax: 619.448.3044
URL: http://www.microspeed.com

NanoPac, Inc.
4823 South Sheridan Road Suite 302
Tulsa, OK 74145–5717
Telephone: 800.580.6086
Fax: 918.665.0361
URL: http://www.nanopac.com

One Hand Typing
URL: http:// www.aboutonehandtyping.com

Origin Instrument Corporation
854 Greenview Drive
Grand Prairie, TX 75050–2438
Telephone: 972.606.8740
Fax: 972.606.8741
URL: http://www.orin.com

Penny + Giles Computer Products
1 Embankment Way
Castleman Industrial Estate
RINGWOOD Hampshire BH24 1EU United Kingdom
Telephone: +44 (0) 1425 463100
Fax: +44 (0) 1425 436111
URL: http://www.penny-gilescp.co.uk

Prentke Romich Company
1022 Heyl Road
Wooster, OH 44691
Telephone: 800.262.1984
URL: http://www.prentrom.com

Research Press
2612 North Mattis Avenue
Champaign, IL 61822–1053
Telephone: 800.519.2707
Fax: 217.352.1221
URL: http://www.researchpress.com

Riverdeep Interactive Learning Limited
(Edmark, Broderbund, The Learning Company)
399 Boylston Street
Boston, MA 02116
Telephone: 617.778.7600
Fax: 617.778.7601
URL: http://www.riverdeep.net

R. J. Cooper & Associates
27601 Forbes Rd. Suite 39
Laguna Niguel, CA 92677
Telephone: 800.752.6673
Fax: 949.582.3169
URL: http://www.rjcooper.com

Sunburst Technology, Inc
1900 South Batavia Avenue
Geneva, IL 60134-3399
Telephone 800.321.7511
Fax: 888.872.8380
URL: http://www.sunburst.com

Tash, Inc.
3512 Mayland Ct.
Richmond, VA 23233
Telephone: 800.463.5685
Fax: 804.747.5224
URL: http://www.tashinc.com

The Learning Company
See: Riverdeep Interactive Learning Limited

Universal Design
URL: http://www.design.ncsu.edu:8120/cud/univ_design/princ_overview.htm

WebQuest Generator
URL: http://web.bsu.edu/wmock/wqg/

GLOSSARY

Absolute cell reference. A spreadsheet cell reference that points to a specific cell address and does not change if the cell reference is copied to another cell. (See *Relative cell reference*.)

Alternative keyboard. A hardware device or software that replaces or works in conjunction with the standard keyboard to meet the specific needs of the user.

Alternative mouse device. A peripheral device that offers the functionality of a standard mouse (e.g., trackpad, trackball, joystick, or touch screen).

Archival copy. Copies made from software to insure uninterrupted software use in case the original becomes damaged; also called back-up copy.

Assisted keyboard. A standard keyboard whose functioning has been modified by software to accommodate diverse needs.

Assistive device. Refers to the whole range of aids, tools, devices, and equipment used by people with disabilities—not just computer adaptations.

Authoring software. Software that allows the user to create computer-assisted lessons and activities without knowing a programming language (e.g., *HyperStudio, IntelliMathics, IntelliPics Studio*).

Automatic scan. A scan method whereby the scan progresses automatically at a predetermined speed. The switch user stops the scan by activating the switch for the desired choice—the opposite of inverse scanning.

Browser. A computer program for accessing web sites (e.g., *Explorer, Netscape, Safari,* or *Mozilla*).

Calibrate. To align active areas of a touch screen to the monitor so that the correct choices can be selected by touch.

Cause and effect. Software in which a response such as a switch press or key press causes something to happen on the screen.

Clip art. Sets of artwork designed to be "clipped out" and pasted into documents.

Communication board. A device to allow expressive communication by pointing or gazing at a printed word, symbol, or picture; usually does not have spoken or written output.

Ctrl-click. A key combination to access a contextual menu on a Macintosh computer. (Windows—see *Right-click*)

Database. A collection of data used to store and organize information. Also the name of a type of software program that enables the sorting, filtering, finding, and matching of data records.

Default. A set of predetermined settings or values in hardware or software that remain in effect until specifically changed by the user.

Document. The product of an application program such as word processing; also called a file.

Documentation. The written instructions that accompany software and hardware to explain their use and maintenance.

Em dash. One of two special dash characters used in typesetting to indicate a change in thought or to equate similar ideas. The em dash is equivalent in length to a capital letter "M" in the selected font face. (See *En dash*.)

En dash. One of two special dash characters used in typesetting to indicate duration. The en dash is equivalent in length to a capital letter "N" in the selected font face. (See *Em dash*.)

219

GLOSSARY

Ergonomic keyboard. Keyboards that offer the user a more natural hand and finger position to help reduce the stress and injury often associated with frequent keyboarding; often repositioning keys and providing wrist support.

Fair Use. A legal term specifying that copyrighted materials can be used without permission of the copyright owner provided that the use is fair and reasonable.

Field. A single type of information in a database (e.g., a name, phone number; also called a category).

Footer. Recurring text that appears at the bottom of every page, such as author name, page number, title, or running head. (See *Header*.)

Graphics software. Software for creating and manipulating images; includes drawing and paint programs in addition to page layout, photo editing, and greeting card/banner software.

Group. An instruction in graphics software to unite multiple lines, shapes, or images into a single object. (See *Ungroup*.)

Hanging Indent. A paragraph spacing where the first line is flush with the left margin and succeeding lines are uniformly indented—a style typically used with reference lists.

Head mouse. An input device attached to the user's head that replaces a mouse by using infrared signals that translate head movement or eye movement into mouse actions.

Header. Recurring text that appears at the top of every page, such as author name, page number, title, or running head. (See *Footer*.)

HTML (Hyper-Text Markup Language). Language that is used to create documents on the web incorporating text, graphics, sound, video, and hyperlinks.

Interface. A device that facilitates the relationship between systems or system components. For example, a switch device connected to the computer via a switch interface.

Internet. An electronic communications network that connects computer networks and computer facilities around the world.

Inverse scanning. A scan method whereby the switch user activates the switch to advance the scan, and releases the switch to make a selection; the opposite of automatic scanning.

Joystick. A peripheral device capable of controlling objects on the screen for applications ranging from games to graphics software. Some joysticks can be used in place of a mouse as an alternative input device.

Keyguard. A plastic or metal sheet with finger-sized holes that covers a standard or alternative keyboard to help people with poor motor control select the correct keys without accidentally activating unwanted keys.

Landscape. A horizontal page orientation selected in Page Layout of most application software. (See *Portrait*.)

Macro. A group of computer commands treated as a unit. When activated, macros execute the set of commands with a single keystroke.

Moisture guard. A thin plastic cover for a computer keyboard that prevents damage from liquids.

Mouse Keys. Utility software that allows the use of the numeric keypad to activate all mouse function; part of the Easy Access Control Panel/Universal Access for Macintosh computers or Accessibility Options for Windows computers.

On-screen keyboard. A software program that places a virtual keyboard on the monitor, sharing the monitor space with other software; activated with any mouse or alternative mouse device, it functions like a standard keyboard.

Overlay. Paper or plastic that fits over a keyboard or alternate keyboard depicting the active areas on the board. Overlays may be blank so that they can be customized to a student's individual needs.

Page Break. Suppression of the automatic flow of text to the next page by inserting a break to force subsequent text to the next page.

Page Setup. Features that differ among computer systems and printer software to select page orientation, paper size, and printer formatting; usually found in the File menu.

Peripheral device. Any of a number of hardware devices that add function to a computer; for example, disk drive, digital camera, printer, scanner, and so on.

Plagiarism. To pass off text, images, and even ideas, from other sources to yourself without crediting the source.

Portrait. A vertical page orientation selected in Page Layout of most application software. (See *Landscape*.)

Presentation software. Software that facilitates the creation of effective presentations that can include text, graphics, sound, video, and animation.

Problem-solving software. Software that offers instructionally relevant problems for students to solve.

Proprietary software. A copyrighted software title whose use is restricted to one computer unless fees are paid for network or lab packs.

Public domain software. Software that has no copyright and can be freely used and distributed. Usually software in the public domain is free and is often called Freeware.

QWERTY. The most commonly used keyboard layout in the United States, named for the first six letters on the top row of letter keys.

Record. A single set of related data in a database, comprised of fields or categories; can be compared to a set of data on an index card.

Reference. Software that offers traditional reference materials; for example, dictionary, thesaurus, or encyclopedia resources.

Reinforced practice. An instructional strategy providing practice, with feedback, of a previously taught skill; a common category of educational software.

Relative cell reference. A spreadsheet cell reference that points to a cell address that changes if the cell reference is copied to another cell. (See *Absolute cell reference*.)

Right-click. A button press to access a contextual menu on a Windows computer. (Macintosh—see *Ctrl-click*.)

Sans serif. Without lines or "feet" at tops and bottoms of characters or font faces. (See *Serif*.)

Scan array. Groups of choices the computer moves through when scanning; can be word, letter, or picture choices on the screen; the computer interprets the selection made by switch activation as a keystroke or mouse click.

Scanning. An indirect method of computer access substituting for keyboard input; the computer steps through choices that the user may select by switch activation.

Search engine. Computer software that searches for specified data or key words across the web.

Serif. Short lines or "feet" at tops and bottoms of characters or font face. (See *Sans serif*.)

Shareware. Software that can be freely copied and distributed. Generally the author requests a small fee for continued use or extended features.

Simulation. A program that allows the user to experience a realistic situation or problem and determine a course of action; for example, *Oregon Trail*.

Slow Keys. Utility software that delays the computer's receipt of a key press, ignoring stray touches by persons with poor motor control; part of the Easy Access Control Panel/Universal Access for Macintosh computers or Accessibility Options for Windows computers.

Software piracy. The unauthorized copying and use of copyrighted software.

Speech recognition. Also called voice input, a process whereby the computer learns to understand discrete sounds or words, and requires special software and hardware, such as *ViaVoice, Naturally Speaking,* or *Dragon Dictates.*

Spreadsheet. A document that contains rows and columns used primarily for calculations. Also the name of a type of software program used for primarily performing calculations.

Step scan. A scan method whereby the switch user "steps" through the scan array by activating the switch for each choice.

Sticky Keys. Utility software that allows single-finger typists to depress keys in succession that ordinarily would have to be pressed simultaneously; available for Macintosh in the Easy Access Control Panel/Universal Access, and for Windows computers as Accessibility Options.

Student utility software. Utility software designed for children to use, such as word processing, database, or spreadsheets.

Switch. An input device that allows the user to operate a computer without a keyboard; requires either a switch interface or a keyboard emulator.

Teacher utility. Software that performs tasks for teachers such as test building, grade books, scoring tests, or calculating readability level.

Text Wrap. The flow of text around an image.

Touch screen. An input device made of transparent plastic and attached to a computer monitor containing vertical and horizontal contact points that can transmit information to the computer by touch.

Trackball. A computer input device holding a ball that is rotated to simulate mouse movement; is stationary and requires less arm movement that a mouse.

Tutorial. Educational software that provides step-by-step instructions to teach new material to the student.

Ungroup. An instruction in graphics software to separate previously grouped objects into their individual components. (See *Group.*)

Universal design. The design of products and environments to be usable by all people, to the greatest extent possible, without the need for adaptation or specialized design.

URL (Universal Resource Locator). A web address.

Watermark. A pale image placed behind text to simulate watermarks produced by pressure on paper.

Word prediction software. Software that speeds up text entry by predicting the word to be typed from the initially typed letters, thus reducing the number of keystrokes necessary to produce text.

Word processing. Computer software that enables the user to produce, edit, save, and print text documents that can simulate typesetting.

Web (World Wide Web—WWW). A part of the Internet accessed through software called a browser and containing documents connected by hyperlinks.

Word wrap. In word processing, the automatic movement of text from one line to the next.

INDEX

absolute cell reference, 45, 46, 49
Accessibility Options, 102, 108
Activity Exchange, 149
Adesso, Inc., 114, 115
Alps Electric, 105
Alps Glidepoint Trackpad, 105
alternative keyboard, 103, 112-117, 124, 130, 131, 141, 152, 154, 159
alternative mouse device, 105-108, 110, 124, 130
ALVA Access Group, 111
Amazon Trail, 78
American Heritage Dictionary for Children, 79
Apple Computer, Inc., 80
archival copy, 88, 90
assisted keyboard, 102, 108-109, 124
assistive device, 122, 124
Assistive Technologies, 106
authoring, 87
authoring software, 76, 81, 90, 126

Balanced Literacy, 77
Behavior Objective Sequence, 79
Big Keys (Plus), 113
BlackBoard, 97
Boardmaker, 79, 137
Bobby, 92
Broderbund, 77, 79
browser, 99

calibrate, 103, 124
cause and effect, 118, 124, 174
CE Software, Inc., 112
Center for Applied Special Technology (CAST), 86
ClarisWorks for Kids, 80
Classroom Suite, 86, 169
clip art, 22, 35, 76, 79
Co:Writer, 111
communication board, 79, 90, 116
Creature Chorus, 77
ctrl-click, 69, 73, 103, 185

DataDesk Technologies, 114
Discover products
    Discover:Board, 116-118, 120, 125, 131, 151
    Discover:Create, 125, 130, 134, 151

Discover:Kenx, 120, 125, 151
Discover:Screen, 110, 120, 125, 131, 151
Discover:Switch, 110, 118, 120, 125, 131, 151
documentation, 85, 90
Don Johnston Incorporated, 77, 80, 90, 107, 110, 111, 118
Dragon Dictates, 121
Dragon Systems, 121

Early Learning I, II, and *III*, 84, 86, 118
Easy Access, 102, 108
Edmark Reading, 76
em dash, 15, 20
en dash, 15, 20
ergonomic keyboard, 114, 124

Factory Deluxe, 79
fair use, 94, 99
field, 50, 53, 55, 67
footer, 20, 40
Freedom Scientific, Inc., 112
Fun, Two, Three!, 81, 196, 197

graphics software, 76, 79, 87, 90
Greystone Digital, 113
group, 29, 30, 31, 32, 35

hanging indent, 6, 7, 20
head mouse, 106, 124
header, 13, 16, 20
HeadMouse, 106
Houghton Mifflin, 79
How Stuff Works, 96
HTML, 19, 20, 99
HyperStudio, 81

IBM, 121
inLarge, 111
Inspiration, 80
Inspiration Software, Inc., 80
IntelliKeys (USB) keyboard, 115-117, 128, 131, 196
IntelliMathics, 81, 130
IntelliPics Studio, 81, 126, 130, 134, 169
IntelliPics Studio Player, 169, 197

223

INDEX

IntelliTalk, 80, 81, 110, 130, 139, 146, 164
IntelliTools, Inc., 77, 80, 81, 86, 90, 110, 115, 118, 169
interface, 118, 120, 124, 152

Jaws, 112
joystick, 90, 106, 110, 124
Joystick (and Mouse) Trainer, 77

Kensington Group, 105
Kensington TurboMouse, 105
Key Stickers, 107
keyguard, 103, 124
Kid Pix Deluxe, 79
Kidspiration, 80
Kid-TRAC, 105
Knowledge Adventure, Inc., 81

landscape, 11, 20
Laureate Learning Systems, Inc., 77, 118
Learning Upgrade LLC, 77
Little Fingers keyboard, 113

Macally Micro mouse, 105
macro, 112, 124
Madentec Limited, 110, 111, 115, 118, 120
Marblesoft, 84, 86, 118
Mavis Beacon Teaches Typing for Kids, 77
Maxis, 78
Mayer-Johnson, Inc., 79, 137
Mix 'n Match, 84
moisture guard, 107, 124
mouse keys, 109, 124

NanoPac, Inc., 112
NaturallySpeaking, 121

one hand typing, 115
on-screen keyboard, 110, 111, 124, 152, 154
Oregon Trail, 78, 83, 90
Oregon Trail II, 78
Origin Instruments Corporation, 106
outSPOKEN, 112
overlay, 115, 124, 136
Overlay Maker, 125, 128, 130, 134, 135, 136, 196
Overlay Printer, 196

page break, 14, 20
page setup, 11, 20
Penny + Giles Computer Products, 107
Penny + Giles Joystick Plus, 105
peripheral device, 50, 67
Picture Communication Symbols, 79
plagiarism, 90, 93
portrait, 11, 20
presentation software, 68, 73
Print Shop Deluxe, 79, 90
problem-solving software, 76, 78, 87, 90
proprietary, 88, 90, 111
public domain software, 88, 89, 90
Puzzle Tanks, 79

Quia, 97
QuickKeys, 112
QWERTY, 5, 20, 77, 113, 115

R. J. Cooper & Associates, 77, 89, 107, 111, 118
record, 50, 52, 53, 54, 67
reference, 76, 79, 87, 90, 95
reinforced practice, 76, 77, 87, 90
relative cell reference, 44, 45, 46, 49
Research Press, 79
right-click, 69, 73, 103
Riverdeep Interactive Learning Limited, 76, 77

SAM Joystick and Trackball, 107
sans serif, 16, 20
scan array, 118
scanning, 118, 120, 124, 154, 196
    automatic scan, 119, 124
    inverse scanning, 119, 124
    scan array, 118, 119, 124
    step scan, 119, 124
search engine, 92, 93, 99
serif, 16, 20
shareware, 88, 89, 90, 111, 119
SimAnt, 78
Simon Sounds It Out, 77
Simon Spells, 77
SimTown, 78
simulation, 76, 78, 87, 90
Slow Keys, 109, 124
Snood, 119
software piracy, 88, 90

speech recognition, 120, 121, 122, 124
Stanley's Sticker Stories, 76
Sticky Keys, 109, 124
student utility, 76, 80, 87, 90
Sunburst Technology, 79
switch, 107, 117-119, 124, 130, 152, 154, 196
Switch Intro, 118
SwitchIt!, 118

Tash Mini keyboard, 112
teacher utility, 76, 79, 80, 87, 90
text wrap, 23, 24, 25, 35
The Learning Company, 77, 78, 79
The Secret Writer's Society, 77
Thinkology series, 77
touch screen, 102, 103, 105, 110, 124
Track IR Head Mouse, 106
trackball, 105, 110, 113, 124
Tru-Form keyboard, 115
tutorial, 76, 77, 84, 87, 90, 196

ungroup, 30, 31, 35
United States Copyright Office, 94

Universal Access, 102, 108
universal design, 85, 86, 87, 90, 118, 169
URL, 93, 99

ViaVoice, 121

watermark, 21, 24, 35
Web Accessibility, 91
Web Monkey, 96
Web Monkey for Kids, 96
WebQuest, 96
WebQuest Generator, 96
Wheels, 89
Word Munchers, 77
Word Munchers Deluxe, 77
word prediction software, 111, 124
word wrap, 10, 20
WordArt, 32
World Wide Web Consortium (W3C), 92
Write:Outloud, 80, 110, 146, 164

ZoomCaps, 107
ZoomText, 112